DEWEY

An American of This Century

STANLEY WALKER

DEWEY

An American of This Century

Whittlesey House

MC GRAW-HILL BOOK COMPANY, INC.

New York   *London*

DEWEY: AN AMERICAN OF THIS CENTURY

Copyright, 1944, *by the* McGraw-Hill Book Company, Inc.

*This book is produced in full compliance
with the government's regulations for con-
serving paper and other essential materials.*

PUBLISHED BY WHITTLESEY HOUSE
A division of the McGraw-Hill Book Company, Inc.

Printed in the United States of America

CONTENTS

CONTENTS

SPEECHES AND ADDRESSES

DEWEY

An American of This Century

"HE FEARS THE FACE OF NO MAN"

THOMAS EDMUND DEWEY has pursued a straight path. Indeed, viewing it all today, there seems to have been a certain inevitable quality about the unfolding of his career. He has stuck with remarkable steadfastness to a forthright course of conduct. He has been unimpressed alike by the portentous warnings of the powerful or the fearful squeaks of the timorous. Respectful of tradition, he has never allowed tradition to cow him. At the end he remains unbossed, his own man— a man who, happily, has no apologies to make.

One evening in the spring of 1944 an elder statesman of the Republican Party, a New Yorker of great wisdom and solid dignity, who has seen the making of much history, fell to talking of the young Dewey as he was when he first entered the lists against the great criminal combinations. He recalled that Dewey seemed almost exasperatingly sure of himself. He respected authority but was curiously unawed. Judges before whom he appeared wondered about this self-possessed young man. Could he really have the stuff? The old gentleman, reminiscing of all this, went on: "He was the perfect example of the right man at the right time. The times called for Dewey. I soon came to understand one thing, and to marvel at it: he feared the face of no man."

Throughout his career there has never been any question of the fundamental honesty and the natural courage of Mr. Dewey. He never asked the odds. He was a disciple of the pugilistic philosophy of the late Robert Fitzsimmons, who enunciated the theory of physics that the bigger they come the harder they fall. Many men, judges and others, came to suspect that what they had first taken for conceit was nothing more than confidence. But whatever it was, many found it hard to swallow at first. On better acquaintance, this quality became understandable, and even rather admirable.

There are probably better lawyers than Mr. Dewey. As a prosecutor, however, he was without doubt one of the greatest ever heard of in New York or anywhere else. His success may be attributed to several circumstances, but, in the opinion of many who observed him closely, two factors are of the first importance:

1. He had an amazing capacity for preparing a case. He was thorough. He would not be hurried. He would take months, sifting hundreds of bank records, talking to scores of witnesses, and wandering through what sometimes were blind alleys, to clinch a case against one man, if he thought that man was worth pursuing.

2. He had self-control. Only the greatest provocation would cause his temper to flare up. He could keep his mouth shut. A prosecutor, especially if he is juggling explosive material, is under an almost unbearable temptation to talk— to a friend, to the press, to somebody. Dewey held himself in leash until his evidence, the witnesses and the documents, were secure, and the accused in custody. Time enough then to talk. And when he talked he had something to say.

Some of Mr. Dewey's friends say that he has changed since those early days. What they mean, chiefly, is that his manner is easier and more congenial. They are right about this, but the change represents no astonishing metamorphosis; it is a change that would come naturally enough to any man who, over a good many years, has had to rub up against all sorts of people, some of whom could be exasperating without half trying. Certainly he has gained in urbanity as the years have gone by. But to try to make him out a new man is stretching things a bit far. They say that as a schoolboy he was sure of himself; he is sure of himself today.

No man is more alert to his surroundings. No one shows a more spontaneous delight at meeting new people. A fresh set of facts, a new slant on an old question, an arresting opinion on a debatable point, will find him enthusiastic— ready to argue, perhaps, but with an open-mindedness which can only be set down as fairness. Time and again he has shown a deep concern for individuals of all colors and creeds and conditions, and this concern had nothing to do with politics or business or high matters of state. The person might be a watchman, a policeman, a chauffeur, a conductor, a storekeeper—no matter what, their personalities and their problems were the important thing.

And yet the gentleman is not a backslapper. From the time he first began to attract public notice he has preserved a curious but consistent attitude, or manner, for which the only word, inexact enough, is dignity. He can be as easy and informal as the next man, but there is a point in his relations with other human beings beyond which he will not go. One of his associates said of him, "I doubt if anyone has more sympathy for what is currently known in many circles as 'the common man' than the Governor. But that never means that the Governor thinks it necessary to become 'common' himself."

The Governor not only has self-respect to a notable degree; he respects the office that he holds. He respects tradition. If it has been the custom to do things a certain way, to observe certain niceties, to issue proclamations at certain times, then, he argues, let us continue to do so, provided there is no urgent reason for changing things. He has a sober regard for institutions, whether religious, political, or social, that have lasted through long generations.

This trait, which amounts almost to reverence for the sound and permanent things, may be observed in his attitude toward the office of Governor of New York. He would never think of doing anything which in the slightest way might tend to debase that office. He knows, as all students of the history of New York know, that some egregious pip-squeaks have at one time or another occupied the Governor's chair, but he knows, too, that in the main the occupants have been good men. He respects the memory of such governors of other times as Samuel J. Tilden, Grover Cleveland, Theodore Roosevelt, Charles Evans Hughes, Charles S. Whitman, and Alfred E. Smith—men of widely differing political views and personal attributes, but all deserving of their peculiar place in the chronicles of their times. They left him an honorable legacy.

New York had another governor once, in a strange period, named William Sulzer, a rabble-rouser who after a few months was impeached and driven from office. Sulzer, in his ascendancy, was sometimes referred to as "the man who looks more like Henry Clay than Henry Clay looked." Because he had once been in Alaska, some of his admirers called him "Klondike Bill." He was the archetype of the spurious "People's Friend."

An old-timer said recently, "I remember Bill Sulzer principally for one thing, and a rather endearing thing it was. He chewed tobacco, and he could hit a spittoon with the most astounding accuracy. My judgment of distance may be a little off, but I should say he could make a bull's-eye at twelve feet. Now if Dewey could only do that, or something like it—"

Alas for "color," Mr. Dewey will never do anything of the sort.

There is a school of political thought which believes that luck is the most important factor in any man's political advancement. On a somewhat higher and mystical plane, it is sometimes held that Fate (or Destiny or something akin to that) puts its finger on a man early in life and marks

4

him for great things. In elucidating such theories, political writers, and even more sober historians, can construct millions of paragraphs of rather fetching buncombe. On the other hand, it may be argued, with somewhat more plausibility, that Mr. Dewey has got where he is by the simple pursuit of a straight path. The path has been straight enough, all right, but the circumstances do weave themselves into a pattern which suggests that Fate may, for all anybody knows, have had something to do with it. Consider the succession of "ifs":

If he had not aimed for high position, he would not have been able to make his record as Chief Assistant United States Attorney.

If he had not had the unanimous backing of a group of other lawyers, Governor Lehman would not have appointed him Special Prosecutor to break up the rackets.

If he had listened to the voice of political logic, he would not have made the race for District Attorney in an overwhelmingly Democratic county.

If, having been in the District Attorney's office only a year, he had heeded the advice of his best friends and declined to make the race for Governor, he would have remained fixed in the public judgment as only a prosecutor.

If, again acceding to some of his friends, he had not put up a fight for the Republican nomination in 1940, he would have remained essentially a local man. His preconvention activities, and his later speeches on behalf of Wendell Willkie, not only taught him much about the country but enabled the country to know him better.

If, in short, he had not done all these things, and in a manner which may at times have suggested foolhardiness, he would not have been in such a commanding position when he was elected Governor in 1942 and placed in a spot where the Republican nomination for President seemed not only logical but inevitable.

There are the "ifs." They probably mean nothing except to students of the vagaries of chance. It is easier to believe that Mr. Dewey followed his own inclinations, most of the time, even when he knew that, on the immediate issue, he would in all likelihood be defeated. In such considerations Mr. Dewey has always been his own boss. He will take advice; he seeks it, and listens to it with infinite care and patience. But all the momentous decisions affecting Mr. Dewey have been his and his alone. To be sure, the pressure on him by his party to make the race for Governor in 1938 was too strong for any reasonable man to withstand, but he was not "forced" to run.

It is a pleasant habit to refer to a luminous political figure as "unbossed" or, more positively, as "His Own Man." There is little reason to change this habit in discussing Mr. Dewey, if one important exception is made: He has never thought it the part of an independent policy, or of ordinary common sense, wantonly to insult the leaders of the Republican Party. The two most powerful New York leaders are Edwin F. Jaeckle of Buffalo, State Chairman, and J. Russel Sprague of Long Island, National Committeeman—both able executives, shrewd politicians, and friends of Mr. Dewey.

These two men have worked closely with the Governor on matters of legislation and patronage. Of the two, Jaeckle is the tougher, a strong man with a vivid vocabulary; Sprague is a diplomat. Both are able. They have an easy relationship with Dewey.

When the Republicans were swept into power in 1942, the patronage problem was acute. Mr. Dewey was the first Republican Governor to be elected since the defeat of Nathan L. Miller by Al Smith in 1922. Hordes of faithful Republicans were hungry for jobs and power. The rush was something like that which occurred at the time of the great run in Oklahoma when the Indian lands were opened for settlement. Some good men were up for appointment; others, to make no bones about it, were party hacks.

Mr. Dewey was in no hurry to dole out patronage. When he was ready, he chose for his more important posts some strangers, and some men he had known for years, without much regard to whether they were important as Republicans. In dealing with the many other appointments, Mr. Dewey subjected every potential appointee to the closest sort of scrutiny—a scrutiny which did not sit well with many a party worker who had assumed that a Republican victory meant automatic entry into the land of Canaan. They did not like the idea of having state troopers checking on their business histories, their habits, and their standing in the community, but the check went on nevertheless.

The scheme, in general, worked this way: A Republican leader would suggest that a man be appointed to a certain office. The Governor's investigation machine would then go into action. If the man stood up under inquiry, the Governor would then get in touch with the man's sponsor and give his approval, saying, "You probably will want to notify him yourself. Then please have him drop in and see me." Thus were the ends of political politeness served, but not until Mr. Dewey had satisfied himself that he was not appointing a man who on some future day might turn out to be an embarrassment.

Few persons will be surprised to learn that some appointments, to relatively obscure posts, went to men who had been sturdy Republicans but whose intellectual attainments and records of achievement were far from exciting. Word was passed to some of these loyal misfits:

"This is not much of a job, but it is one you can handle if you'll buckle down. It is the best we can do for you. From now on, remember, you are on your own. No Republican leader can save you if you fizzle."

An old schoolteacher back in Owosso, Michigan, once

said to young Dewey, "Young man, you must learn to get along with people." Good enough advice, no doubt, but it took the young man many years to learn it, by which time it seemed to come naturally rather than by precept. He gets along with the leaders, he gets along with the men in key positions in the state government, and for the most part he gets along well with the members of the Legislature. When a complicated legislative program was under consideration, he would hold conference after conference with men of divergent points of view, hoping that once the general objective was settled upon some agreeable means could be found of reaching it. Actually Governor Dewey has enjoyed more cordial and sympathetic relations with the Legislature than any Governor of New York in recent history. He has shown unusual talent for persuading men of opposing views to reconcile their differences and work together.

This is not to imply that Mr. Dewey and other strong-willed men, especially in the Legislature, have always managed to iron out all their differences. Far from it. To many Democrats and to a few Republicans, he is a difficult, hard-headed fellow, and all the conferences in the world cannot alter their opinion. Nonetheless, results have been obtained; Mr. Dewey has proved that conciliation and cooperation are usually possible among men of good intentions; the flare-ups of spleen and vituperation have been few.

Judges who used to preside over the Dewey trials, as well as the men and women who have seen him in action as Governor, have alluded to his ability to keep a tight rein on his emotions. Instances of extreme exhilaration and of extreme depression are so rare as to be unimportant. When a mistrial was declared in the case of the *People v. James J. Hines,* and it appeared that Dewey might have suffered a damning defeat, he went into his inner office long enough to hang up his hat, then came out and said to his dejected assistants, "Never mind. We'll try him again, on the same indictment, and next time we'll win." At the Republican Convention in Philadelphia in 1940, after Willkie had won the nomination, Dewey saw a tired young party worker sitting in a corner, head down. He went over, lifted the man's chin, and said, "Keep it up, young fellow." Dewey has been pleased at some of his victories, but never to exuberance. He has usually been content to dictate a brief statement of thanks to those who had helped him, giving them the credit; then he might allow himself to hum a tune and go off to a restaurant for a quiet celebration.

Mr. Dewey himself is a high-powered, ebullient machine, though he rarely seems to be hurried. He finds time to learn of the private troubles and ambitions of the people in his offices whenever he thinks such knowledge will be of any help. He has performed many acts of kindness that have never received a line of publicity, and probably never will. One will be enough:

An assistant came into his office in New York to tell him that one of the girl stenographers, whom Mr. Dewey knew and whose work he had liked, had been away for a month, ill.

"I believe," he said, "that the law requires that I take her off the pay roll."

"Has she any other source of income?" asked the Governor.

"No," said the assistant, "and she is at Saranac with tuberculosis."

"I don't think," said Mr. Dewey, "you will find anything in the law requiring you to take her off the pay roll."

Like most men who are eager for facts, and who have the knack of holding on to facts tenaciously, Mr. Dewey on infrequent occasions has given new acquaintances the impression that he might, just possibly, also have a knack for butting into matters that were none of his business. Once, at the home of a friend, he met a couple who were about to sail for the Orient, where the husband had an important new job. Mr. Dewey began asking questions: What had he paid for tickets? Did he have a contract? And so on. The husband, alarmed, cornered the host and whispered, "Who is this fellow? What's he trying to do?"

"Why," explained the host, "that's just old Tom Dewey, trying to help you. And he probably can help you, too. Go ahead and tell him everything and see if I'm not right."

The host, luckily for friendship's sake, happened to be right. Mr. Dewey's gratuitous advice saved the couple a considerable amount of money and endless trouble. But this habit may become trying. Take the celebrated case of Mrs. Hogan and her beans. Mr. and Mrs. Carl T. ("Pat") Hogan, long friends of the Deweys, have a place near the Dewey farm at Pawling, New York. One summer evening Mr. Dewey wandered into the Hogan kitchen and found Mrs. Hogan busily canning green beans. As she tells it:

"I had both hands full, was in a hurry and in no mood for talk. Tom didn't know the first thing about canning beans. Apparently he had never seen a pressure canning outfit in operation. I had to explain everything. He asked a million questions. I had to think fast for some of the answers—for example, why this and why that? But I'll say this for him—when he had finished he knew as much about pressure cooking, and canning beans, as I did. What's more, he'll remember it."

Likewise, the Governor became interested in a freezing unit at Pawling. He soon became an eloquent booster of freezing, which is part of his gospel for the postwar life.

II

THIRTEEN YEARS

By the summer of 1944 Thomas Edmund Dewey had completed approximately thirteen years in the public service. Even during those few months when he was back in the private practice of law he was busy at least part of the time handling matters of public concern. Two periods, therefore, are roughly parallel: Mr. Dewey's career in public office, and the era covered by what is usually called the New Deal Administration in Washington.

It has been a long time, as such things go, since Mr. Dewey, a young lawyer whose personal qualities and legal abilities were known to only a few of his friends and associates, was picked out of relative obscurity, placed in the office of the United States Attorney of the Southern District of New York, and set upon the path where he was to become one of the most discussed men of our time—a man capable of arousing bitter disagreement, hysterical envy, as well as a singular degree of loyalty, admiration, and respect.

True enough, when he first emerged as a public figure, his prominence came almost overnight. He moved quickly into the spotlight, propelled there by the inexorable nature of events. Those were dramatic times; sending underworld overlords to prison and exposing great fraudulent combinations were dramatic business. It is equally true that his present standing before the country has come after hard years of unremitting work, of intense application to whatever job was at hand, and a course of conduct which has been remarkably consistent.

Mr. Dewey, in short, is anything but a political morning-glory. Politics have always fascinated him, as they fascinated his father and grandfather before him. As a young man in the New York of the 1920's Mr. Dewey began as one of the humblest of party workers, ringing doorbells and performing all those chores which are necessary if a party organization is to be kept alive. A Republican in New York in those days was something of a rarity, almost a freak. Tammany, the gray iniquity, controlled the city. The Republican Party was tired, accustomed to defeat, expecting defeat, and at times almost inviting defeat. Mr. Dewey was one of that group of young men, many of whom were born outside the domain of the Tammany Tiger, who revitalized the party in the city, later in the State of New York, and finally in the nation itself. Accidents happen in politics. It is no accident that the symbol of this revitalization came to be the figure of Mr. Dewey himself—the alert, unterrified gentleman with the black mustache, the foe of corruption and inefficiency wherever they were found.

The definitions of politics are many, and some are brutal. The high-minded Aristotle said that "the good of man must be the end of the science of politics," but there are those who deny that it is a science at all. In our own time the Baltimore savant, Frank R. Kent, has referred to "the great game of politics," a cynical but not altogether inaccurate description. Whatever politics may be, it is neither mysterious nor repulsive to Mr. Dewey. He believes in the preservation of the party system as surely as he believes in the preservation of the republic. No one ever caught him apologizing for "politics" as such. Moreover, he has never said anything to indicate that he believes "realist" and "idealist," in the conduct of public affairs, are necessarily mutually exclusive terms.

Examined solely with the political eye (and this is of course only one legitimate form of examination), Mr. Dewey is important at this time primarily because he has demonstrated that he can carry elections. He is the man that people vote for, often to the astonishment of veteran prognosticators who seem to have forgotten Bismarck's very sensible dictum that "politics is not an exact science."

"He was elected, wasn't he?" was once Mr. Dewey's own reply to a friend who had observed that a certain officeholder had no political acumen.

Observers have long realized that Mr. Dewey, for whatever reason, or probably for a great variety of reasons, has a tremendous strength at the polls. It has been called a "hidden strength," which is doubtless akin to that hoary political phenomenon "the silent vote." Respectable figures have taken to the radio to oppose him; talk on the streets has been that "he didn't have a chance"; campaign-scarred bosses and analysts have argued, with maps and charts and records of past performances, that he could not get the vote. But somehow the votes were there. That is why the Republicans see in him a new and powerful champion; that likewise is why his opponents—and these come in many shades, from the most calloused big-city bosses to the most hysterical professional friends of the underdog—fear him and are eager to turn against him every weapon in the arsenal of political invective. By none of this is Mr. Dewey astonished. He expects it. He knows his politics.

The record of Mr. Dewey's drawing power is plain, and usually it has surprised even his most enthusiastic supporters. For example, when he ran for District Attorney of New York County in 1937, he had behind him a solid list of achievements as a prosecutor, but few persons thought he had more than an outside chance. He was elected by 109,000 votes. The next year his party insisted that he make the race for Governor. It was a curious campaign. The chief argument against him was that he should not be elected because he was the best prosecutor in the world; many Republicans held to this view. And yet he was defeated by only 64,000 votes. This defeat, far from lessening his political strength, made him the most powerful Republican in the state. Next time, in 1942, he was elected Governor by 647,000 votes. No one laughs off figures like those.

Maybe it is crass to allude to the obvious—that such figures have an appeal to Republican leaders in all parts of the country. By 1944 it was clear that he was far in the lead for the Republican nomination for President, even though, to keep the promise made when he was elected Governor, he did not lift a hand to obtain that nomination.

But votes, in the mass, are cold things, fit subjects for the Warwicks who pore over their graphs in political headquarters. Behind Mr. Dewey's vote getting is something else of far more immediate importance: that is the simple fact of public confidence. People have discovered that his word is good and that he can get things done.

As a prosecutor Mr. Dewey performed in a spectacular field. It even had its touches of romance. True, showmanship was not his strong point, and his methods were far different from those of the more theatrical type of prosecutor. But partly because of this very difference, and because of the intrinsic melodramatic qualities of many of his cases, he soon became a national figure. Much of the hair-raising literature of the period, as well as the motion pictures, was suggested by the deeds of Dewey in New York. Other cities, depressed and brought to the verge of hopelessness by their own little Tammany Halls, or whatever they were called, saw in Mr. Dewey's effective work in New York an intimation of how they also might achieve some semblance of reform.

Mr. Dewey did not "clean up" New York in the sense that he made it chemically pure. He did not abolish all playing of policy games or all betting in poolrooms; he did not put an end to all prostitution, nor did he put behind bars all the men who live upon that ancient racket. He failed to make many evil men see the light. He improved the city, but if any of his more extravagant supporters try to promote the idea that he brought moral perfection, or anything closely resembling it, to New York, then these admirers are going far out on a limb. For he did nothing of the sort; he never even tried. If old Anthony Comstock or old Dr. Charles Henry Parkhurst, the great reformers of another age, could see New York today, they no doubt would find much to alarm them—and with good reason. On the other hand, if Boss William Marcy Tweed should walk among us once more (not a pretty thought) he would surely be astounded by the change in the direction of decency. It all depends on the viewpoint.

What Mr. Dewey accomplished in his years as a prosecutor may be summed up, and perhaps oversimplified, in these two statements:

1. He demonstrated that it was not necessary for any citizen, any businessman or any householder, to submit to extortion or any form of terrorism. Gangs usually thrive because the victim is afraid to complain. When a prosecutor is complaisant or lazy or corrupt, this fear has a very real and sometimes terrible basis. Mr. Dewey protected his complainants and his witnesses. It was his first task to gain confidence. People learned—and these people might be small shopkeepers or members of labor unions or anybody else—that when they took a case to Dewey's office they were not going to have their heads bashed in the next day.

2. He proved that no criminal-political combination, no matter how strongly entrenched, no matter how encrusted with age and custom, was above the law. He showed that there were ways of getting at these people. No Man Higher Up could claim immunity because of his power or because

of the ostensible respectability of his friends. Was the guilty man esteemed a "good fellow" among the boys? Did he have pious pretensions? Was he a welcome visitor in the homes and offices of the mighty? No matter. If he was a crook, Dewey's relentless machinery of prosecution was set in motion. Sometimes it was slow and heartbreaking work. Many of these men were sent to prison; others, on the political side of the picture, were driven from office; still others walk the streets of New York today, discredited and stripped of influence.

Those were the main accomplishments. They were the sort of thing that appealed to the imagination of the people of that time and place. Some observers whose memories are short, and who may have developed the belittling habit as a convenient pose, have intimated that Dewey's work as prosecutor was little more than a cops-and-robbers game. This is an easy dismissal of a feat which at first seemed so stupendous as to be impossible. The enforcement of the law had reached a shocking state; Mr. Dewey proved that the statutes still had teeth in them.

As to his own qualities, Mr. Dewey demonstrated something else during his years as prosecutor, and that is that he knew how to pick good men and delegate authority. His job was largely one of organization. At one time and another he directed the work of hundreds of men—lawyers, accountants, and detectives for the most part. He appeared in court only in certain important cases when he thought his presence was necessary. He did not personally conduct loud door-smashing raids; he did not procure indictments just for the fun of the thing or for whatever publicity he might have got; he did not tear his hair or bite his nails. He sat usually at his clean desk, a thoroughly businesslike executive in charge of what probably was the most successful and smoothly operating crime-smashing machine every put together in the United States.

Those who saw Mr. Dewey in action as a prosecutor did not need to be told that when he became Governor he would pursue the same vigorous but unflustered methods of doing things. He surrounded himself with good men. He gave them responsibility. He let them work. There were many things about the previous administrations of which he did not approve. He made certain changes promptly, but he waited for other changes until he was sure of his ground. He was the first Republican Governor in twenty years. Those years had seen the administrations of Alfred E. Smith, Franklin D. Roosevelt, and Herbert H. Lehman (not counting the twenty-eight days which Charles Poletti, the Great Pardoner, served after Governor Lehman left office in December, 1942). Mr. Dewey came into office with considerable respect for many of the policies and accomplishments of his Democratic predecessors, although he had made telling attacks upon certain examples of what he called dry rot, inertia, and muddling.

His job, he felt, was to take over the machinery of the state government, complex in many respects but admirable in design, and make it work better. There were certain pressing wartime problems, some of which required special legislation. He saw his program carried through—and with a minimum of bickering. He proved once more that he could cooperate without sacrificing any of the essential principles to which he might be devoted.

An unusual thing about Mr. Dewey, as Governor and politician: He might attack some of his Democratic forerunners as faulty administrators, for tolerating certain corrupt bosses or for being lax in other matters, but he never denounced them as crooks (which they were not) or even as wholly incompetent. Likewise, he did not pretend that the former occupants of the Governor's chair had done everything backwards. He simply argued that he could do it somewhat better, a great deal better in some ways, and set about doing

17

it. It is generally conceded, except, naturally, among the fringe of malcontents who see no good whatever in the man, that he has made an excellent Governor.

The pomposities of politics are as varied as they are amusing. Politics attracts stuffed shirts and even ersatz stuffed shirts. There is one stock question, asked about Abraham Lincoln, Grover Cleveland, Theodore Roosevelt, and Alfred E. Smith, among dozens of others, and propounded with a portentous solemnity, sometimes in a whisper, to wit: "Is he a big man?" So far as the records show, no entirely satisfactory answer to this terrific poser has yet been evolved. A yes or no answer only encourages the inevitable retort: "How do you know?" or the even more withering: "Would you recognize a big man if you saw one?"

In Mr. Dewey's rather special case, the time-honored question is often propounded, with the usual answers, and it is usually coupled with another question: "Has he grown?" That, also, is a tough question. Often it may be merely a part of our political cant and deserves whatever answer will preserve the amenities of civilized conversation; on the other hand, it may be a fairly sensible question, deserving of a serious answer.

Those who have known Mr. Dewey best throughout his public career are quick to say that he has developed steadily, which, it may be assumed, is what is meant by "Has he grown?" The old argument that he was "too young," which carried much weight at one time, has been just about forgotten; at the age of forty-two he can plead guilty to maturity. As for his knowledge of affairs, his friends point out, and very plausibly, that it would be rather remarkable if a highly intelligent young man in his position, whose curiosity is unlimited, who soaks up and digests information quickly, and whose mind is naturally retentive and logical, had stood still in his development for the last five or ten years.

The facts, from which anyone may draw any inference desired, are these: When Mr. Dewey first arrived in New York he knew little about the city; the time would come when no one would know more. Time was when he was far from being expert on the people, the history, and the government of New York State; today few persons, if any, are as well informed. At one time it could have been said that his knowledge of the country was not broad; he has cured that defect, if it was a defect, by many trips, by his acquaintance with leaders in every state, and by his constant habit of study.

This habit of study, the insatiable quest for information, is firmly fixed in Mr. Dewey. At various times over the last several years he has dug deep into finance, taxation, diplomacy, foreign affairs, agriculture, social legislation, and a dozen other subjects. He is not afraid of books, but usually he prefers to talk to men who know what they are talking about. As a result, he is hard to fool.

Like all governors, Mr. Dewey on occasion has to listen to men of large ideas, often exceedingly gaseous in content. One gentleman, heralded as one of the world's deepest thinkers on monetary matters, got in to see him one blustery day last winter. The Governor talked pleasantly for a few minutes, listened patiently, and then a look of discomfort came to his face. He got rid of the visitor as quickly as possible and then said to his secretary, Paul E. Lockwood, "That's no expert. That's a faker."

What does the man believe? First, he believes in courage and honesty, which he practices. On most other issues he has made himself clear enough. Last winter Forrest Davis, the eloquent, bearded journalist, published a magazine article entitled "The Albany Enigma." When Mr. Davis's opulent verbiage was sifted down, however, it became apparent that by "enigma" he meant only that Mr. Dewey was keeping his mouth shut about the presidency, a policy to which he had adhered scrupulously since his election as Governor. Actually Mr. Dewey is no more of an enigma than the multiplication table. Indeed, he seems to be singularly devoid of the psychic disturbances which make many rising statesmen so interesting and so troublesome. He is even, so far as can be determined, innocent of self-hypnosis. Naturally enough, he has attracted certain idolators; when one of them refers to Mr. Dewey ominously as a "man of destiny" the Governor is among the first to wince.

Mr. Dewey believes in the Republican Party and thinks that it can accommodate men of many shades of thought— so-called liberals, middle of the road devotees, and conservatives. He himself is as far removed from the left-wingers as he is from the most standpat Republican of the Rollin Kirby cartoons.

He believes that the form of government under which the American people have grown and struggled is the best yet devised and that within its framework the country can carry on.

He believes that our potentialities of development have by no means reached their limits and that new frontiers, however unpredictable their nature, lie ahead of the people.

He believes that it is better to have a sound government than an amusing one, that it is better to be honest than crooked, that thrift is preferable to extravagance, that facts are necessary even when not beautiful, and that the truth is better than a lie. Far from being obvious, these doctrines, he holds, are actually a bit sensational in this generation.

He also believes in Thomas E. Dewey. As he once asked, when chided for being a young man, "Is that wrong?"

III

THE BEGINNINGS

THOMAS EDMUND DEWEY was born at seven o'clock in the morning of March 24, 1902, over a general store on the edge of the Shiawassee River, a small stream which meanders through the town of Owosso, Michigan. Owosso, which at that time had a population of 8,000, lies about halfway between the busy manufacturing city of Flint and the state capital, Lansing. The town has grown considerably since Dewey's birth; it is a quiet, pleasant place where the people's yards are filled with trees and flowers.

Dewey would have been born at Lansing, where his father was assistant to the State Auditor General, but the parents of his mother, who lived above the red brick store at Owosso, insisted that the event should take place there.

It is well established that as far back as the 1500's the progenitors of Thomas E. Dewey were Huguenots who spelled the name "Douai." Soon after leaving France and settling in England, they changed the spelling to "Duee," which later became "Dewey," a form which has been standard both here and in England for several centuries. This first American Dewey was also named Thomas; he took the Freeman's Oath at Dorchester, Massachusetts, on May 14, 1634. A short time later, probably finding the strait-laced attitudes of his neighbors a bit stifling, he moved to New Hampshire, where he raised a large family. One of his sons, Josiah Dewey, served as a sergeant in King Philip's War, and among Josiah's descendants was the American hero, George Dewey, who served under Farragut in the Civil War and achieved lasting fame when he led his fleet to victory in the Battle of Manila Bay in 1898. Admiral Dewey was the third cousin of George Martin Dewey, the grandfather of the present Thomas Edmund Dewey.

Thomas Edmund Dewey came by the "Thomas" in his name, not from that first American Dewey who came to Dorchester but from his mother's family. She was Anne Thomas and was born in Owosso in July, 1877. She is still alive and vigorous, a woman of wit and high spirits. Her father was Alfred Thomas, who came to the United States from Canada. He was of English descent. He married Augusta Corrigan, of the noted clan of County Cork Corrigans, the daughter of a professor in the University of Dublin who migrated to Canada. Alfred Thomas was one of the pillars of the community of Owosso for many years. He belonged to the Episcopal Church, had the best garden in town, and ran the general store, above which, in a seven-room apartment, he lived with his family. Thomas Edmund Dewey remembers this grandfather as a man of singular gentleness and dignity. Indeed, he was so dignified that, although he was in the merchandising business, he would not allow his name to appear in advertisements.

George Martin Dewey, the paternal grandfather of Thomas Edmund Dewey, was a delegate to the convention held under the trees at Jackson, Michigan, in 1854, where the Republican Party, as we know it today, was formed. All his life he was devoted to politics. He was a good speaker and stood high in the councils of the party. He attended Harvard but was never graduated; in his senior year he went instead to South America with a Harvard scientific expedition. He later settled in Hastings, Michigan, where he founded a newspaper called the *Banner*. He soon started another paper at Niles, and operated both, along with a fraternal organ, the *Michigan Odd Fellow*. Later he sold his

Hastings and Niles papers and moved to Owosso, where he established the *Times*.

Of the six children of George Martin Dewey, one, a daughter, died young. The others were named, in the order of their birth, Henry Bingham, Edmund Otis, George Martin, Jr., Emma Grace, and Mary Hannah. Henry Bingham Dewey was Commissioner of Education for a time in the state of Washington. He later moved to Boston, where he was associated with the publishing firm of Houghton Mifflin. He died in 1931. Edmund Otis Dewey (it was from him that Thomas Edmund Dewey got his middle name) was a Republican county leader and for many years postmaster of Owosso. He died in 1918. Emma Grace Dewey was graduated from Wellesley and became a college teacher; when she was forty-five she decided, rather inexplicably, to become a certified public accountant. She was for a long time an examiner of corporate income-tax returns. It was this determined, able woman who first told Thomas Edmund Dewey, when he was six years old, that he was going to be a lawyer, a prophecy which appeared highly improbable at the time. Mary Hannah Dewey was graduated from the University of Michigan and married Dr. Howard Sprague Reed, who is noted for his work in biology and plant physiology at the University of California.

Thomas Edmund Dewey's father, George Martin Dewey, Jr., was born at Hastings, Michigan, in 1870. He went to West Point, where he had a high standing. In his junior year he was injured in the gymnasium. The injuries, while not particularly serious, made it impossible for him to meet the strict physical requirements of the regular army. He was six feet tall and considered exceptionally good-looking. After leaving West Point he worked a year as a reporter on the *Ledger* in Tacoma, Washington, and then he went back to Owosso and worked on his father's paper, the *Times*. There he met Anne Thomas and they were soon married.

They moved to Lansing, where he had a position in the Auditor General's office; in 1905 he went back to Owosso to take charge of the *Times* and to manage its job printing plant. After his brother Edmund died he became the postmaster at Owosso, a post which he held until his death in 1927.

Thomas Edmund Dewey remembers his early years in Owosso with much fondness. He knew just about everybody in town. He had the run of the newspaper plant and came to like the smell of ink and the noise of the presses. He had a high admiration for his parents. His father, he recalls, never spanked him, but left that occasionally necessary chore to the mother. The family lived on a good street. Life was pleasant and comfortable, even though the annual income of George Martin Dewey, Jr., was only about $1,800. Thomas Edmund Dewey inherited his mother's medium stature and her nose, but his eyes are like his father's, brown of such an intense cast that they may as well be called black.

When he was eleven years old Thomas Edmund Dewey began to exhibit the first faint stirrings of business ambition. He sold *The Saturday Evening Post* and other publications of Cyrus H. K. Curtis. It was not long before he began to show some executive ability; when he was thirteen he had ten boys working as his agents. Then he took on the local distribution of the *Detroit Daily News,* meeting the 4:15 train, splitting the papers among his young assistants and sending them on their routes. Some of the boys who worked for him in those happy times remember him as a rather exacting boss, punctilious in all matters but eminently fair. When he was fifteen he worked several months in a drug store; the life, though it had its social advantages, did not greatly appeal to him.

In the summer of 1918, at the age of sixteen, Thomas Edmund Dewey had his first taste of farm life. It was far from easy, but this experience did give him a feeling for the manifold satisfactions to be found on the soil. He worked for Earl Putnam, a competent farmer who had a place near Ovid, Michigan. He rode rollers, drilled beans, milked cows, hitched and curried horses, fought thistles, hauled barley, herded sheep, and slept on a straw mattress. All his life he has had an appreciation of good food, and to this day he remembers the Putnam table as excellent.

Hardened by the work on the farm, he played on the high-school football team. He was a pretty good player, fast but a bit too light. He took part in the high-school plays, appeared in the minstrel shows of 1918 and 1919, made the debating team, became a lieutenant in the cadet corps, and, in his last year, was editor of the school yearbook *Spic*. In this book the following curious lines appeared under his photograph:

> First in the Council Hall to steer the state
> And ever foremost in a tongue debate.

In the summer of 1919 he went to California. He visited Dr. and Mrs. Reed in Riverside, went fishing off La Jolla, camped in the San Bernardino Mountains and had a fine time generally. That fall he entered the University of Michigan at Ann Arbor. By hard work and a good deal of prudence he had saved $800, and he was able to pay all his expenses the first year. He worked on the *Michigan Daily* (one of the best college papers in the country, then as now). He was a reporter part of the time, and telegraph editor. He was disappointed because his lack of heft prevented him from making the football team. For recreation he played chess and bridge.

It was not long before the talk went around the Ann Arbor campus that young Dewey had an exceptionally good voice, a baritone of which great things might be expected. Soon he was leading the glee club and acting in college plays. He became a member of the musical fraternity Phi

Mu Alpha. William Wheeler, head of the voice department, saw promise in the Dewey voice and urged him to study. He was a soloist in the Ann Arbor Methodist Church; honorarium, $7.50 a Sunday, which was good money in those days.

He devoted his senior year to the study of law at the University of Michigan Law School. He kept up his singing studies under Mr. Wheeler. He played the star role in the annual college opera and won first prize in the Michigan State Singing Contest. This was more like it. His prize entitled him to go to Asheville, North Carolina, and take part in a national singing contest, where he won third prize. He got back to Michigan in time to be soloist at the commencement exercises and to receive the Bachelor of Arts degree.

The summer after graduation he went to Chicago on a scholarship which entitled him to attend, tuition free, the Chicago Musical College, where the New York teacher, Percy Rector Stephens, was conducting classes. Stephens encouraged Dewey still further. Meanwhile, apparently pointed toward two careers at the same time, the young man read law and did odd jobs in the office of Litsinger, Healy and Reid. Leonard Reid, a member of the firm, was the cousin of Dewey's mother.

This Chicago interlude was of the greatest importance in determining the course of Thomas Edmund Dewey's life. One incident was of more than passing seriousness: He met an attractive young woman named Frances Eileen Hutt, a mezzo-soprano from Texas and Oklahoma. The home town opinion had been that Miss Hutt was remarkable both as a person and as a singer; in this opinion young Tom Dewey, after less deliberation than is customary for one who is supposed to have the judicial temperament, concurred. At the time Dewey met her she was acting as secretary and studio manager for Stephens, the teacher. Miss Hutt, though she only half suspected it at the time, was to become Mrs. Thomas E. Dewey.

Miss Hutt was going to New York in the fall. Stephens urged Dewey to come along and continue his musical training. Dewey did not want to abandon his law studies. He had thought of the Harvard Law School; the Columbia University Law School in New York, however, accepted Michigan credits. He had to make a decision, and it was not very difficult. He would go to New York, study law at Columbia, study singing under Stephens, and keep Miss Hutt under strict surveillance, thereby settling three problems with one neat stroke. In 1923 he had been elected national historian of Phi Mu Alpha for a two-year term; for the next two years he edited the fraternity's quarterly national magazine.

What to be—lawyer or singer? The question was not pressing. There was plenty of time, and meanwhile he could pursue both torts and bravuras. He headed for New York. He was young, and the world itself seemed young and peculiarly attractive.

YOUNG MAN IN NEW YORK

THOMAS E. DEWEY arrived in New York in the fall of 1923, a time when the forces of the underworld were just beginning to lay the foundations of their vast illicit combinations. The old gangs, the plug-uglies who formed such groups as the Hudson Dusters, the Gophers, the Whyos and the Dead Rabbits, were generally regarded as extinct, though some of their battle-scarred members were still active. A new type of criminal was arising who was to apply the principles of big business to every form of nefarious activity, from bootlegging to prostitution, from dope peddling to stock swindling.

It seems strange, viewing it now with the wisdom of hindsight, that the public and the press and the political leaders were not more fully aware of what was going on. True, there was talk that the prohibition law was "bringing all law into disrepute," that an era of lawlessness might be developing, and that evil men were making a great deal of money trafficking in alcohol. And yet the widespread nature of this fantastic growth was not generally recognized. Dreadful things were going on, but for the most part they were kept under cover—and New York rocked along conforming in most matters to the philosophy of the late Mayor William J. Gaynor, who observed that the sole responsibility of law-enforcement officials was to preserve "outward order and decency."

Al Smith was Governor, and people were saying that he had a good chance for the Democratic nomination for President the next year; others said William Gibbs McAdoo would get it. John F. Hylan, affectionately called John ("Faithful") Hylan by the Hearst press, was Mayor, but even Tammany was beginning to tire of him; there were rumors that a "New Tammany" was rising and that it would put a better type of man in office. A State Senator and former song writer, James J. Walker, was being discussed as one of the hopes of this "New Tammany." The dashing Herbert Bayard Swope was running the *World*. Frank A. Munsey had not yet sold the *Herald* to the *Tribune*. The town sage was the venerable Chauncey M. Depew, to whom reporters went on dull days for opinions and reminiscence; the old gentleman was still able to make a few graceful remarks when pressed. After-dinner speaking, virtually ruined by prohibition, was practiced only by such die-hards as Patrick Francis Murphy, Wilton Lackaye, Augustus Thomas and Job E. Hedges, and even those talented orators were not very funny at dry banquets. The old Waldorf Astoria stood, seemingly immutable, at Fifth Avenue and 34th Street, but the magnificent bar was no longer the meeting place of the country's wit and brains. Dewey was, much later, to become counsel for the old Waldorf and a member of the board of directors of the new one.

On the surface, the town was pleasant enough. Even prohibition was bearable, what with floods of bathtub gin, frequent cargoes of passable whisky landed in the night, and truckloads of very palatable Canadian ale. A little digging, however, would have turned up some revolting material. Al Capone, not yet famous, was just getting a start in Chicago as a protégé of Johnny Torrio. Owen V. Madden, the great conciliator of gangdom, had convinced himself that violence did not pay and was getting ready to go into the brewery business, making a beverage known as "Madden's Number One"—not a bad beer compared with most of the slop turned out during prohibition. Frankie Uale (Yale) and Arthur Flegenheimer ("Dutch Schultz") and William V. ("Big Bill") Dwyer and Joe Masseria ("Joe the Boss") and a long list of other notables, some brainy and some stupid, were only at the beginning of their varied careers.

With all this, young Thomas Edmund Dewey, fresh from Owosso, Michigan, was little concerned. He was busy with his singing and with his courses at Columbia Law School.

And yet he knew New York fairly well. The place had considerable charm. Down in Greenwich Village, Barney Gallant, the first man in New York to be arrested for violating the prohibition law, was struggling along with a little night club. Mrs. Mori had a fine restaurant on Bleecker Street, and there was Mother Bertolotti's on Third Street. Raymond Orteig ran two of the best dining rooms in town at the Brevoort and the Lafayette. But Dewey had not the time, money or inclination to become one of the Village playboys, or even a diner-out except on special occasions.

When he could find time, he devoted himself assiduously to courting Miss Frances Eileen Hutt, whose own singing career was coming along well. When they went out together they usually attended concerts; they could not afford to be regular theater-goers. For a long succession of Sundays she would go over to Plainfield, New Jersey, to sing in the Plainfield Methodist Church. At the same time Dewey would be singing solos in the Episcopal Church of St. Matthew and St. Timothy, for which he received $15 a week, exactly twice what he had been paid for singing in Ann Arbor. He was definitely getting ahead in the world.

Soon after he entered Columbia Law School, Dewey was invited to join the legal fraternity, Phi Delta Phi. His parents still sent him money throughout his law school studies, but the money he earned by singing also helped out. A faintly amusing, though rather snide, undercover campaign was started against Dewey as late as 1942, when he was running for Governor. This horrendous tale, spread not only by word of mouth but by industrious letter writers, was to the effect that Mr. Dewey, in his early years in New York, had sung in a synagogue. No less! It was never made quite clear just what might have been disreputable about singing a solo in a synagogue, but there was the charge. Well, the charge happens to be true, if it makes any difference. He was a professional. He sang in a great many places, so many that he cannot begin to remember them all. Moreover, the money situation being what it was, it is probable that, for the proper inducement, he would have been delighted to lift up his rich baritone at a convention of the Improved Order of Red Men, a Tammany clambake, the Union League Club, the cops' beefsteak dinner or a flag raising in Union Square.

The time came when he began to neglect his singing. For one thing, he had to have an operation on his throat, which, though not serious, set him to thinking how it might not be wise to depend for a career upon such a tricky thing as a voice. He realized, moreover, that although he might become a passably good singer, or perhaps a little better than that, he could scarcely hope to become a de Reszke. With cool objectivity he faced the truth. During his last year in law school he took no lessons.

His absorption with the law increased. He turned to it with a single-mindedness which ruled out virtually every other interest. He made many friends at Columbia among the faculty and his classmates; most of these friends are his friends today. Another place where he made more friends was the Columbia University Club, on West 43rd Street, where he attended a night seminar on economics. He and some friends organized a moot court of their own. They named it after Judge Burdick, and it became a leading moot court at Columbia. Anything about the law, its science, its growth, and its mysteries, held his rapt attention.

Dewey was graduated from Columbia in 1925 with the degree of Bachelor of Laws. He wanted to practice in New

York, an ambition that for many long decades has been held by many bright young men—perhaps too many, for there is notoriously an overproduction of lawyers in New York. And the lot of a young lawyer in New York is usually exceedingly hard if he expects to eat on his salary. He is, and always has been, in a slightly more difficult position than the young newspaper reporter who has no family bank roll behind him.

Before seeking out an office where he could start work, Dewey decided to see Europe, an idea that verged closely upon the impractical. He had only a little money; his family gave him a little more, but it was not enough to make a grand tour. He and a friend from Michigan, A. Ward Jenks, landed in England at Plymouth. They paid $130 for an old Ford and, with a young Cambridge University man who was employed in the navy yard at Plymouth, they scooted over the roads of rural England. In London they sold the Ford, wandered about the city for a short time, inspecting a few barristers at a respectful distance, and then crossed to France and bought bicycles. They liked bicycling about France well enough, but they found themselves short of money. Luckily they had round-trip tickets and were able to get back to New York. On the trip from New York to Michigan, they actually did not have enough money to buy food. They tightened their belts, and Dewey finally reached Owosso, famished.

The trip to Europe may have been important for what is known as "broadening," but its principal historical value lies in the fact that while abroad Dewey raised a mustache—at first a tentative, unpromising wisp, but soon full-blown and bristly. From that day forward he kept the mustache There is no way of knowing how much it has helped to fix the personality of Tom Dewey in the public consciousness. Certainly it has been of inestimable help to the political cartoonists, who, according to their inclinations, can draw it so as to indicate either a powerful, aggressive, dignified gentleman or a near-buffoon. From the first Dewey liked the mustache and did his own trimming; Miss Hutt approved it also. Today it would be as hard to visualize a mustache-less Dewey as a toothless Theodore Roosevelt.

After a visit with his parents in Owosso, Dewey returned to New York, arriving on September 1, 1925, and started as the most junior of the clerks in the law offices of Larkin, Rathbone and Perry, a tremendous and rather frightening establishment where there were twelve partners and twenty-eight associates. His salary to start was $1,800 a year. His work was the usual work of the fledgling New York lawyer: he did research, hunted out documents, looked up points of law, answered court calls, and served papers. He remained with this firm fourteen months and then joined MacNamara and Seymour, a smaller firm which had only three assistants, one of whom was Dewey. Here he started at $2,000 a year, and in four months was raised to $2,400.

Dewey was beginning to know his way around New York. His Republican father and grandfather had early impressed upon him that Tammany Hall was the great symbol of political wickedness, and he saw little in his observation to change that early opinion. Soon after entering practice he met another young lawyer, Sewell T. Tyng, who was a Republican captain in the Tenth Assembly District. It was Tyng who really started Dewey in practical politics; he set him to running the often menial errands connected with politics—visiting voters, helping with the office work at headquarters, and keeping a watch at the polls on election day. He joined the Young Republican Club, became head of committees, and finally was elected chairman of the board of governors.

With both the law and politics to engage him, Dewey was working hard. When his father died in 1927, he went back to Owosso for two weeks to be with his mother. Returning to the city, he plunged once more into his work, much of which was sheer drudgery. In 1928, his salary was raised to $3,000 a year, enough, he decided, to enable him to marry Miss Hutt. The ceremony was performed in the chapel of St. Thomas Episcopal Church, Fifth Avenue and 53rd Street, on June 16, with the Rev. Dr. Roelif H. Brooks officiating. They went to live in a two-room walk-up apartment on the upper East Side.

In 1929 the Dewey salary was $3,600, and in 1930 he was raised to $4,200 and given a share of the firm's profits, which made his income for that year $6,400. The next year he was making $8,000. Such advancement, while not exactly astonishing and by no means unique, was unusual enough to indicate that the young man definitely was getting ahead.

A turning point in the course of the Dewey career came in December, 1930, when one of the firm's clients, a trust company, was sued by a woman for $20,000. Although it was felt her case was weak, it was nevertheless decided that outside counsel should be called in. Dewey got in touch with George Z. Medalie, a trial lawyer of long experience and great resourcefulness who had served as an Assistant District Attorney of New York County and as Assistant Attorney General of the State. Dewey made an appointment with Medalie for ten o'clock in the morning; they talked until two the following morning. Together they prepared the case, and Dewey sat at the older man's elbow during trial. Medalie lost the case, then won it on appeal—but all that is not relevant here.

The important point is that Dewey had met Medalie and impressed him by his thoroughness, his alert manner, and his logical mind. The trial of the trust-company suit was just drawing to a close when William D. Mitchell, Attorney General of the United States, telephoned Medalie and urged him to accept the appointment as United States Attorney for the Southern District of New York. Medalie accepted, though he realized it meant the interruption of one of the most profitable legal practices in the city.

Medalie asked Dewey to help him recruit able young men for the office staff. He offered Dewey a place and, when Dewey hesitated, offered to make him head of the criminal division. Dewey still hesitated. The pay was not much, and he had had no experience whatever with criminal law; indeed, at that time he felt that criminal law was something entirely outside his plans. His closest friends urged him not to go into the United States Attorney's office.

Medalie finally offered Dewey the post of Chief Assistant, at the head of an office of sixty lawyers, many of them older than he. No one as young as Dewey had ever held the post of Chief Assistant United States Attorney in New York; moreover, he was wholly untried in criminal law. Dewey accepted on March 15, 1931, just nine days before his twenty-ninth birthday. The salary was $7,500 a year. It was a stroke that Medalie never regretted. Today, when asked to put his finger on Dewey's dominant strong point, Medalie says, "Common sense. He was born with it."

MR. MEDALIE FINDS A CHAMPION

"I DROPPED him in the cold water and let him swim out," said George Medalie later in describing what happened during the first few months after Thomas E. Dewey's appointment as Chief Assistant United States Attorney. Medalie was sure of his man, but not even he could know that he had picked a prosecutor who combined the two great gifts—organizing ability and an extraordinary, seemingly natural, sense of how to try cases.

The Southern District of New York, beginning at the lower tip of Manhattan Island and extending northward to include eleven counties, has long been by all odds the most important in the United States. The cases handled by the Federal prosecutor's office are bewildering in their complexity and variety and often astonishing because of the money involved or the prominence of the defendants or the victims. To this district come the graduate sharpers of the world.

Medalie was boss of the prosecutor's office; there was never any doubt of that. But to Dewey fell the task of carrying on the bulk of the executive work. Some dead wood went out. Dewey gathered about him sixty lawyers, most of them young, in whom he had confidence. Out of this group, several stayed with Dewey during his later career, and most of the others have gone on to gain distinction. They were early picked for their abilities and enthusiasm; they were "comers."

In his new job Dewey had to master the structure of the

Federal government. In disposing of criminal cases he worked with those fine man hunters, the postal inspectors, the Treasury Intelligence Unit, the Secret Service, the Federal Bureau of Investigation, the narcotics experts, the customs men, as well as with the New York detectives; in civil cases he had to keep in touch with virtually every department of the Federal government as well as with state and municipal agencies and large corporations. There were cases involving international trade, steamship companies, the President's power to stop the hoarding of gold, the interpretation of treaties, taxes, the tariff, immigration and dozens of other matters.

However, naturally enough, the criminal cases attracted the most attention. Crime, especially when much money is involved, gets the headlines. One of the first cases was that of the Manhattan Electrical Supply Company, listed on the New York Stock Exchange. Its stock was manipulated by a pool operating through forty different brokers; the stock was boosted artificially from $20 a share to $56, then allowed to drop to $6. In this one example of skulduggery, it was estimated that investors lost $10,000,000. Jacob J. Rosenblum, one of the most devastating young prosccutors ever to set foot on Manhattan Island, was the one of Dewey's assistants who tried the case. He sent questionnaires to 1,000 Stock Exchange Houses seeking the accounts maintained by the operators of the crooked pool. This case, known among lawyers as the famous case of *United States v. Brown,* exposed many devices that later were outlawed by the Securities Exchange Act; but even without that act it had been proved that the old laws could get results.

Another case involved something called the National Diversified Corporation, which, with a show of respectable intentions, had been raising money for the production of a motion picture to be called "The Life of the Blessed Virgin." Many good and eminent men were bamboozled into

37

lending their names to this bogus promotion, and stock was sold widely among poor people whose emotions were easily stirred. No picture was ever made; thirteen of the promoters went to prison.

Then there was the case of the dollar-loving policeman, James J. Quinlivan, who, assigned to the vice squad, had a yearly income of $80,000. But he had never paid an income tax. He also had another quaint practice: he would confiscate liquor in a raid and have it taken over to a speakeasy he owned. Quinlivan was sent to prison for three years.

In August, 1931, Dewey had his first brush with that cruel, weak-lunged little killer, Jack ("Legs") Diamond, who survived so many bullets from the guns of assassins that he earned the title of "Clay Pigeon of the Underworld." Dewey supervised the trial, which resulted in a fine of $11,000 and a sentence of four years in prison for Diamond. The charge: operating a still. Diamond's pal, Paul Quattroccio, was fined $5,000 and sentenced to two years.

Patrick Commerford, head of a union of hoisting engineers, had hoisted his own bank account by calling his men off of certain jobs, shaking down the employers, and then letting the men go back to work with no increase in pay. Notwithstanding timid witnesses, who were afraid to tell the truth, Dewey built up his case. Commerford was indicted for evading the payment of income taxes on $63,000, was fined $2,000 and sent to Federal prison. Dewey was to prosecute many another crooked labor leader. On a few such victories he was hailed as one of the best friends of labor; usually, however, the epithet "labor-baiter" was used against him.

A case with rich overtones involved the Tammany Cupid, James J. McCormick, Deputy City Clerk in charge of the marriage-license bureau in the New York Municipal Building. This fabulous buzzard had piled up $222,388 by running his Little Chapel down the Corridor as a racket. He would put the evil eye (known sometimes as "the whammy") on bridegrooms who, in the confusion and elation of the moment, were usually glad enough to slip him $5 or even more. McCormick sneered at $1 tips. He had thirty-four bank accounts. When he heard that he was under investigation, he cleaned up his income tax, which weakened the case against him. Nevertheless Dewey convicted him. McCormick was fined $15,000 and sent to prison for four months— the first man of any importance in Tammany to feel the Dewey bite.

The United States Attorney's office also brought to trial Charles E. Mitchell, banker and one-time millionaire, on charges of having evaded payment of income taxes amounting to $657,152. Medalie conducted the actual prosecution; Dewey had prepared the case. Mitchell was acquitted of the criminal charges; later, Dewey helped obtain a judgment of $1,000,000 for the government against Mitchell.

It was in May, 1931, that Dewey, studying income-tax evasions, began to learn something of the "policy game" or "numbers racket," which was played principally in Harlem and which was protected by criminals and politicians who made it impossible for an honest policeman to get convictions. Dewey went after one of the powerful Harlem "policy kings," one Henry Miro, and proved that Miro's unpaid tax was more than $130,000 on an income taken mostly from poor Negroes. Dewey got on the trail of another "king," Wilfred Brunder, and presented evidence to show that Brunder had, in two years, made profits of $390,721 and $603,363 —and had paid no taxes. Brunder pleaded guilty. He was fined $45,000 and shipped off to the penitentiary.

In the investigation of Henry Miro, Dewey and Medalie stumbled upon a fact that made them wonder: Miro had been sending gifts to James J. Hines, the Tammany district leader who controlled much of Harlem. Why should Miro be sending silk shirts to Jimmy Hines? The end of this trail

would have to wait. At the same time they found enough to
make them suspicious of J. Richard ("Dixie") Davis, "The
Kid Mouthpiece," friend of Hines and counsel for the policy
racket operators. But Davis, like Hines, would have to wait.

Three months after he had gone to the Federal Building,
Dewey assigned four assistants to delve into the careers of
two of the most infamous of American criminals—Arthur
Flegenheimer ("Dutch Schultz") and "Waxey" Gordon, a
former pickpocket whose real name was Irving Wexler.
Work on this case consumed more than two years. The
canny Dutchman, learning that Dewey was scrutinizing his
operations, went into hiding. Schultz, charged with evading
the tax on an income of $481,000, holed up in an apartment
and waited until Dewey had left the United States Attorney's
office before giving himself up. He was then acquitted,
though he did not live long. The guns of his enemies got
him.

Waxey Gordon also heard that Dewey was closing in on
him, but at last he was captured in May, 1933, and held in
$100,000 bail. Meanwhile, in 1932, Medalie had taken time
out to make the campaign for United States Senator and
had been defeated in the Democratic landslide; while he was
making the race, Dewey was Acting United States Attorney.
In November, 1933, Medalie decided it was time to go back
to his private practice. President Roosevelt and Homer S.
Cummings, the new Attorney General, had not yet agreed
upon his successor. The nine Federal judges elected Dewey
to serve as United States Attorney; at thirty-one, he was the
youngest man ever designated to serve in that office in New
York. When Medalie announced his resignation, Dewey had
been conducting the trial of Waxey Gordon for two days.
He left the courtroom long enough to be sworn in, and then
hurried back to continue his masterful presentation of the
evidence against the underworld boss.

The Gordon case, probably more than any other, clinched

Dewey's rising reputation as the nemesis of gangsters. Gordon was an authentic nabob. It was said that, in two years, his illegal enterprises had made him a profit of $4,500,000, on which he had paid a tax of $2,010. He had accounts in 200 banks. To catch him, Dewey and his assistants interviewed more than 1,000 witnesses. They went through stacks of bank records. They followed up the telephone slips on 100,000 telephone calls.

This Gordon was suspected of many crimes. However, as in the cases of so many other gangsters, the income-tax law was the only one that could be invoked with much hope of success. The killings laid to Gordon's mob have been estimated variously, from a mere score or so to a hundred. He himself, more than once, was marked for death. Once he hid in a bed in a hotel in Elizabeth, New Jersey, while gunmen killed two of his associates, after which Waxey slipped down a fire escape.

How bizarre seems the career of the great Waxey, considered today. More than one banker fawned upon him, and connived with him or his agents in the falsification of records. He had three breweries—at least. He owned two hotels on Broadway. He ran a night club. He backed theatrical productions—sometimes he even made a little money on them—and it was common talk in the theatrical district at the time that more than one show girl got her chance in a Gordon-backed show because she was the friend of one of Gordon's mobsters.

This dark, pudgy, unimpressive but generous man had come up from nothing, but he had brains, of a sort. And, like other high-class thugs, he yearned for the finer things of life. He lived in a ten-room apartment on West End Avenue. He wanted his children to have the best, so he sent them to expensive private schools. When winter came to Manhattan, Waxey went to Florida. He had a library that had cost him $4,000. It was impressive to see, but no one had ever read any of the books. Whatever else may have been said against Waxey, he was no pedantic bookworm.

Nailing down a strong case against Gordon long seemed impossible. The aged and gentle District Attorney of New York County, a Tammany Sachem named Thomas C. T. Crain (a pious man, part of whose income came from the ownership of a burlesque house), had made a few characteristically fumbling motions in Waxey's direction, but he quit the trail. He couldn't find witnesses, he said. Witnesses often were very quiet in those days, and sometimes they died suddenly.

Dewey brought droves of witnesses before the Federal Grand Jury. He protected them all. When one refused to tell of transactions with Waxey, he was sent to prison for contempt. The backbone of Dewey's case, however, was the bank account—the witness that is beyond all intimidation. With the aid of Treasury Department men and his own expert accountants, together with handwriting experts, Dewey gradually and with infinite care built up a picture of the structure of the Gordon empire.

But, besides the figures, there were a few living witnesses, and some of them were brave. There was, for example, the waitress, Helen Delbeck, who worked in a lunchroom near one of Gordon's garages and who was of value in tracing beer trucks. Some of the insiders in the Gordon organization "broke" and came into court for the trial; Gordon had not been expecting them.

The Gordon case had enormous complications. The financial maze was beyond the abilities of the ordinary layman to comprehend. Dewey prepared a large chart on which were shown the links between Gordon and his many enterprises; here were traced bank transactions, telephone calls, and the entire setup. This scheme, making a case so graphic that any juror can at least get the gist of it, was used by Dewey many times in later prosecutions.

Complex though the case may have been, the jury deliberated only fifty-one minutes before bringing in a verdict of guilty. Waxey was fined $80,000 and sentenced to prison for ten years. He was one of the biggest of all the mushroom financiers who came along during the prohibition era. His conviction in the fall of 1933 came within just five days of the repeal of prohibition; he toppled while legitimate liquor came back. Today Gordon is out of the Federal prison. He lives a furtive life. The New York police are under orders always to pick him up on sight as a vagrant, which they do with pleasure. The twilight of an ex-Big Shot can be dismal indeed.

The conviction of Gordon made a deep impression. From the bench, Judge Frank J. Coleman said, "It is my firm conviction that never in this court or any other has such fine work been done for the government. If ever again I hear the criticism that there are no longer enthusiastic and able young men in the government service, I shall refer the speaker to this case."

Dewey issued a warning: "If any witness in this case is ever touched by reason of his testimony, the Federal government will never stop until the responsible parties are punished to the full extent of the law."

There was one of Dewey's basic tenets, the reason for much of his success—the protection of witnesses. After the verdict Dewey, though undoubtedly delighted with his own part in the prosecution, issued this statement, which is similar in spirit to statements he has made many times since:

"This case could not have been presented or won without the brilliant and faithful work, for days and nights and on Sundays during several months, of Assistant United States Attorneys J. H. Terry, G. S. Tarbell, Jr., Barent Ten Eyck, Nicholas Rogers, Jacob Grumet, and the special agent in charge of the intelligence unit of the Treasury Department and his remarkable staff."

Dewey had held the office of United States Attorney five weeks when President Roosevelt and Attorney General Cummings decided upon a Democrat, Martin Conboy, for the office. Conboy, long prominent in the Democratic organization in New York, had served as counsel to Governor Roosevelt in the trial of Mayor James J. Walker at Albany— the trial at which the squirming Walker made such an unimpressive showing that even his most steadfast admirers were downhearted. Conboy was sworn in on December 27, 1933. The oath was administered by Judge Martin T. Manton, one of the outstanding whited sepulchers of all time. For many years newspapermen and a few lawyers had known that something was wrong with Judge Manton, but the full extent of his infamy was not brought to light until 1939— and Dewey made the exposure. This money-mad judge, who was not above selling decisions, dishonored the bench, his innocent friends, and his church, and went from his high place to a prison cell. He snarled as he went, for, although he could make gracious gestures when it served his purpose, his ill temper showed itself in his hour of disgrace.

Dewey went back to private practice, opening a law office in the Equitable Building, 120 Broadway. So far as he or anyone else could discern at the time, he had finished with public service. He had proved himself, and made a reputation for being both sound and brilliant. The clients, he assumed, would be coming in.

44

SPECIAL PROSECUTOR

---

*"A racketeer is a man who preys on so-called legitimate busi-
ness."—From the sayings of Owney Madden, philosopher and
ex-racketeer, now retired.*

*" 'Racketeering' is a much-abused and overworked word.
It should be limited to the systematic extortion of money
through intimidation by an organization conducted for that
purpose. Only in the cruder and more primitive rackets are
violence and threats still necessary or the shakedown plain
and brazen. Legal means are customarily used to achieve illegal objectives; and illegal means are used to achieve otherwise legal objectives. Every large racket is based upon the
successful intimidation of dozens or hundreds of separate
businessmen."—From a speech by Thomas E. Dewey, 1935.*

Clients did come to Mr. Dewey. Life was easier. He could
live better. He could play more. He was making money. A
profitable and even distinguished career seemed to be opening up.

But at this time the tom-toms were beginning to beat.
It was not enough that Jimmy Walker, who had the gifts of
the angels and the weaknesses of the least of his human
brethren, was no longer Mayor. There came the stirrings of
that odd phenomenon—something resembling a civic consciousness in the City of New York. New York for generations has been notorious for its lack of civic pride. Tammany thought it knew its people and knew how the city

lived and what the city wanted. "Honest graft" was accepted as reasonable and tolerable.

Dewey attended to his practice, but he had other matters dumped into his lap. There was the curious and sordid case of Harold L. Kuntsler, a judge of the New York City Municipal Court, who was weak in money matters. The New York Bar Association had finally entertained charges against Kuntsler. Their case was not regarded as complete. Dewey was called in and served as counsel to the Bar Association, without compensation. In April, 1934, Dewey was ready for trial; he petitioned the Appellate Division to remove Kuntsler, charging him with five offenses. Two months later the trial began. Dewey played his ace: documents that forced Kuntsler to admit that in three years he had laid aside $126,000 more than his salary as a judge. The blustering Kuntsler put up an argument, but eventually he resigned on the conventional grounds that his "usefulness had been impaired" by the attacks upon him. Exit Kuntsler.

Other public matters claimed Dewey's attention. Together with Edward S. Greenbaum, he was appointed a Special Assistant Attorney General to get a judgment against Charles E. Mitchell, the banker. He had to do his part to combat the appeal of Waxey Gordon, for the old racketeer was still fighting his conviction. Meanwhile he had been made chairman of the Committee on Criminal Courts, Law and Procedure of the New York City Bar Association. He recommended many reforms designed to make the enforcement of the law speedier, getting rid of much litigiosity and innumerable delays. One suggestion, if carried out, would have forbidden lawyers to work for rackets. On most of his ideas he got nowhere.

But back to the tom-toms of the good conscience. The District Attorney of New York County was William Copeland Dodge, a former city magistrate who was decidedly not in the glorious tradition of dragon slayers. The whisper was true (though not proved until much later) that he was the political creature of James J. Hines, the toughest of the Tammany bosses. The ancient "policy racket" was up for investigation before a grand jury. Dodge assigned the greenest member of his staff, Lyon Boston, to present the evidence. The grand jury was disgusted. Its foreman, an upright citizen named Lee Thompson Smith, led the revolt against Dodge and all his works. Following Smith's leadership, the grand jury on May 13, 1935, excluded Dodge and his assistants from its deliberations and demanded a new prosecutor.

Dodge seemed amenable to the idea. The jury suggested six names; the name of Thomas E. Dewey was at the head of the list. Dodge offered instead to appoint a former associate of Max D. Steuer, one of the brainiest of Tammany lawyers. The grand jury said no. Clarence J. Shearn, president of the Bar Association, suggested Dewey amid a deep silence. The grand jury appealed to Governor Herbert H. Lehman to assign a special prosecutor. The fog was getting thick. On June 24, Governor Lehman suggested to Dodge that he appoint, as special assistant, any one of four Republicans: George Z. Medalie, Charles Evans Hughes, Jr., Thomas D. Thacher, and Charles H. Tuttle. These men declined the appointment and then, on Medalie's suggestion, recommended that Dewey be appointed. Lehman argued against the idea, saying that Dewey was not well enough known. Medalie, who knew his Dewey, retorted that soon, if appointed, Dewey would be one of the best known men in America. The Governor named Dewey as Special Prosecutor. As a matter of pure technicality, Dodge was Dewey's superior, but the Governor had made it clear that Dewey was to have a free hand.

Meanwhile J. Richard Davis, the shyster, had gone to Dodge and warned him against Dewey. Word had got around New York that Dewey was not a man to trifle with. District Attorney Dodge, thus pushed into a corner, politely invited Dewey to a conference and formally offered him the post of special rackets prosecutor. Dewey took the job. He took it understanding perfectly that it was an up-hill job. For police he would have to look to that crotchety little man, Mayor Fiorello H. La Guardia; for funds he must depend upon a Board of Estimate made up principally of Democrats.

Going the whole way to give the Republicans a chance to put up or shut up, Governor Lehman appointed as the presiding judge of a special term of the Supreme Court a man belonging to one of this country's finest families, "The Fighting McCooks." This man was Justice Philip J. McCook of the New York State Supreme Court, who served in the Spanish-American War and the First World War and whose probity and courage were above any hint of suspicion. The jesters might call McCook "Fighting Phil" and Dewey "The Boy Scout." But soon there was to be no more joking. An atmosphere of doom seemed to hang over the underworld; little Don Skene, the old boxing writer, who had a large acquaintance in strange social circles, remarked that "every time one of the mugs sees a stocky gent with a mustache he goes up and says, 'Yes, Mr. Dewey, I'll come along quietly.'" Damon Runyon also had a story of a poor sap with a mustache, who merely wanted to borrow a dollar, and who was mistaken for Dewey by a man about town; the touchee said, "Guilty."

A glance at Dewey's methods in launching his great investigation of New York rackets will indicate the man's temper and method. He was exceedingly careful of every person on the jury panel. He went to Washington and got the promise of aid from the Treasury Department. He conferred with Lewis J. Valentine, the almost painfully honest Commissioner of the New York Police Department, and from him obtained a group of able men, including Deputy Inspector John A. Lyons, Captain Bernard A. Dowd and

Sergeant William J. Grafeneker. He chose his helpers—
Sewell T. Tyng, who had first introduced him to politics in
New York; Frank S. Hogan, who, years later, was to become
District Attorney; Paul E. Lockwood, the amiable giant from
Brooklyn; William B. Herlands, one of the most careful
investigators ever heard of; A. J. Goodrich, the expert ac-
countant who had worked with him on the Kuntsler case;
Barent Ten Eyck, who had been associated with him in the
United States Attorney's office; Mrs. Eunice H. Carter, a
Negro woman lawyer; Murray Gurfein, a young man with
a gift for getting at the truth. And there were many others.

Dewey wanted a separate setup. He obtained space on the
fourteenth floor of the Woolworth Building, a place of
many entrances, and put a day and night guard about the
building. On this fourteenth floor were many waiting rooms.
The cabinets had special locks. The telephone cable could
not be tapped. Finally he felt that the machine was ready.
Then, before one malefactor had been caught, or even questioned, he made a radio speech to the people of New York,
the city that may or may not have a conscience.

He told the people that he did not expect to be a talking
prosecutor, but he wanted to define what he had in mind.
"If this were merely an attempt to suppress ordinary prostitution, gambling and lottery games," he said, "I think I am
safe in saying that the Governor would not have ordered it
and I know I would not have undertaken it. . . ." He promised that the investigation would deal only with vice where
it existed in organized form. He charged that there was
scarcely a business in New York that did not somehow pay
tribute to the underworld. He alluded to the associations, set
up as "corporations" with bylaws and other flummery, which
posed as "protectors" of businessmen. To labor he said:

"The underworld plays no favorites. Organized labor has
been one of its most recent and most tragic victims. Some
originally honest and sound labor unions have been slowly

but surely infected with the virus of organized crime. Today, certain corrupted leaders operate as extortionists upon both industry and the members of their own unions. Just as surely as public office is a public trust, so labor leadership is a public trust."

He appealed to the public to come to his office with information. He promised secrecy; he promised protection to complainants. He warned against rumors. He said he and his staff hoped to "vanish" from the public eye until cases were ready. It was a straightforward plea, sensible and eloquent. And what happened? Hundreds of eccentrics visited the Woolworth Building; that was about all. But Dewey and his staff were not greatly disappointed. They knew, in a general way, where their quarry was. They went on studying, adding a touch here and there, and making their organization perfect. Without publicity, they also were bringing in reluctant witnesses through the side doors.

It was a correct assumption that Dewey would pick up the trail of Dutch Schultz. The threads of the Dutchman's life went far back; he had left his tracks, faint at times, in many of the more profitable rackets. But the executioners of the underworld, probably from the Unione Siciliano, cheated Dewey; they found Schultz in a restaurant in Newark, New Jersey, on the night of October 23, 1935, and filled his body full of slugs. Apparently Schultz and his whole gang had been marked for assassination. The brave "Lulu" Rosencrantz, a Schultz gunman; Abe Landau, another able pistol shot; and "Abadaba" Berman, Schultz's financial wizard, were killed in the restaurant at the time Schultz was shot; at about the same time Martin Krompier, another Schultz gangster, was shot in a New York barber shop, though he survived his wounds. In the sudden wave of killings many other of Schultz's friends disappeared.

Before he died, in delirium, Schultz seemed to be trying to talk, and out of his ramblings may be pieced together a crazy pattern of fear. But none of it made a great deal of sense. The oddest thing the Dutchman said in his ravings was:

"A boy has never wept nor dashed a thousand kim."

Gibberish? Probably, but it was poetry too. For years after the Dutchman's death, detectives and students of literature tried to find out if he had quoted the line from some obscure work, or whether he had made it up, and, if so, what it could have meant. It remains a mystery.

Even after his death Schultz was important to Dewey, who continued to pick up clues here and there linking Schultz with higher-ups. On the broad front of his inquiry, Dewey took his time. He put a few stubborn witnesses in jail; most of them talked, and some turned over valuable records. Then Dewey surprised everybody by rounding up, not gangsters, but a group of loan sharks. He caught thirty-seven Shylocks who were held on thirty-seven indictments in bail totaling $174,500. These harpies had been arrested by fifteen squads of policemen, pulled out of the ratholes where for years they had sucked in the savings of people in acute distress. Dewey obtained thirty-six convictions.

The machine was beginning to hum. While several collateral lines of inquiry were proceeding, Dewey was diverted into a field he had hesitated to touch—the organized prostitution racket. Mrs. Carter and Murray Gurfein found the early tips, and Dewey told them to go ahead. It was established that prostitution had been caught up into one close-knit combination. The "bookers" (the agents who routed the girls from one house to another) were brought under control. They had to deal with Joe Levine, Benny Spiller, and Ralph Liguori, each of whom was distinguished by ability as either a strong-arm man or a slick collector of money. Over these was Jimmy Frederico, a sort of general manager; and over him were Tommy Pennochio ("The Bull") and Abie Wahrman. Above these was a director,

"Little Davie" Betillo. The rest of the staff consisted of about twenty-five men, including collectors, bondsmen, and two lawyers. The girls themselves were swindled outrageously.

On the last night of January, 1936, Dewey's raiders struck. From many different parts of the city the police rounded up not only the girls but the bosses and took them to the Woolworth Building. Odd names some of them had: Jennie the Factory, Sadie the Chink, Frisco Jean, Nigger Ruth, and Gashouse Lil. Justice McCook set bail for the madams and girls at $10,000 each as material witnesses: they were put in the House of Detention, treated decently and given medical service, which many of them needed. Some of them finally began to talk to Dewey's men. Some of the others talked also, among them Dave Marcus, a booker, who happened to mention the name "Charlie."

All along the investigators had felt that, although they had a fairly accurate picture of the prostitution racket's setup, there was something missing. Who was the ultimate power, the big man at the top? The name "Charlie" supplied the answer.

This "Charlie" was the notorious "Lucky" Luciano (real name, Lucania). He was supposed to be the head of the Unione Siciliano in the East. He was known at the race tracks and in the gambling houses. He had never figured much in the newspapers. Once, in October, 1929, he was kidnaped in Manhattan and taken for a ride to the woods of Staten Island, where he was tortured and threatened, beaten up, and left in a ditch. Legs Diamond was supposed to have engineered this ride. But Lucky never talked about it when he came back. On the lower East Side he was generally known simply as "Lucky"; in politer circles uptown he sometimes went under the name of "Charles Lane." He was registered at the Waldorf Astoria as "Charles Ross" and lived in sybaritic ease on the twenty-ninth floor.

As soon as Dewey had the evidence he needed, he sent two detectives to Hot Springs, Arkansas, a favorite meeting place for the more prominent racketeers. They arrested Luciano in front of a gambling house. But Luciano was hard to hold. He came very near escaping to Mexico. However, after much delicate legal hocus pocus, he was brought back to New York. In asking high bail, Dewey said to Justice McCook:

"His business is far-flung, and brings in, to my certain knowledge, a colossal revenue. He is one of the largest beneficiaries of the policy racket. His henchmen operate a number of industrial rackets as well as drug importing and bookmaking. He is one of the biggest illegal importers of drugs in the country. He is head of a large syndicate with sources and amounts of income far in excess of any bail you might set."

The court fixed Luciano's bail at $350,000. He and his men were now held in a total bail of $1,175,000. Now a word about the so-called "joinder indictment," or "Dewey Law," which had been passed by the Legislature. This law authorized the joinder of connected or similar offenses in one single indictment; it is essentially the same scheme that had been used in the Federal courts for many years. In arguing for this law, Dewey said:

"Today crime is syndicated and organized. A new type of criminal exists who leaves to his hirelings and front men the actual offenses and rarely commits an overt act himself. The only way in which the major criminal can be punished is by connecting to him those various layers of subordinates and the related but separate crimes on his behalf.

"As the law now stands, there is a procedural strait jacket which prohibits the trial of these offenders together (except in conspiracy, which is a mere misdemeanor), though they all coordinate the acts of the master through his subordinates. Although the organization is conceived and functions to prey upon hundreds of men in the same states, each of its offenses must be tried separately before a separate court and a separate jury."

Dewey's joinder law was attacked by many lawyers, although it was upheld by the State Court of Appeals. Objections to this law, indeed, have been so twisted that many well-meaning persons even today apparently are convinced that, because of it, in some strange way, Dewey has made himself "the foe of civil liberties."

The trial of Luciano and his satraps started May 11, 1936. Three "bookers" had pleaded guilty, leaving "The Boss" and nine other defendants. Anticipating the arguments of the defense, Dewey said to the jury:

"Frankly, my witnesses are prostitutes, madams, heels, pimps, and ex-convicts. Many of them have been in jail. Others are about to go to jail. Some were told that they would be prosecuted if they did not tell the truth. I wish to call to your attention that these are the only witnesses we could possibly have brought here. We can't get bishops to testify in a case involving prostitution. And this combination was not run under arc lights in Madison Square Garden. We have to use the testimony of bad men to convict other bad men."

Dewey presented his case, a long list of frowsy witnesses. Most of them stood up well enough under cross-examination. One witness deserves special mention: the woman called Cokey Flo. She had been the sweetheart of Jimmy Frederico, and when Jimmy was caught in the big raid she went to his lawyer and offered help. The lawyer snubbed her, and soon after Cokey Flo was picked up for soliciting. Brooding in the House of Detention, she talked with some of the other girls, who told her that Dewey and his men were "on the level." She did not like Luciano; she blamed Tommy the Bull for starting her on the dope habit. She offered to help. Dewey put her on the stand. Sick, frail, not too bright, she was still a wonderful witness. She tied Luciano to the prostitution business, and nine hours of cross-examination failed to damage her story.

In this trial Luciano and his counsel made a grave mistake. They tried to affirm that Luciano was wholly unacquainted with any of the mob except Little Davie Betillo. A chambermaid from the Waldorf Astoria and then six other members of the hotel staff (people who made their money decently) went on the stand to testify that Luciano had been visited by these very men whom he had tried to call strangers.

The picture of Luciano that his lawyers tried to paint was of a rather romantic fellow, a man about town, a generous spender—but the boss of a prostitution racket, never! Luciano took the stand with apparently complete assurance. He swore he had never taken a cent from prostitution. He said he was a successful gambler. He admitted that when he was eighteen years old he had peddled narcotics. Dewey took him in hand and brought up the fact that, long before, Luciano had betrayed another dope peddler in order to save himself. "You were a stool pigeon then," observed Mr. Dewey.

Dewey recalled Luciano's delightful record of brushes with the police. The witness confessed that he had obtained pistol permits under false pretenses. He said he had carried two pistols, a shotgun, and forty-five rounds of ammunition in an automobile "to shoot birds with."

"What kind of birds?" asked Dewey.

"Peasants," said Luciano, who was rattled, though he may not have been above taking a pot shot at a peasant, at that.

"Shooting pheasants? In July? With a pistol?" asked Dewey. The courtroom smiled, and Luciano was uncomfortable. Luciano continued to deny his own intimates; Dewey produced records of telephone calls to such gangsters as Louis Buchalter (the great Lepke) and Ciro Terranova, once the "Artichoke King." Luciano's showing on the stand, taking it all in all, was hardly successful.

There was much speechmaking to the jury. The defense charged that Dewey, by giving immunity to his witnesses, had "legalized prostitution." Dewey admitted that he had not intended to stop all immorality; he was gunning for Luciano and his henchmen. He called Luciano "the greatest gangster in America." Justice McCook's charge to the jury lasted two hours. He sent the jury out at 9:30 on the stifling evening of June 6, 1936, a Saturday. It was almost dawn on Sunday morning when the jury reported back. It had found Luciano guilty on sixty-one counts. His codefendants likewise were found guilty.

The three "bookers" who had pleaded guilty were sentenced to from two to four years each. Another of these, Jack Eller, who had stood trial, was sentenced to from four to eight years; Ralph Liguori, seven and a half to fifteen; Jimmy Frederico and Tommy the Bull, twenty-five years each; and Betillo, twenty-five to forty. Justice McCook, in sentencing Luciano to from thirty to fifty years, remarked, "I am not here to reproach you, but, since there appears no excuse for your conduct or hope for your rehabilitation, to administer adequate punishment."

Mayor La Guardia, who over the years has been alternately enthusiastic and critical when Thomas E. Dewey was concerned, was jubilant. He remarked that Luciano could never have run his rackets without the knowledge of "some of the very people entrusted with law enforcement." "I recommend," said the Little Flower, "that at least six public officials commit hara-kiri." The fine old custom of hara-kiri, however, is one that has somehow never taken hold in New York.

In the midst of the general praise of Dewey, certain persons, notably lawyers, raised a sour note. They did not like the joinder indictments. They even argued that, since prostitution was not Luciano's main racket, so far as they could determine, it was wrong to take such an advantage of him. These criticisms persist today in some quarters. Others, on the moralistic side, were angry because Dewey had freed a horde of prostitutes, many of whom were well heeled with their accumulated witness fees.

The convictions of Luciano and his gang were affirmed on appeal. Martin Conboy, who had left the United States Attorney's office, used all his skill, the quality of which was always open to debate, but the Court of Appeals not only upheld the convictions but approved the joinder law with the observation that "we must not be so backward as to make our legal procedure a hindrance instead of a furtherance to justice." Another lawyer, Moses Polakoff, tried an appeal to the Supreme Court of the United States. Without success. Lucky Luciano, after a brief time at Sing Sing, was taken to Clinton Prison at Dannemora and put to work in the laundry.

On June 30 the special grand jury resigned in order that its members might resume their private affairs. These men recommended that two grand juries be appointed to carry on the heavy work; in July, Governor Lehman ordered that two special grand juries be impaneled. He continued Justice McCook with one of the juries. To the other he appointed Justice Ferdinand Pecora of the New York Supreme Court, a Democrat with long experience in investigations and prosecutions. The quest of the rackets was resumed at double speed.

VII

THE LIBERATION OF A CITY

THE case of the sinister Lucky Luciano, notwithstanding its significance in the history of crime prosecution and its gaudy appeal to newspaper readers, was actually something of a side issue, a bypath into which Dewey had been diverted by evidence that was largely unexpected. Dewey's most noteworthy accomplishment as Special Prosecutor was his tracking down for the first time of the great, sprawling industrial rackets in their various patterns—and stopping them. While Luciano was in the headlines, Dewey's men were pushing their inquiries along other channels.

Dewey subpoenaed their records from unwilling and terrorized employers. He tried, sometimes with success, to put a little backbone into businessmen, some of whom were not merely spineless but corrupt in the bargain. He pried into more than a dozen rackets. He saved the people millions, for the rackets touched the pocketbooks of virtually every citizen, whether the citizen knew it or not. He gave labor unions that had become the captives of terrorists and thieves a chance to be honest—and not all of them, so perverse is human nature, thanked him for their freedom. The great garment industry was only one victim of the rackets; it was being milked of $1,000,000 a year by one group. Dewey's men seized the records of this group and carried them off in a truck and five taxicabs. This was only the beginning of the tedious campaign to unhorse two monstrous figures, two smooth · ex-hoodlums known as Lepke and Gurrah, the gorilla boys. "Lepke" is a diminutive for Louis, and this man's full name was Louis Buchalter. He came of a decent but poor East Side family, the other members of which have lived honorable lives. Lepke was meek, almost apologetic in manner, but he was no man to trifle with. He is gone now, having been put to death in the electric chair at Sing Sing in the spring of 1944 for having instigated a murder in Brooklyn back in 1936. His partner, the one called Gurrah, was a coarse and brutal roughneck, two years older than Lepke. The name Gurrah was a contraction of his angry, slurred command, "Get out of here!" Gurrah, in 1944, is in prison, and will doubtless remain there for the rest of his life. Their trail was slimy and devious.

Back in the 1920's Lepke and Gurrah were free-lance muscle men, sluggers who would sell their services to the highest bidder. Later, as they grew more powerful, they took over whole industries; they would even force a legitimate businessman to take them in as partners. Among the enterprises they controlled were the flour-trucking and baking industries.

On the night of September 13, 1935, a group of men, most of them connected with the Flour Truckmen's Association, sat in a room just off the main dining room of Garfein's Restaurant, down at the lower end of Avenue A. Among these men were Meyer Luckman, who soon afterward killed his own brother-in-law, Sam Drukman, in Brooklyn; and Max Silverman, a partner of Lepke and Gurrah. A chair had been left vacant for William Snyder, president of Local 138 of the Flour and Bakery Drivers' Union. Snyder came in. He was greeted by "Wolfie" Goldis, vice-president of the union. There had been some feeling against Snyder because of his slowness in following orders. At about ten o'clock a man came in and shot Billy Snyder in the back, Snyder turned, and was shot again. The killer got away. Billy Snyder was taken to a hospital by Max Silverman. He lived two days. The police traced the killer's getaway car, which had been rented by a young man named Tratner, and Tratner told the police that Morris Goldis, brother of Wolfie, had given him the money for the rental. Two witnesses told the police that the picture of Morris Goldis, taken from police files, was the man who had walked out of the room at Garfein's, pistol in hand, and got away. But when they saw Morris Goldis face to face they refused to identify him. In Homicide Court, Tratner also changed his tune, and Morris Goldis went free. Wolfie Goldis was elected president of the union, taking the place of the slain Billy Snyder; he put his brother Morris on the pay roll.

The temporary freedom of Morris Goldis and Tratner had been obtained by a lawyer, Charles A. Schneider, who was an Assistant State Attorney General. He received a $2,000 fee. Schneider was a power in the Eighth Assembly District. Dewey later blasted him into oblivion.

Dewey kept an eye on the strange murder of Billy Snyder. Barent Ten Eyck, one of Dewey's assistants, came across the name of Max Silverman and recognized him as one of the lieutenants of Lepke and Gurrah, which indicated a racket killing. Soon it was established that the gorillas had taken over the flour-trucking union. Employers submitted to a shakedown of more than $1,000,000. Dewey seized the books of the Flour Truckmen's Association. Max Silverman knew something was in the wind. He left his home at Sea Gate and vanished. Long afterward he was caught by Dewey's chief investigator, a slim young man hunter, in California and brought back to New York.

The crushing of the mob took a long time. But with most of the mobsters either in custody or in hiding, the flour-trucking and baking industries were able to operate without terrorism. The prosecutions of the mobsters—sometimes for extortion, and sometimes for homicide, were long delayed. Max Rubin, an employee of Lepke and Gurrah, turned state's evidence; he was waylaid and shot through the head after he had refused police protection, the only one of Dewey's witnesses ever to suffer harm. He recovered, to his own surprise, and took the stand against the mobsters. In April, 1940, in the Court of General Sessions, Lepke was sentenced to from thirty years to life for extortion. The sentence meant little, for he was already serving a sentence for violating the Federal narcotics laws—and then, while serving that sentence, the Brooklyn prosecutor got him for murder and sent him to the chair. Wolfie and Morris Goldis pleaded guilty to first-degree manslaughter and told of their part in the flour racket. They were sent to prison. Max Silverman, who suffered from both diabetes and heart disease, was sentenced to from thirty years to life. The killing in Garfein's had been cleared up, and the racket broken.

Then there was the restaurant racket, the brains of which were Dutch Schultz and Jules Martin. Martin's real name was Mogilewsky. He was a big plug-ugly and dreamed of going back to Russia sometime as Commissar of Transportation. His pals called him "Julie" and "Commissar." He had a little restaurant on West 46th Street where mobsters gathered. He and Schultz; two of his employees, Aladar Retek, a former officer in the Imperial Army of Austria; Charles Baum; and a Montenegrin waiter named Paul N. Coulcher, got the idea of organizing a restaurant racket. They took over Local 16 of the Waiters' Union and Local 302 of the cafeteria workers, which covered Manhattan above Fourteenth Street. Jules Martin, with two of his right-hand men, Sam Krantz and Louis Beitcher, a collector, went to work. They rooked the waiters and they shook down the restaurant keepers. Encountering an argument, they would settle it with strikes or stench bombs. One of the most dexterous of the bomb tossers was one "Mully" Kramer, chauffeur for Krantz.

The mob tried to extend its control below Fourteenth

Street, where, to their astonishment, they encountered Benjamin Gottesman, head of Local 1 of the Waiters' Union—an unterrified gentleman whose like they had never seen before. Benny wouldn't scare and he could not be bribed. He went to Thomas E. Dewey, and furnished information which helped in the case against the racketeers.

Meanwhile Schultz and Martin organized the Metropolitan Restaurant and Cafeteria Association and charged an initiation fee of $250, with dues of $5 a week. One chain-restaurant owner was cowed into joining and paying $45,000. The association had offices at 1819 Broadway; Philip Grossel, a former silk salesman, was in charge of the headquarters, and Harry Vogelstein and Abraham Cohen attended to legal details. Beautiful plaques, testifying to membership in the association, appeared in the fronts of restaurants. Jack Dempsey, the old mauler, joined on behalf of his restaurant and had his picture taken signing up—a good piece of promotion for the racketeers.

These membership plaques were manufactured at a plant operated by Julie Martin at Elkhart, Indiana, where the dreaming "Commissar" turned junk into gadgets. The ambitious Julie was losing money, and Dutch Schultz was tired of advancing him cash. Schultz summoned him to Troy, New York, accused him of stealing, and then killed him by shooting him in the mouth. J. Richard ("Dixie") Davis later said he was near by at the time of this killing. Martin's body was found in the snow. A visit to the headquarters at 1819 Broadway was revealing. Among Martin's papers was a notation—"Call up Jimmy Hines."

William B. Herlands, a Dewey assistant, found enough evidence to tie up virtually all the leaders of the racket. The entire scheme became clear. The mob was running both the unions and the restaurants. One of the mob, the sly Montenegrin waiter Coulcher, had become quite a personage. He talked to NRA hearings in Washington, was appointed to an NRA board, and was guest of honor at dinners where he was applauded as a friend of labor.

After fourteen months of the most difficult work, Dewey obtained indictments against thirteen men—two lawyers, six labor leaders, and five gangsters. Schultz and Martin, both dead by this time, were named as coconspirators, along with two dead labor leaders. Again Dewey was denounced in some quarters as an enemy of labor. The Communist *Daily Worker* screamed about an "anti-union drive."

Louis Beitcher, the collector, was captured. He confessed. Another defendant, Max Pincus, a vice-president of the Waiters' Union, jumped to his death from a tall building. Most of the prosecution, which started in January, 1937, was conducted by William B. Herlands, who was assisted by Milton Schilback and Charles D. Breitel. One of the questions that Dewey asked the members of the jury panel was the simple but startling one, "Do you know James J. Hines?"

But the time of Jimmy Hines had not yet come. The trial was tough. Scores of witnesses were presented by both sides. Herlands in his summation to the jury said:

"This is the first time that a full industrial racket has been presented in a single case. If there is anything that is important to the community today, it is a warning that rackets can be prosecuted and broken. If we cannot get a conviction in this case, there never again will be a like opportunity."

The seven defendants (all who were on trial) were found guilty. Coulcher, who had tried to conceal the fact that he had cached large sums of cash with various friends, was sentenced to from fifteen to twenty years in prison. The others were sentenced by Justice McCook to terms of five years and more.

Next in line in the path of Mr. Dewey's juggernaut was

the puissant and highly aromatic Charles ("Tootsie") Herbert, the czar of poultry. The nickname, it was said, was derived from the fact that Herbert, like so many underworld characters, was a sucker for the delights of the barber shop, with a special weakness for sweet-smelling unguents and tonics. The ineffable Tootsie was business agent of the Chicken Drivers, Chauffeurs and Helpers Union, Local 167, and high in the National Councils of the Teamsters International. He was arrested early in 1937 with David Diamondstone, president of the union, and Harry Frankel, an ex-convict who was secretary and treasurer. They were charged with stealing nearly $40,000 from their own union.

Herbert's union handled the trucking for more than three-fourths of the kosher slaughterhouses, and he also was the dominant figure in the nonkosher markets of New York. He began his career as a dance-hall bouncer. He early formed a team with Joseph Wiener, a safecracker. They came to control the poultry unions and the industry as well. One of their profitable dodges was to rent coops, which cost $1.65 each, to poultry dealers at the rate of 65 cents a day per coop.

The Federal government had once got after Herbert and his henchmen and had convicted sixty-seven out of ninety-nine defendants for violating the antitrust law. This was a good stunt, but, because violation was only a misdemeanor, Herbert served only eight weeks in jail. When he got out, he and Joey Wiener showed the poultry industry how they could really operate if they tried. Among other things, they made themselves stockholders in the Metropolitan Feed Company, elected themselves vice-presidents, and let word get around that it was a good idea to buy feed from them.

Tootsie and Joey had their generous instincts. Tootsie loved to send flowers to his friends; and, when James J. Hines, the Tammany leader, made his annual distribution of turkeys to the poor, Joe furnished the turkeys.

The evidence in the poultry racket was collected by Dewey's assistants, in this case principally by Jacob Rosenblum and Sol Gelb, lawyers, and the accounting wizard, A. J. Goodrich. When the case came to trial in August, and the evidence began to pile up, the defendants pleaded guilty to grand larceny and were sent to prison. Herbert, who was sentenced to from four to ten years, turned back to the union $25,000 which he had embezzled from their funds.

Justice Ferdinand Pecora, who had presided at the trial, remarked at that time, "If racketeering is to be stamped out in this community, it will only be through the splendid type of prosecution conducted by Thomas E. Dewey and his associates."

The list of Dewey's effective blows at the rackets is long; each case is different, and yet they all follow a similar pattern—patient and relentless investigation, the building up of an airtight case, a break usually in the ranks of the defendants, and the extraordinarily competent conduct of the trial itself. Among other rackets were the collusive bidding among electrical contractors, a racket in brick, and the relatively minor but vicious racket in the garment-trucking industry. The racket had kept itself in power by intimidation and sometimes mutilation and murder. Threats to cut off a victim's ears were common, and usually persuasive. The trial of the two ringleaders, John Dioguardio (usually called "Dio"), and James Plumeri, alias Jimmy Doyle, started on June 2, 1939. When the prosecution rested after four days of damning evidence, Dioguardio and Plumeri pleaded guilty on all counts.

All through 1937 came suggestions that Dewey make the race that fall for the office of District Attorney; the general feeling was that, since he was doing the work the District Attorney was supposed to do, he might as well have the office. He ran and was elected. But the story of his smash-

65

ing campaign, his organization of the District Attorney's office, and his unsuccessful race for Governor in 1938, must wait upon the strange tale of the rise and fall of that square-jawed and rather pleasant crook, James J. Hines—sometimes known with a touch of levity as the "Honest Blacksmith."

VIII

THE HONEST BLACKSMITH

"JIMMY," said an upright police inspector once to James J. Hines at 110th Street and Central Park West, "I like you in many ways but I do not like the company you keep."

"That's all right," smiled Hines.

"Nevertheless," went on the police officer, "if you lie down with the dogs you will get up with fleas."

Excellent advice. James J. Hines, the genial, glad-handing ex-blacksmith, powerful in Tammany, with a voice in national affairs, smilingly refused to believe that he could possibly get into trouble. His early labors at the forge and at horseshoeing in his father's blacksmith shop had developed his physique. He had not been afraid to stand up against Charles Francis Murphy, the greatest of modern Tammany bosses, in a fight at the polls. When he went into Jim Moore's bright and crowded eating place in West 46th Street he always found many who were eager to shake his hand; but he was seen also in the dark places. He was generous, but where did he get his money? He had some vague connection with horse racing; just what, no one appeared to know. He was always given the Broadway accolade—that is, he was said to be a "quick man with a buck." Where the buck came from hardly anyone cared. On some mornings his apartment was crowded with people asking favors—a job here, a "fix" there, a little loan in an emergency, and so on. He had influence at the White House and considerable to say about Federal patronage in New York. He was a conspicuous figure at Democratic National Conventions. And yet—something was wrong.

It was whispered that he "controlled" certain officials, magistrates among them; it was said that he could "break" a policeman if he cared to; it was said his advice was sometimes heeded at the Parole Commission; it was hinted also that, far from being a clean-living, home-loving soul, he was actually the intimate of underworld characters. For a long time New Yorkers had heard these intimations and were not shocked. Few would have been greatly shocked if they had been shown that the stories were true—which they were.

The facts in the case go back to the garish life and times of Arthur Flegenheimer (Dutch Schultz). For all their ramifications, the main outlines are simple enough. Schultz, who was inordinately fond of money and who had a good business head, decided to "move in" on the Harlem policy games.

For a few months, when the mean-tempered Dutchman was getting control, there were many instances of violence in Harlem, but, so persuasive were the methods employed that soon most of the old operators—such people as Henry Miro, Alexander Pompez, "Spasm" Ison and Wilfred Brunder—were working for Schultz. Several women were in the business and one white man named Maloney, a friend of James J. Hines. While Schultz was taking over, Hines was in Hot Springs, Arkansas. When he returned, he arranged a truce between Schultz and Maloney, and while he was about it he took the newly reorganized policy racket under his protection. Actually, he went to work for Schultz. This partnership was arranged in 1932. When Dewey, making his first tentative jabs at the policy games, prosecuted Henry Miro for income-tax evasion in the Federal court, he found the suspicious item relating to gifts of silk shirts which Miro had made to Hines. Suspicious, yes, but it required years to prove that any tangible link existed between Hines and policy.

At the time Schultz entered the policy business, the gross income of all the games in Harlem was probably not more than $25,000 a day; later, when the Dutchman had got things as he wanted them, the daily gross was $63,000. People put up their money and picked three numbers that might range from 000 to 999; the numbers at first were chosen from clearinghouse figures, later from total Stock Exchange figures, and still later from certain horse-racing figures. The person guessing the correct combination was paid 600 to 1. Those who played the game wrote their guesses on slips of paper that were picked up by collectors and delivered to central offices, or "banks." On some days so many persons would guess the right number that the "bankers" would be ruined. Dutch Schultz, who didn't like to lose, made the game into a racket.

Schultz found a way to control the winning figures. He engaged a mathematical genius, Otto Berman, known around the race tracks as "Havasack" or "Abadaba," a handicapper, and paid him $10,000 a week. Berman used part of this money to place last-minute bets at the track, thereby changing the pay-off figures if it appeared that a heavily played number seemed likely to win. Some other number, because of Abadaba's shenanigans, would win, thus saving the "bank" from heavy losses.

In 1933, when a new District Attorney was to be elected, Hines backed his friend, Magistrate William Copeland Dodge, for the office. Dutch Schultz contributed handsomely to Dodge's campaign fund. Dodge, no mental giant but respectable enough, was elected. All these arrangements did not mean that the policy racket was immune from annoyance by officials. The police made occasional raids. Even Dodge made some motions toward prosecution; but many cases were dismissed, and the bosses of the racket were never molested. Schultz, under indictment, had to go in hiding much of the time, but, using an ingenious system of signals and codes of his own invention, he retained control of policy. Schultz, reappearing after Dewey had left the United States Attorney's office, was acquitted of the charge of income-tax evasion at a trial at Malone, New York. He was still fearful of Dewey and kept in moderate seclusion up to the time of his murder in Newark in the fall of 1935. But the policy games went on, and so did Dewey's patient inquiry.

At the beginning of Dewey's rackets investigation in 1935, he assigned an assistant, Charles P. Grimes, a vigorous young lawyer from the West, to work with a squad of detectives on the policy situation. It was not until January, 1937, that Grimes and his men were ready to go into action.

The old Claremont Inn, on Riverside Drive, near the tomb of General Ulysses Simpson Grant, was city property and was closed for the winter. Dewey, with the assistance of Robert Moses, Park Commissioner, converted the resort into a secret super police station. Police Commissioner Valentine supplied a large group of police, including many rookies. Captain Dowd and Sergeant Grafeneker made the assignments, and the policy raids were on. Some strange people were brought into the Claremont Inn that night, and none of them could be sure what was going on. The "bankers" Ison and Pompez were out of the country, but their banks were seized. Pompez, in Mexico, fought extradition, but Dewey's men were able to bring him back in September.

The sixty-five witnesses caught in the January raid were sent to jail in separate batches. Some of them began to talk. Helping Grimes on the details of this case were Harry Cole, Sol Gelb, and Mrs. Eunice Carter. In July indictments were returned against Ison (he who was called "Spasm"); Pompez; Harry Schoenhaus, the Schultz comptroller; George Weinberg, another old Schultz mobster; and, most important of all, J. Richard Davis, the "Kid Mouthpiece." Davis and Weinberg were in hiding. Dewey broadcast a reward for Davis, offering $5,000 for "the young New York lawyer who betrayed his profession and turned gangster." This young lawyer had achieved success of a sort; his office occupied a floor at 1450 Broadway, costing him $13,000 a year; he had sixteen suits of clothes costing $165 each; he had three "homes," one on West End Avenue, another on Park Avenue, and a penthouse in East 92nd Street. He was a highroller, a Good Time Charlie of the first rank.

Dewey got a tip that Davis and his glamorous sweetheart, Hope Dare, were hiding in a Philadelphia apartment. Miss Dare was loyal to the Kid Mouthpiece. She had been a showgirl and a rodeo performer. Her hair was naturally red; she dyed it black and went with Davis into seclusion. Following up his tip, Dewey sent detectives to Philadelphia, where they found not only Dixie Davis and Hope Dare, but George Weinberg, who was asleep on a couch in the living room. Davis's wife hurried to Philadelphia to offer help, but Davis refused to see her. He was sticking to Hope Dare. Since there were no charges against her, Miss Dare was allowed to depart for New York, where she tried, without success, to raise money to help her sweetheart. One of those who turned down her pleas was James J. Hines. Davis and Weinberg were brought back to New York and placed in Tombs prison. The Kid's bail had been reduced from $150,000 to $75,000, but he still could not meet it.

George Weinberg was the first to indicate that he would talk. After a few conferences with Grimes he promised to plead guilty and tell his story. Then Harry Schoenhaus surrendered and also promised to turn state's evidence. Davis still held out, but he was weakening. Then, on May 25, 1938, the news broke that Dewey had grabbed Hines.

The complaint against Hines, signed by Grimes, accused the Tammany boss of influencing and intimidating judges and police so that rackets could operate. Hines went to Dewey's office and surrendered and was held in $20,000 bail. The day after Hines's arrest he was indicted; it was charged that he was an actual member of the Schultz mob, from which he received a salary. Other defendants were Davis, George Weinberg, Schoenhaus, John Cooney, Sol Girsch, Harry Wolf, Martin Weintraub, and "Bo" Weinberg— Weinberg the gunman, whose body, according to underworld legend, lay even then in a chunk of concrete at the bottom of the East River.

The former District Attorney, Dodge, now proclaimed his faith in the innocence of Hines and said he "would never desert a friend." Nobody cared much at this time what Mr. Dodge thought. Hines procured the services of an able though somewhat old-fashioned lawyer, Lloyd Paul Stryker, and began to fight. The staff now helping Dewey on the Hines case also included Herman McCarthy, Frank S. Hogan, and Livingston Goddard.

Hines and Davis appeared before Justice Pecora and pleaded not guilty on July 11, 1938. Meanwhile Dewey's office was working on Davis. He finally agreed that he would plead guilty and would furnish much information privately, but he still declined to testify in court. Then it became public knowledge that Davis, accompanied by detectives, had been allowed to leave the Tombs prison on many occasions —to go to restaurants, to consult his doctor, and to visit Hope Dare's apartment for changes of clothing. Justice Pecora, angry at this disclosure, refused to permit Davis to leave the Tombs any more. But Davis was thinking; he figured he was probably ruined, and perhaps marked for assassination, no matter what he did. So he decided to go all the way and testify in court. He went before Justice Pecora and pleaded guilty. The judge paroled him in the custody of Dewey, who sent him to a secret hiding place to be guarded, along with George Weinberg and Harry Schoen-haus.

Justice Pecora now ruled that Dewey must give a bill of particulars as to just what officials Hines was accused of influencing. Dewey named former District Attorney Dodge, Magistrate Hulon Capshaw, and Magistrate Francis J. Erwin, who had died not long before. Before selecting jurors for the trial, in August, Dewey asked for and obtained a severance in the case of Martin Weintraub, saying that his trial would take only a day or two. This left Hines alone.

In his long address to the jury on August 17, opening his case, Dewey said that he had reduced the number of his witnesses to fifty-five, that some of them were unfriendly to him, and that some of them would undoubtedly lie on the stand. Stryker, in his opening speech, said that Dixie Davis, by turning state's evidence, had taken part in a low conspiracy to implicate "an innocent man who has lived in this community with his family all his life."

Dewey had intended to build up his case against Hines in chronological order, but Stryker attacked this plan of procedure, and Justice Pecora sustained the objection. Dewey immediately called Weinberg to the stand and let him tell his story: the story of being present at a conference with Hines and Schultz in Schultz's apartment when the protection arrangement was agreed upon, of how Hines had said he could "handle" the police of the Sixth Division in Harlem, of how he was sure of the magistrates, of how Hines had given Schultz permission to use his name where it would do the most good. Weinberg said he had been instructed to pay Hines $500 a week, as well as other "reasonable amounts." This salary was later cut in half, he said. He described how policy arrests had been reduced and how troublesome policemen had been transferred. Stryker was fighting Weinberg's story hard, but the main outlines stood up well. Weinberg told of hearing Magistrate Capshaw tell

Hines, when some policy cases were to come before him, "I have never failed you yet. I will take care of it." He told of handing $30,000 of Schultz money to Hines to help in the campaign of Dodge for District Attorney.

Detectives testified that Hines had often called up Davis to get his weekly payments. Harry Schoenhaus swore that he also had paid money to Hines. The master of a Connecticut riding school took the stand to describe meetings between Schultz and Hines at his place. Police testified that they had been transferred after raids on the policy games. John F. Curry, who had been leader of Tammany Hall during much of the alleged conniving, unhappily testified that Hines had frequently obtained transfers of policemen.

Dixie Davis told his story. He described how District Attorney Dodge, in 1935, had thrown the grand jury (the famous "runaway grand jury") off the trail of the policy racket. He said he had warned Hines that Dewey must not be appointed Special Prosecutor. Another witness, James D. C. Murray, the criminal lawyer, corroborated Davis on this point. Max Steuer, the lawyer who was one of Tammany's brain trust, testified that Hines had attempted to have him settle Schultz's income-tax difficulties. There were other witnesses to piece out the story. On the seventeenth day of the trial, Dewey announced that he had completed his case.

Stryker moved for dismissal of all charges. He made a hard fight, speaking for more than three hours. He argued, among other things, that the case was outlawed by the statute of limitations—that the racket had ended with the murder of Schultz in 1935. He attacked Dewey violently, accusing him of trying to ruin Hines to help his own political future. Justice Pecora admitted his doubts; Dewey argued against dismissal and presented a brief to support his views. The next day Justice Pecora denied Stryker's motion, and the trial continued.

Stryker placed on the stand Lyon Boston, who had been

on the staff of District Attorney Dodge and who had been assigned to present policy racket evidence to the grand jury. He said he had tried conscientiously to do this. Stryker told him to "go ahead" and tell "the entire story" of his relations with the grand jury. He said, among other things, that some of the grand jurors had shown "a desire to indict Mr. Hines." On cross-examination, Dewey forced Boston to admit that he had had no experience whatever with criminals "except as a child detective" during the First World War. Dewey showed that Boston was the lowest paid man on Dodge's staff. Moreover, he proved that Boston knew very little about the workings of the rackets or about Dutch Schultz. Dewey, trying to get at the "whole story," referred to the testimony of William Fellowes Morgan, Commissioner of Markets, and Lewis J. Valentine, Police Commissioner, before the grand jury. Turning to the Morgan testimony, Dewey asked, "Don't you remember any testimony about Hines and the poultry racket there by him?"

Stryker, after a quick bit of prompting by an assistant, jumped up and demanded a mistrial. Dewey replied that the subject had been opened by the defense when Stryker asked Boston to tell the "whole story." After some heated argument, Justice Pecora said to Dewey, "There was no such subject opened up, and I think you should not refer to it in any way, shape, or form."

This happened on a Saturday afternoon. Justice Pecora said he would take Stryker's motion under advisement and announce his ruling Monday. Both Dewey and Stryker worked on briefs that were submitted to the court. On Monday, Dewey and Stryker argued for two more hours in the judge's chambers. Finally, in the afternoon, Justice Pecora delivered a two-hour disquisition, at the end of which he granted Stryker's motion for a mistrial.

The Pecora decision raised much controversy. Lawyers, laymen, editors, and the public debated its soundness. The general feeling seemed to be that Justice Pecora, taking advantage of a questionable technicality, had not only wasted the time and money of a great many people but had once again demonstrated the ancient axiom that the law is an ass. Some held that, even if Dewey's question had been improper, no harm would have been done if the bench had merely instructed the jury to disregard it; others, particularly certain lawyers who had watched Dewey's progress with dismay and jealousy, were quick to say that the Pecora decision proved that Dewey was not the lawyer he was cracked up to be. Some of these arguments still rage. Right or wrong, the fact remains that Justice Ferdinand Pecora, who had appeared to be on the road toward eminence in public affairs, lost his glamour after this decision. The gentleman may have injured himself straining at a gnat.

Hines, walking out of court after the mistrial, was cheered by his friends and lobbygows. When Dewey came out of the courtroom, some people booed. Asked for comment back at his office, Dewey said, "Make no mistake about it. Hines will be brought to justice. I will move for a new trial at the earliest possible date. It will be the same identical indictment." He asked that Justice Pecora yield jurisdiction and transfer the Hines case to General Sessions; Pecora kept in his own hands the sentencing of Davis, Weinberg, and Schoenhaus, but he did agree to the transfer of the retrial to the other court.

Meanwhile Dewey ran for Governor and was beaten; whether the mistrial had much effect on the result is something that no one can say with certainty. Probably it helped him, but who knows?

The new Hines trial opened before one of the most distinguished and experienced jurists of modern times, Judge Charles C. Nott, Jr., in the Court of General Sessions, on January 23, 1939. This time the trial moved with speed and without the long debates on petty points of law. The Judge ruled as questions came up, and the trial proceeded in businesslike fashion. Dewey put in his old evidence, with a few added touches. Very early Stryker insisted that before the trial proceeded Dewey must prove conspiracy, and he alluded to Justice Pecora's ruling on this point. Judge Nott said, "I don't know any way you can prove a conspiracy except by conversations between the conspirators." He also said, "I do not consider myself bound by every ruling that Justice Pecora made."

Then the repentant mobster, George Weinberg, whose importance to Dewey's case was incalculable, almost ruined the case. He killed himself. Weinberg, with Schoenhaus and Dixie Davis, had been concealed under guard in a rented house in White Plains. Weinberg was ill, and brooding over many things, among them the killing of certain mobsters who, he assumed, might have been helping Dewey. Whatever went on in his mind, he obtained the pistol of one of his guards, who had carelessly left the weapon in a closet, and shot himself. What of his testimony? Stryker fought hard against the admission of a transcript in the second trial, but Judge Nott ruled that it was admissible. The judge himself informed the jury of Weinberg's suicide.

Dewey put on the stand all his old witnesses and a few new ones, including the widow of Dutch Schultz, who said that her husband had introduced her to Hines and then told her to forget that she had seen him. She said she had also met Hines with Davis when Schultz was a fugitive. Dewey rested his case after he had put on a parade of forty-seven witnesses.

For the defense, the three important witnesses were Magistrate Hulon Capshaw, former District Attorney Dodge, and James S. Bolan, who for a brief period had served as Police Commissioner. Bolan, under Dewey's cross-examination, made a particularly pitiful witness. Among other things he said he did not know Hines well, although Hines frequently visited him at headquarters. Bolan fumbled on the stand; he did Hines no good. Magistrate Capshaw, one of those up and coming Southern gentlemen for whom Tammany has for decades had a fondness, was wilted by the time Dewey had finished with him. In pathetic bewilderment, he admitted that, although thousands of policy arrests had come before him, he "didn't know what a policy bank was." Dodge was as weak a witness as the others. Dewey made him admit that he and Hines had been friends for twenty years; that, in assigning Lyon Boston to inquire into rackets, he had known he was assigning the least experienced member of his staff. The old story of the Hines contributions to Dodge's campaign fund was gone over again. Lyon Boston took the stand; he was little help to Hines.

It had been expected that Hines would take the stand in his own defense. Dewey was ready for him; the Honest Blacksmith chose to sit it out. He wanted none of Dewey's cross-examination.

The summations of Dewey and Stryker were vastly different in content and style, but each had its dramatic qualities. Stryker, a veteran of the bar, was a master of grandiloquence; he knew much of literature, and he was a gifted courtroom actor. Out of his occasionally delightful fustian, however, there came his main plea—that Hines, a fine example of the spirit of democracy, was being persecuted for political purposes by a young prosecutor who had to rely upon the testimony of underworld rats to accomplish his ends. Dewey, in his turn, made one of the most effective speeches of his career. He spoke for the most part quietly. He went through the evidence, and its obvious implications, so clearly and logically that no one could misunderstand. It was a picture of what he called "the inevitable march of truth." Toward the end he said:

"It is not a pleasant task for a District Attorney to go through a case like this. . . . The important thing is that you declare to the people of New York, the police of New York, that they are free; that they will no longer be betrayed by a corrupt alliance between crime and politics; that that alliance is going to be smashed by this jury and branded as something we won't stand for, because we want to keep the kind of system we have in this country and we don't want it polluted by a betrayer. We don't want protection of gangsters by political leaders."

The jury was out seven hours, returning at 7:14 on the evening of February 25, 1939. The verdict was guilty, on all thirteen counts in the indictment. A reporter asked Hines how he felt.

"How would you feel," asked Hines, "if you had been kicked in the belly?"

This time there were no cheering lobbygows outside to whoop it up for good old Jimmy Hines. And there were no catcalls for Dewey. Dewey gave out the following statement:

"The members of the jury are entitled to the thanks of the whole community. By their verdict they have reasserted the ability of democracy to clean its own house and cast out those who betray it. I cannot praise too highly the work of the men who have been responsible for the investigation and presentation of the evidence in this case, Assistant District Attorneys Charles P. Grimes, Sol Gelb, Frank S. Hogan, and Herman McCarthy, as well as the police officers and investigators who have worked so hard on the case for many months."

At this time Hines was sixty-three years old. Judge Nott sentenced him to from four to eight years. Hines fought hard to keep out of Sing Sing. He called in the aggressive young lawyer, Martin W. Littleton, a former District At-

torney of Nassau County. Hines lost his appeal and went
up the river, a felon. Hines aged greatly in prison, and his
health was not good. And in New York, so swiftly does time
erase memories of power and glory, he is remembered today
as a somewhat obscure boss who lived—yes, it must have been
a long time ago.

MR. DISTRICT ATTORNEY

SOME great men, some preposterous mountebanks, and some dreary drones have held the office of District Attorney of New York County. Charles S. Whitman went to the governorship after his term as District Attorney. After the murder of the gambler Herman Rosenthal, outside the old Hotel Metropole, Whitman sent to the chair the crooked police lieutenant Charles Becker and those illustrious gunfighters and bruisers—"Lefty Louie," "Dago Frank," "Gyp the Blood," and "Whitey" Lewis. Before Whitman's time, in the Harry Thaw era, the office was held by William Travers Jerome, a scholar and a fighter whose personality so impressed itself upon his city that men still living recall him with a wistful admiration.

Jerome was remarkable as an individual, superb as a prosecutor. Jerome would throw dice with the boys across the street for drinks, and sometimes he would drink too much; at least once he was photographed asleep at his desk; he was a man about town, many-sided in his interests, as brave a man as ever walked; he was the beau ideal of prosecutors, and even his eccentricities and weaknesses aroused admiration. His smile could be a benediction, his snarl something terrible. Tom Dewey was the first District Attorney since Jerome to combine personal color and a devastating effectiveness. True, the men were cut to a different pattern and came of different backgrounds. But Dewey in action reminded the older generation of Jerome at his best. Both

81

were, in a sense, reformers; neither had an ounce of prudery in his make-up. Jerome, when he took office, threw out the accumulated deadwood of many years and got down to serious business; Dewey did the same. Jerome brought into his office many competent and ambitious young men; his scorn for political hacks was sublime. To have served with Jerome was to have a mark of distinction. The same was true of Dewey and the men he gathered about him. Neither man "cleaned up" New York in the sense that they made of it anything resembling the Utopia of the bluenoses; both demonstrated that strongly entrenched and illicit political-criminal alliances could be broken up and that neither power nor money need place a malefactor beyond the law.

One of the first suggestions that Dewey run for District Attorney was made early in 1937 by Mayor F. H. La Guardia, at a time when Dewey was in the full swing of his work as Special Prosecutor of the rackets. Mr. La Guardia has a pet tune—he hates politicians. No one has ever been fooled by this. The little man, unpredictable though he may be, is one of the smoothest of all politicians. He had been elected Mayor in 1933 because the Democrats were split. Now, in 1937, if he expected to run again, he was up against a Democratic machine that was showing signs of revival.

Three of the leading members of the Fusion Party, Samuel Seabury, Charles C. Burlingham, and Thomas D. Thacher, conferred with Dewey in June, 1937, and urged him to run for District Attorney. He might not be elected, they agreed, but they argued that without him on the ticket, La Guardia and the cause of clean government in New York might be lost for another generation. The regular Republicans also came out for Dewey. Dewey promised to back La Guardia for reelection, but he was cool to the idea of running for District Attorney. The American Labor Party came forward and, at the last minute, agreed to support Dewey if

82

he would make the race. If ever a man was "drafted" to stand for public office, that man was Dewey in 1937. He accepted the nomination and said:

"As a result of the work of the rackets investigation, it has become clear to me that there is an alliance of long standing between crime and certain elements of Tammany Hall. For twenty years Tammany Hall has controlled criminal prosecution in this county and for twenty years the power of the criminal underworld has grown. This alliance must be broken."

Dewey's opponent was the Tammany wheelhorse, Harold Hastings, who for many years had been an Assistant District Attorney. Mr. Hastings, relying upon tradition, decided to take things easy. He went on a vacation that lasted until the end of September, and when he returned he found that the Dewey movement was very hot indeed.

In organizing his campaign, Dewey selected Millard H. Ellison, a lawyer, as campaign manager. Hickman Powell, a shrewd newspaperman, was made publicity director; Harold Keller, also a newspaperman, was put in charge of research. Two thousand young men went to work for him in every part of the county. Many Democrats came over to Dewey's side, among them Clarence J. Shearn, former president of the Bar Association, who became head of a committee of lawyers. Shearn said, "One factor of influence ought to be what the enemies of society, what the criminals themselves want. Every racketeer, every vice profiteer, every loan shark, gunman, blackmailer, fugitive from justice, crook, and convict wants to see Dewey defeated. We all know why."

Dewey, who had before been sneered at as a labor baiter, accepted the American Labor Party's nomination in a speech at Carnegie Hall. One quotation:

"The workers need no longer accept the crumbs which drop from the tables of vote-seeking politicians. . . . There can be no advance in our industrial society without collective bargaining. There are still businessmen who regard a picket line as a signal for a criminal investigation. The gangster has been the second obstacle to industrial progress. The racketeer is in no sense part of the labor movement. He is no more a labor racketeer than a business racketeer. Never again must the criminal underworld be permitted to sit between the employer and worker, extorting from the one and beating down the wages of the other."

Dewey talked everywhere and he talked often—to Negro groups, Armenian groups, Italian groups, to the Young Women's Christian Association, and so on and on. People at last came to know him by sight. He was an effective speaker before all these groups; a little later in the campaign he was to demonstrate his strong and persuasive abilities as a speaker over the radio. He took much pains with the radio, rehearsing, listening to advice, and playing recordings back to himself.

It was over the radio, on the evening of October 24, 1937, that Dewey unlimbered his big guns. It was startling. He started this way:

"Tonight I am going to talk about the alliance between crime and politics in the County of New York. I am going to tell you about a politician, a political ally of thieves, pickpockets, thugs, dope peddlers, and big-shot racketeers; Albert Marinelli, county clerk of New York, powerful leader of half the Second Assembly District, dominates the whole. He attained power by staying in the dark and keeping his mouth shut. Tonight we turn on the spotlight."

Dewey went on to charge that Marinelli had been assisted to power by "Socks" Lanza, a markets racketeer, and old Johnny Torrio, the gangster who put Al Capone in business in Chicago. He charged that Marinelli had attended the Democratic National Convention in Chicago in 1932 with Lucky Luciano, that he and Luciano were together in the

Drake Hotel and at the local race tracks. He gave the police records of thirty-two of Marinelli's henchmen.

To these charges Marinelli said, "No comment." In other speeches Dewey made grave charges, documented charges, and dangerous if he had not had his facts secure, against other Tammany figures. He denounced Charles A. Schneider, the Assistant State Attorney General who had interceded for the killers of Billy Snyder in Garfein's Restaurant. Nothing so blunt, so meaty, had ever been heard on the air in a New York campaign.

But was all this enough to beat Tammany? As for the city-wide race, James A. Farley, then Postmaster General, predicted a La Guardia defeat by 400,000. As to Dewey's chances, that other able leader, James J. Hines (whose indictment and prosecution came the following year), on the night before election, said, "Well, there is a vibration in the air that seems to say La Guardia and Dewey. If it's a true guide it's a sweep. When a sweep comes there is nothing you can do about it. Dewey is a very nice young fellow."

Another prophet, an old gambler, stood at Broadway and 59th Street, the meeting place of the sports and gaming world's raffish wisenheimers, and predicted a Dewey defeat. He said, "I have been in New York a long time. I know this town. It's an easygoing place. New Yorkers will not elect a man who has the reputation for putting the neighbors' children in jail."

Neighbors' children? True enough, he had sent many of them to prison; some of them were mere striplings forty or fifty years of age. However, silly as it sounds, the old gambler expressed an idea—the instinctive dislike of many persons for a prosecutor.

La Guardia, in carrying the city that year, had a plurality in New York County of 91,989; Dewey carried the county by 109,019. His grand total of 326,351 votes broke down this way: Republican vote, 187,411; American Labor Party, 92,-

584; Fusion, 38,800; Progressive, 7,556. As soon as he was sure of the returns, Dewey said:

"In the campaign just ended, I made but one pledge to the public. I promised that, beginning January 1, the people would be protected by their own District Attorney and by a staff of lawyers who owe their allegiance to the people. We shall restore criminal justice in this county. We go ahead with a deep sense of responsibility to the people of New York."

Although Dewey was not to take office as District Attorney until January 1, 1938, he had to face some of the repercussions of some of his campaign charges. Charles A. Schneider quit his post in the Attorney General's office; his feelings seemed hurt. A committee of citizens, referring to Dewey's speeches attacking Marinelli, demanded that Governor Lehman remove Marinelli as County Clerk. The Governor forwarded the charges to Marinelli, who replied with a blanket denial. He also remarked, "They are trying to crucify me. If it's a crime to help the underdog, then I'm guilty."

Governor Lehman called upon Dewey for proof. Dewey sent out subpoena servers for 300 of Marinelli's followers, and then, bolstered with still more detailed evidence, he drafted a statement to the Governor in affidavit form, so that "in the event you desire to treat these statements of facts as formal charges there will be no delay."

Governor Lehman asked Marinelli for a reply, and after a week of soul-searching Marinelli quit his $15,000-a-year job. He said he would not ask for a public hearing to establish his innocence, because it might cause some of his friends needless suffering. At this development it was now Dewey's turn to say, "No comment."

Before he went into the office of District Attorney, Dewey was full of plans for reorganization. He had worked out a system under which his own rackets inquiry could be carried out as a part of the regular work of the District Attorney's office. He gave a dinner to the nine judges of General Sessions to talk about his office. He also conferred with the sixteen justices of Special Sessions. He obtained some WPA workers and set about renovating and rearranging the physical layout of the office even before Dodge's term was up. He was particularly insistent that witnesses could be questioned where spies could not know what was going on.

As everybody had anticipated, he cleaned out much dead timber—the loafers, the politicians, and the incompetents. He dismissed Dodge's sixty-four assistants, with the exception of three; one was a man who would be eligible for a pension in a few months; another was John MacDonnell, whose record in both war and peace was excellent; the other was Felix Benvenga, head of the appeals bureau, and later a Justice of the New York Supreme Court.

Dewey's knack for building a workable organization, for picking the right man, for distributing responsibilities and duties, could be observed in his first days in the District Attorney's office. A few of his stand-bys: Paul E. Lockwood, with whose strong qualities and extraordinary tact Dewey was familiar, was made executive assistant; Sewell T. Tyng, his old friend, who had gone into private practice, came into the organization; Jacob J. Rosenblum, shrewd and tenacious, was made head of the homicide bureau; Sol Gelb and Mrs. Eunice Carter took over the Special Sessions Bureau, which handled fourteen thousand misdemeanor cases a year; a fraud bureau was placed under the direction of Barent Ten Eyck and later was headed by Frank A. F. Severance; the indictment bureau was in charge of Stanley H. Fuld at first, and later Robert H. Thayer; the rackets bureau was directed by that assiduous bloodhound, Murray I. Gurfein; the complaint bureau was under Thomas B. Gilchrist, Jr., and Edward S. Joseph; the bail bureau, working in a field where so many abuses had existed, was in charge of Ernest

Lappano; an accounting staff was placed under the direction of the wizard, A. J. Goodrich. There were many others. John F. O'Connell, whose abilities Dewey knew well, became chief investigator. The detectives assigned to the office were in charge of the two men in whom Dewey had learned to place the utmost trust—Captain Bernard Dowd and Lieutenant William J. Grafeneker. As his secretaries, he chose the two go-getting young New York reporters, Harold Keller and Lamoyne A. Jones. And, naturally, he kept with him his personal secretary, Miss Lilian Rosse, who, then as now, combined just about all the qualities of all the good secretaries since recorded history—an appraisal that is by no means extravagant.

More than 5,000 young New York lawyers wanted to work with Dewey. He and his chief assistants sifted this group, investigating the most promising ones thoroughly. Each man chosen was required to promise to give up all private practice and live on his salary. In all, Dewey had 225 persons on his pay roll, including eighty assistant attorneys, a number that represented what was necessary when he merged his own Special Prosecutor's racket staff with the regular District Attorney's corps. And, although he had more lawyers than his predecessor, Dewey's first year in office actually showed a saving of $388,274.

When, in May, 1938, Dewey had finished putting the last touches to his machine, he called his people together and made a long speech—one of his best—explaining not only his theories of enforcing the law but also his ideas on the relationship of the District Attorney's office to the community. He was not disturbed, he said, by the fact that many of his assistants were young. He said, "The way to run a prosecuting office is to have men whose futures are ahead of them and not behind them." He told them to learn to "get along" with the members of the bar, the judges, and the public. He warned them against thinking they could become experts overnight. "I have spent ten years on one assignment," he reminded them, "and still have a lot to learn." He advised them not to complain of long hours, or of night work, adding that he knew of "no New York lawyer who amounted to anything who didn't work ten or more hours a day." He warned his assistants, as a matter of both sense and taste, not to let photographs be taken of them with defendants—"Remember the sheriff who had his picture taken with one arm about Dillinger." He asked them not to discuss their cases outside the office. He said:

"Bear in mind that every public official is sold out by the man he spoke to on the street corner. Bear in mind that there are people who would give a few years off the end of their lives to be able to get something on any assistant attached to this office."

The instructions were clear, explicit, direct. They got results. "Consecration" is a lofty word to describe the attitude of a group of eager and loyal young men; being realists, most of them would have smiled at the description. But they swung into the battle with all their energies. William B. Herlands, who had been with Dewey in his rackets inquiry and who left to become Commissioner of Investigation for the La Guardia administration, said in talking of this point, "Dewey's outstanding quality is his ability to inspire endless personal loyalty as well as official loyalty. I don't think the rackets investigations would have been successful unless the men had sacrificed time and health and merged their own personalities in Dewey's."

Results soon began to show in the figures. At the end of his first six months Dewey was able to show the highest percentage of convictions in General Sessions in all the history of that court, better even than the record of the great William Travers Jerome, who up to that time had led the lists. It was a record that was to improve through the years.

The vast bulk of a District Attorney's work does not show

in the headlines; however, in the course of Dewey's tenure there were many cases of unusual public interest. One of the first was the astonishing case of Richard Whitney, a former president of the New York Stock Exchange, whose firm had failed for $2,000,000. Whitney, a big, dark man, who came from a fine family, was one of the most spectacular fools, one of the most consistently wrong guessers, in the whole history of New York finance. He had a weakness for putting money into dubious enterprises—business schemes that seemed ludicrous to the investigators who poked through the ashes of his tangled affairs. For example, at a time when people for the most part had stopped drinking applejack (a powerful potion once in high favor in New Jersey), he chose to invest large sums of money in the applejack business. Among other things Whitney had thrown away a trust fund of $105,000 belonging to his relatives. He had also got away with securities worth $103,000 belonging to the New York Yacht Club. He was, clearly, an adept at the fruitless pastime known as borrowing from Peter to pay Paul, and throwing good money after bad. He was arrested, indicted; he pleaded guilty and was sentenced to Sing Sing for from five to ten years. At Sing Sing it was said he was one of the most agreeable, democratic, hard-working and well-behaved men who ever served time there; even the grimiest thugs liked Whitney.

It was also during 1938, at a time when Dewey was running for Governor, that his office found an indictment against Charles A. Harnett, the State Commissioner of Motor Vehicles, who was serving in this office under Governor Lehman, Dewey's opponent. The indictment charged that Harnett had accepted large bribes, and would have been a political bombshell. But Dewey would not drop it, though it is often said that it would have elected him. Then, as in other cases, he refused to allow his office to be used for political purposes—his own or anyone else's—even though it involved delaying the indictment until after election. When the truth came out he was praised in most quarters for his courtesy and decency; others, however, cynically remarked that Dewey had been afraid to make the indictment public during the campaign because Harnett was "popular." As for the unfortunate Harnett, he had gone crooked in an attempt to hold onto some of his real-estate investments; he was one of those odd financiers who seem to be land-crazy. He was never prosecuted because he became mentally unhinged and was sent to an institution.

Then there was the strange case of the subway nickels. In January, 1939, a story broke in the newspapers concerning the theft of $25,000 by employees of the city's Independent subway system. The Board of Transportation, of which John H. Delaney was chairman, planned to hold departmental trials. Dewey saw instantly that the situation called for criminal action. Delaney tried to make it appear that the thefts were trifling; soon Dewey's office reported that the figure should be in the neighborhood of $1,250,000. The thefts were carried out by a scheme between station agents and maintenance men, and they had been going on for years. Thirty-six men were arrested, and twenty-nine of them pleaded guilty. The thefts of nickels in the subway stopped.

Stealing nickels may have had its amusing aspects; the case of Martin T. Manton, senior judge of the United States Circuit Court of Appeals, was profoundly shocking. Dewey had long suspected Manton. For one thing, in 1937, when the precious pair, Lepke and Gurrah, were under investigation by both the Federal authorities and Dewey, the two mobsters were caught and brought into Federal court on an antitrust charge. They were willing to serve time on these charges rather than wait for whatever it was Dewey had in mind for them. Dewey went before Manton and asked for high bail, saying he would soon have enough against them to "send them away for a thousand years." Manton told Dewey not to worry, and then he secretly released them on low bail. Lepke and Gurrah went into hiding, as Dewey had known they would, and the tedious process of catching them had to be gone through again.

Manton's doings began to turn up in other places. Dewey found, in the investigation of the garment rackets, that Manton had borrowed $25,000 from a man with whom he was not well acquainted. As District Attorney, Dewey quietly pressed his inquiry into the business-judicial operations of the dollar-grabbing jurist. Before he was quite ready with his findings, the *New York World-Telegram* began a series of well-documented articles showing that Manton had engaged in grossly improper business deals. Hatton W. Sumners, the bald eagle from Texas, as chairman of the Judiciary Committee of the House of Representatives, announced he would look into the case. On that week end (it was one of the week ends of the second Hines trial) Dewey and his assistants put together a complete report of what they had found out about Manton. It was a story of almost unbelievable corruption; it involved Manton in cases in which, for large sums of money, he had sold what passed for justice. In his letter to Representative Sumners, Dewey gave credit to his assistants, Murray Gurfein, Frank S. Hogan, Aaron Benenson, Victor J. Herwitz, and Lawrence E. Walsh, and offered their services to Congress in the pressing of impeachment charges. He made his charges public; they would have been highly libelous if he had not been sure of what he was doing. Manton quit. Dewey had done his part. Prosecution of Manton was the business of the Federal government. Frank Murphy, the United States Attorney General, who said he had been "secretly negotiating" with Manton for his resignation, proceeded with the inevitable business of putting Manton where he belonged, in prison.

It was an unpleasant chore for the Democratic administration, but it had to be done.

Fritz Kuhn, the arrogant Bundist and admirer of Hitler, should not be forgotten. In May, 1939, Dewey subpoenaed the Bund's books, arousing the Bund's newspaper to print the headline, "Jew York Democracy in Action." Kuhn was indicted for stealing funds from his own Bund; he went on trial not as a traitor or as a potentially dangerous Fuehrer but as a common thief. Herman McCarthy of Dewey's staff prosecuted. The defense unexpectedly called Dewey himself as a witness and asked him whether he had "personal animus against Kuhn." Dewey said he looked upon the defendant as "a nuisance to the community and a possible threat to civil liberties," but that his personal feeling had nothing to do with the case. "If it did," he said, "I should be removed from office." Kuhn was convicted and sent to prison.

Then there was George Scalise. This former associate of the Capone mob was accepted for several years in New York, as well as nationally, as a bona fide labor leader. Mayor La Guardia was among those who treated him as such. William Green, president of the American Federation of Labor, was a defender of Scalise. The truth about Scalise was known to a few newspapermen, who did not have the evidence to justify publication of their knowledge, and to a few other persons with long memories. Now he was the president of the Building Service Employees International Union, which was making great membership gains and pulling elevator strikes in big buildings. Westbrook Pegler dug up and printed the fact that Scalise, as a young man, had served a sentence for pandering. Immediately the cry of "Peglerizing" went up; William Green sent out a printed statement denouncing Pegler for bringing up this "youthful indiscretion" and praising Scalise as a credit to the labor movement.

Dewey conducted a long and patient inquiry into the af-

fairs of the union and found that Scalise—"youthful indis-
cretions" or not—was a thief. He had stolen large amounts
of money from his union. He lived in fancy style. This fat,
swarthy, and suspiciously oleaginous gangster was especially
enchanted by the raising of rhododendrons, which he culti-
vated in lush profusion on his large estate at Ridgefield,
Connecticut. He was convicted and in October, 1940, was
sentenced to from five to ten years in Sing Sing for grand
larceny. Many a hard-headed New York businessman who
had found Scalise "not a bad fellow, really," as well as several high officials who had been pleased to have their pictures taken with him, felt a bit foolish when Scalise started
the trip up the river.

Another leader of Scalise's union, James J. Bambrick,
president of Local 32-B, the New York group that had been
built up to 20,000 members, was next in line. Bambrick
pleaded guilty to second-degree larceny in stealing $10,000
in union funds. The prosecutor told the court that Bambrick, who up to that time had a good reputation as a labor
leader, had been led into his peculations by Scalise and
other former members of the Capone mob. Bambrick,
though undoubtedly guilty, was no mobster at heart; indeed,
at one time he had the courage to stand off the murderous
Lepke and Gurrah combination, which wanted to take over
his union. The looted Local 32-B decided to clean house.
One of their moves for reform was to engage as counsel
Victor Herwitz, their nemesis in the District Attorney's office, who in 1942 left the prosecutor's office after a notable
career.

The District Attorney's office under Dewey became a
model for the country. Justice was speedy, and it was efficient. At the same time Dewey took the part of more than
one person who had been unjustly accused, or brought up
on a faulty case; one of these was a Negro boy who had been
framed by a policeman. He organized a voluntary defenders'

group, composed of many of the ablest lawyers in New York —men who ordinarily would have thought going into the criminal courts undignified—to take the cases of defendants who were without funds.

American prosecutors have Dewey to thank for the so-called "Dewey indictments." There are more than 100 of these, drawn to fit many crimes. With the aid of Stanley H. Fuld, of the indictment bureau, Dewey rewrote the old wordy legal forms, which were masterpieces of mumbo jumbo and almost unintelligible periphrasis. Of these streamlined indictment forms, which are now widely used, the *Harvard Law Review* commented in 1939:

"Although less spectacular than its successful drives against organized crime, the recent revision and simplification of its indictments by the District Attorney's office in New York County promises to be a significant step toward a more rational criminal procedure."

In the fall of 1941, Dewey announced that he would not be a candidate for reelection as District Attorney. He had done most of the things he had set out to do. He believed that the office was one in which rotation was the best policy. He said he was by no means indispensable—that there were many men, at least four of them in his own office—who could qualify for the job. Then came an astounding move from Tammany: Christopher D. Sullivan, the gray little leader, said that he believed the office of District Attorney should be kept out of politics, and offered the Democratic nomination to Frank Smithwick Hogan, a Democrat, long one of Dewey's aces, one of the four whom he had named for his post. Dewey advised Hogan to accept the nomination. The Republicans fell in line with the idea, and Hogan went into office with the good wishes of all parties and with Dewey's able staff practically intact.

How well Mr. Hogan has justified the faith of the community may be seen in his report, published in June, 1944, showing that, for the last year, of 2,038 persons brought to trial, a number amounting to 97.7 per cent was convicted. In Mr. Hogan's previous year the percentage was 97.5—better even than Dewey's 94.3 per cent, which was regarded as notably high. One factor, of course, lies in the fact that in recent years fewer indictments were returned. Discussing the Hogan record (and, incidentally, Mr. Dewey), the *New York Sun* said:

"More important than any record, however, is the manner in which it was made. Governor Dewey, with whom Mr. Hogan first was associated in the District Attorney's office, set high standards for investigating evidence and presenting it in court. Mr. Hogan has advanced on the same course, giving his office a record for thorough, painstaking administration of the law of which New York can be especially proud. The high percentage of convictions represents no vindictiveness. As a matter of fact, the number of indictments returned was substantially lower last year than in 1942, reflecting a disinclination to make charges unless there was evidence to back them up. Furthermore, the prosecutor took full advantage of the new Youthful Offender Law, the passage of which he advocated, to drop indictments against teen-age violators who might have been convicted, but who, through the provisions of this law, may be rehabilitated. Incidentally there have been only three violations of parole by those who thus escaped the stigma of felony convictions. Not least important is the fact that this fine record has been made at less expense to the taxpayers than in the previous six years."

District Attorney Hogan sits today in a fine office in the new building in the magnificent group that was erected to replace the tragic old fortresslike prison called the Tombs; the dilapidated and dangerous old Criminal Courts Building, and the dreary old barn where Dewey first worked as District Attorney. The physical surroundings are vastly changed. But Dewey's example is still remembered in Centre Street. All this would have delighted that droll, quizzical man of action, the late William Travers Jerome.

THE FORLORN HOPE

In the spring of 1938, Thomas E. Dewey was being mentioned as the Republican candidate for Governor of New York in the election to be held that fall. He discouraged the boom. When the Young Republican Clubs, meeting at Niagara Falls, proposed to draft him, he asked them to desist, saying, "Any attempt to inject my name into politics prejudices my work in the performance of my official duties."

The Dewey talk, however, continued. Many of Dewey's closest advisers insisted that in no circumstances should he permit himself to be diverted from the District Attorneyship to which he had been elected only the previous fall. Some felt he would be accused of trying to get ahead too fast. Others agreed with Dr. Nicholas Murray Butler, who said, "Dewey should not allow himself to run for Governor, or President, or Emperor, or anything else. He should remain at his post to clean up the city and make it a different place for our children to grow up in."

Governor Herbert H. Lehman, a tremendous vote getter, was tired of Albany. He wanted to go to the United States Senate. Dewey had been informed reliably that Lehman positively would not run for reelection as Governor. At the Republican State Convention at Saratoga at the end of September, Judge William F. Bleakley of Westchester County, who had been defeated by Lehman in the campaign of 1936 (the Governor's term was for only two years at that time), made the nominating speech for Dewey. There were no other nominations; it was all Dewey. In his acceptance speech, Dewey said that, by declining the nomination and "playing safe," he would have been "shirking the bigger job, the harder fight." He said that "politics has been made the biggest racket of them all" and that the very word "politics" had fallen into disrepute. It was a vigorous speech, and it brought enthusiasm, especially when he said, "Without meaning to be so, any Democratic Governor is perforce the good-will advertising, the window-dressing for what is in part at least a corrupt machine."

In those words he set the key of his campaign. He could not call Governor Lehman by the same terms he would have used to describe the more disreputable elements among the Democrats, for the Governor was a highly respected gentleman; he could, however, argue with great force that evil elements dominated much of the organization to which Lehman owed his position.

James A. Farley went before the Democratic Convention at Rochester the day after the Republicans had made their nomination and announced with pleasure that Governor Lehman had been prevailed upon to run again. In his acceptance speech Lehman made the expected—and in many respects plausible—arguments against Dewey, terming him "entirely inexperienced in either administrative or legislative activities." The charge was not precisely true, but it carried weight. He also said:

"I did not believe that Mr. Dewey would abandon, almost before it started, that important work for which he was chosen by the people less than a year ago and for the consummation of which he accepted an obligation to the people. Every man and woman knows of my interest in clean, honest government and in law enforcement, of which the designation by me of Mr. Dewey, as Special Prosecutor to act against racketeering and corruption in New York City, was only a part."

Here the Governor may have oversimplified matters, but in those few words he called the tune for the campaign of the Democrats against Dewey. It was an argument that could be easily understood and remembered.

Three months before the conventions, at Dewey's suggestion, the Republican State Committee had appropriated $15,000 to be spent in research on the affairs of the State of New York. When he was ready to make the race for Governor he was able to make use of this material. The odds against him seemed hopeless; the wisest of the Republican prophets conceded him only an outside chance. President Roosevelt, running for his second term, had carried the state by 1,100,000 votes in 1936. And soon came more bad news for the Republicans. The American Labor Party, which had supported Dewey for District Attorney, would have none of him for Governor. The A. F. of L. and the C.I.O. came out for Lehman. Down in New York's City Hall Mr. La Guardia decided that he, also, must support Lehman.

Although much of his time was occupied by affairs in the District Attorney's office, Dewey went into the campaign with a dash shown by few Republican candidates in generations. He outlined the principal issues as: (1) the corruption in the Democratic machines of New York City, Buffalo, and Albany; (2) Governor Lehman's questionable record on civil service; (3) the delays and inefficiencies in unemployment insurance; (4) the weakness of the regulation of public utilities; (5) failure to carry out a housing program; (6) a state of looseness, even chaos, in the state budget.

To most of the charges amplifying the issues directly affecting the state administration, it was generally considered sufficient for the dignified, pipe-smoking Governor Lehman to answer with a patronizing calmness that the young man must have been "misinformed." Nevertheless, Dewey tore into the administration of the State Unemployment Insurance Act, in force since 1935, and presented evidence to show that there had been confusion and delay—more than 122,000 claims unpaid. As to housing, he accused Governor Lehman and the Democrats of inaction, and he said of Lehman, "His record is one of the passage of time, not of achievement." On the charges affecting the budget, which is a hard subject for the voter to grasp at any time, Dewey and Lehman exchanged sharp words. In later years, Dewey was to prove that his charges, although some of them might involve bookkeeping technicalities, had been in the main based on simple arithmetic.

But these subjects, to most voters, are dry. The dominant note of the Dewey campaign—and he spoke from one end of the state to the other—was that the Democratic machine, notwithstanding its idealistic pretensions, its constant reiteration of its concern for the underdog, and the attractive personalities of many of its leaders, was at bottom one of the most evil organizations in the country. He pilloried Edward J. Flynn, the Bronx boss, as "unofficial boss of the State Civil Service Commission." He referred to the morally scabrous cohorts of Al Marinelli, the Tammany boss on New York's lower East Side. He went to Albany and denounced the O'Connell machine, which had been powerful in Albany for sixteen years. "Their system of politics for profit," he said, "has become one of the worst in America."

Dealing with the O'Connells, Dewey referred to a story told by James A. Farley of how Dan O'Connell, of the Albany O'Connells, had sat "on a bed" in a Rochester hotel begging Governor Lehman to "make the sacrifice" and run again. A few days later Farley replied that O'Connell had sat not on a bed, but on a chair. "I stand corrected," said Dewey. "I said he was sitting on a bed. He was really sitting in an easy chair."

Then there was the passage about Dutch Schultz and his pistol permits. Governor Lehman referred to a former Republican sheriff in Cayuga County who had given the gangster a permit. In reply, Dewey said that there was no need to go as far as Cayuga County—he might have talked about the Bronx. He held up a copy of the record of Dutch Schultz's appointment as a deputy sheriff in the Bronx. The date was July 31, 1925. Dewey went on:

"Let's see who was sheriff of the Bronx in 1925. Who appointed the man who at that time was a trigger man for Legs Diamond and Owney Madden, and was preparing to build up his own vast racket empire? Let's see the name at the bottom of the certificate—the name of the sheriff who made the appointment, administered the oath, and gave the badge of a law-enforcement officer to this notorious Dutch Schultz. Let's see the name. Here it is. Edward J. Flynn."

(At the time of this speech Flynn was Secretary of State of New York at $12,000 a year by appointment by the Governor. Later he became National Chairman of the Democratic Party. He was involved in a scandal because he had used city labor and Belgian paving blocks belonging to the city of New York to improve his country home. He is the same Flynn who, nominated by President Roosevelt as envoy to Australia, was found unacceptable by the United States Senate.)

Through all this and other issues Dewey was obviously becoming stronger. The big guns from Washington began opening up on him. Harry Hopkins gave out an interview predicting a Democratic victory, saying, "And that means that Sir Galahad will stay home." A thrust of doubtful value.

President Roosevelt felt moved to deliver a talk from his home at Hyde Park pleading for a continuity of "liberal government" and the election of Wagner and Mead to the Senate and Lehman to the governorship. He could not bring himself to mention Dewey's name, but it required no Pinkerton to know whom he meant when he spoke of a candidate who "had yet to win his spurs." This man, he said, had prosecuted a few "underworldlings" but had taken no

part in the greater fight against "the lords of the overworld."
He said the candidate was too young. With an almost paternal note in his voice, the President recalled that, at the
age of thirty-six, when he was Assistant Secretary of the
Navy, he had been urged to run for Governor of New York
but had declined because he did not think he had sufficient
"knowledge and experience of public affairs." A few sticklers
for complete accuracy pointed out that just two years later,
when he was thirty-eight, Roosevelt ran for Vice-President
of the United States. But no matter. The President had
spoken.

In a speech the next night at the Academy of Music in
Brooklyn Dewey said, "I stand before you accused of one
crime: I was born in the twentieth century. To that charge
I plead guilty. I am of the twentieth century. We look forward, not backward. . . . It was well said by the President
last night, and I quote his words: 'By their promoters ye
shall know them.' In this campaign I am promoted by no
man. No man or group of men told me what office I could
not run for. No man or group of men on an easy chair, on
a bed, or otherwise, told me what office I could run for. 'By
their promoters ye shall know them.'"

In his last speech of the campaign, on November 7, the
night before election, he alluded in friendly fashion to "the
personal honor" of his opponent, and then reviewed the issues of the campaign.

Throughout the campaign both Dewey and Lehman had
kept the discussion on a relatively high plane; it was inevitable, however, that various undercover innuendoes should
have gone around, some started by the usual crop of dolts
who annoy people during an election year, and some by
more sinister troublemakers. One day Dewey wrote out this
statement and gave it to the press:

"Whispers concerning racial and religious preferences
have been injected into this campaign on both sides. The

103

man or woman who votes for a candidate because of his race or religion or votes against him for such a reason is a disgrace to American citizenship. I condemn and despise any support based on racial or religious prejudice.

"There are some things more important than being elected Governor, and one is a spirit of religious and racial good will. I would rather go down to defeat than be elected by votes based on race or religion."

On election day, Mr. and Mrs. Dewey and Mr. and Mrs. Lehman voted and submitted to the hallowed American custom of being photographed while doing so. Nothing to do now but wait for the results. For several hours after the polls closed, the count showed Dewey and Lehman running about even. Then a late block of votes from Brooklyn came in which meant defeat for Dewey. He telegraphed Governor Lehman: "Heartiest congratulations on your re-election. I wish you every success and happiness. With best personal regards. Thomas E. Dewey."

Governor Lehman said: "My opponent Mr. Dewey can rejoice in having waged a vigorous and strong fight. To him I extend my wholehearted support in the exacting task that lies before him as the District Attorney of New York."

On the evening after election, Mr. and Mrs. Dewey and Mr. Dewey's mother went to the theater to see the comedy "Leave It to Me." They encountered the Governor and Mrs. Lehman in the lobby, and the photographers did their stuff while the two men shook hands. So far as anyone knows, there was never any personal feeling between the two, and each has expressed respect for certain abilities possessed by the other.

An analysis of the vote: Out of a total of 4,821,631 votes, Lehman polled 1,971,307 Democratic votes and 419,979 American Labor Party votes. Dewey had 2,302,505 Republican votes, and 24,387 more from the Independent Progressive Party. Thus the Republican votes for Dewey exceeded Lehman's Democratic total by 331,198, which meant that the Republicans went back to first place on the ballot for the first time in sixteen years. Lehman's plurality was 64,394 votes; that of Charles Poletti, Democratic candidate for Lieutenant Governor, 229,361; that of Senator Robert F. Wagner, 438,414.

Other notes on the aftermath: The American Labor Party clearly held the balance of power that defeated Dewey. It was demonstrated that Lehman was the only candidate who could have defeated Dewey—which was generally suspected all along. Dewey carried fifty-six of the fifty-seven counties outside the five counties of New York City. He lost Albany, the nest of the powerful O'Connells, by about 20,000 votes. The Communist Party had not put up a candidate for Governor, but its leaders supported Lehman. The Communist vote was about 100,000, and without it, Lehman would have been counted out by about 36,000.

Dewey went back to his office to continue his aggressive campaign against criminals high and low, fantastic and dull —the frightened Charlie Harnetts and the devious Musicas and a hundred other types of miscreants. And the second Hines trial was coming up. As soon as he was sure he could safely do so, he and Mrs. Dewey, accompanied by Paul Lockwood, sailed to Bermuda for a vacation of three weeks. He was more than half convinced at this time that his defeat by Lehman had ended whatever chances he had ever had for high political office. Perhaps, he reflected, it was just as well. When his term was up he could go back to private practice; not a bad idea, since he had two sons now.

When he came back to New York on December 13, 1938, he found that, far from being a political dead pigeon, he was being boomed all over the country for the Republican nomination for President in 1940. The straw polls, the newspaper comment, the opinions of politicians in many sections—all had a good word for Dewey and his magnificent race against such crushing odds. In defeat he had become a national political figure, regarded now not simply as a very good local prosecutor but as a man who could discuss great issues intelligently, conduct a forceful campaign, and attract enough votes to frighten the Democrats.

More, he was now the undisputed leader of the Republican Party in the most populous state—and this after what they had called defeat.

DEFEAT IN PHILADELPHIA

THE movement to make Thomas E. Dewey the Republican Presidential nominee in 1940 began growing as soon as the significance of the 1938 New York vote had seeped through the nation. Straw votes were beginning to show him as the favorite. The Associated Press, in listing the most significant news developments of 1938, included the James J. Hines trial, the Dewey-Lehman campaign, the sentencing of Richard Whitney, and the capture of Dixie Davis—all Dewey "stories."

There had already been a clamor in many of the larger cities, notably in boss-ridden Kansas City, where fat Tom Pendergast had ruled so long, for "another Dewey," and sometimes this clamor got results. In addition, now, a nationwide feeling, just beginning to grow articulate, would make Dewey presidential timber. In December, the month after the New York election, Dewey went to Washington as the honor guest of the Gridiron Club, that select and high-spirited group of newspapermen which usually manages to put on a show with a balanced mixture of seriousness and jocularity. Dewey made a good speech, terse and graceful. Many Republicans, eager to size him up, visited his room at the Mayflower Hotel, wondering whether they would encounter a coming champion or merely another New York freak.

At the beginning of 1939 the Dewey boom gained attention. On January 4, at a "party unity" dinner given by the

Republicans in Albany, Dewey made a speech in which, without making specific proposals for the revival of the party nationally, he said:

"There is room in the Republican Party for men of good will of every kind of political opinion—liberals, middle-roaders, and conservatives of every shade of belief. Our strength is that we can harmonize our differences in conference and then go forward and give the people what they want—that is, good, clean, honest government."

Oswald D. Heck, Speaker of the Assembly, was specific: He said that Dewey was the logical candidate for the nomination.

As early as March 12, at a meeting of Republican leaders in Washington, Kenneth Simpson, then the Republican National Committeeman from New York, made it clear to those present that he was doing all he could to promote the Dewey cause. After the conviction of Hines in February, he had received hundreds of letters, from many states, favoring Dewey. The Gallup poll also showed Dewey gaining since the Hines trial.

Mr. Simpson was not always to be so favorable to Mr. Dewey. His case was a curious one and perhaps can never be fully and satisfactorily explained. His moods were impossible to predict. At times he was a hard-hitting, thoroughly alert and ingratiating political leader; at other times he could be moody, depressed, or choleric. Much of the time his health was not good. It will be sufficient here to say that the time came when he and Mr. Dewey did not see things in the same light; Mr. Simpson is dead and therefore we will discuss neither side of the argument.

Throughout the summer of 1939 the Dewey talk continued. Clubs were springing up in many spots. The boom began to take on a serious aspect when, in August, Mr. Dewey was presented to more than 200 Middle Western party leaders at a garden party on the lake-front estate of his mother's cousin, Leonard C. Reid, at Lakeside, Michigan. Mr. Reid was the lawyer in whose Chicago office Dewey had read law. On this trip Dewey avoided discussing politics in any of his remarks; still, politics was in the air, thicker than any pea soup. He visited his old home town of Owosso and made a speech to the citizens who had assembled to meet him—a speech which, following an introduction by Judge Joseph E. Collins, began in this fashion:

"Judge Collins, neighbors and friends, former playmates who taught me to use my fists, former teachers who tried to get me to study, businessmen who tried to get me to work— it is a joy to me to see in this gathering so many persons who taught so many things to one small boy."

At about this time, talk began going around that Mr. Dewey had formed a "brain trust" patterned somewhat upon that group of professors which in the early days had fluttered about Mr. Roosevelt. It was not a "brain trust"; it was, he explained, a research bureau. There were some things he wanted to find out about. What he found out (and it was a great deal) formed the basis of a series of powerful attacks upon the national administration—speeches which were effective then, and which, for the most part, are good reading to this day.

Leaders began coming to see Mr. Dewey to announce their support. One of them, and by no means the least important, was Mrs. Ruth Hanna McCormick Simms, the daughter of Mark Hanna and perhaps the shrewdest woman politician of them all. Strong, brilliant, with a gift for speaking her mind, she came early to Dewey's side and has been his friend and ally ever since. She operated two ranches, Los Poblanos near Albuquerque, New Mexico, and La Trinchera in southern Colorado. Leaving her cattle and turkeys, she went East and offered her services to Mr. Dewey, who was delighted with her. In a speech to the Women's Republican Club in Boston, in November, 1939, she said:

"Tom Dewey is that rare phenomenon that occurs once in a generation. . . . It is clearly demonstrated that the country wants young men without fear in its government today, and further, that it wants someone whose leadership is directed against corruption, waste, and graft; a man who can be an able administrator as well as a two-fisted fighter, a practical man as well as colorful. In Dewey we have the dynamic leader who has packed into his thirty-eight years as much experience as most men of fifty. . . . If anyone can slash through the maze of bureaucracy in Washington and cut down the forest of patronage, inefficiency, and waste, so that the American people can begin to see the three big trees of constitutional government again, the legislative, judicial, and executive oaks of America, it is Dewey, the man who gets things done."

The formal start of the Dewey campaign began on December 1, at a meeting of New York State Republicans at 100 East 42nd Street, New York City. J. Russel Sprague, the Nassau County leader and member of the state executive committee, told Mr. Dewey on behalf of the state Republican organization, "It is my privilege to tell you that you are their candidate for President of the United States." Mr. Dewey replied briefly, saying he would be glad to make the fight.

Mr. Sprague, a sure-footed politician, a deft organizer, became Mr. Dewey's campaign manager. Thousands of invitations had been received from cities that wanted to hear Mr. Dewey. It was decided he should make many speeches, in as many places as possible. The first speech after he had become an avowed candidate was delivered at Minneapolis on December 6, 1939. Speaking on the theme, "America Is Not Finished," Mr. Dewey got off to an excellent start. It was an attack on defeatism. He quoted President Roosevelt's remark, "Our industrial plant is built." He went on:

"In effect, he says there is no place in this country for the

110

people who are growing up in it. And the tragedy is they are beginning to believe him."

"Is it true," he asked, "that America is matured and completed and overbuilt and incapable of further expansion and new achievements? Is it true that all we can do from now on is to administer the achievements we already have? I do not say no temperately. I say no with resentment and anger."

This speech, an eloquent broadside, was delivered before what was described as the largest preconvention rally ever held in Minnesota. Many came to see the famous gangbuster; others came to cheer his attack. The speech brought generally favorable comment and laid the basis for a long series of more detailed castigations of the Democratic administration.

The Dewey speeches were full of spirit, well larded with figures and quotations. He attacked the economic vacillations of the New Deal in a speech before the Pennsylvania Society in New York on December 19. In Boston, on January 3, 1940, he talked about "the price of the New Deal—and who pays for it." Later he made a great swing over the country. In Helena, Montana, he spoke on basic economic fallacies and accused the administration of incompetence. In Louisville, Kentucky, he made a detailed exposition of the results of the New Deal's economic maneuverings. "The record," he said, "is a stunning series of failures." He tackled the farm problem in a speech at Lincoln, Nebraska, and derided the contradictory policies of the New Deal. In St. Louis he made an eloquent address on "Erosion of Character in Our National Government." He spoke at Chicago; at Wichita, Kansas; at Dallas, Texas; at Winston-Salem, North Carolina, and in many other places.

In more than one speech he alluded to the precarious position of the United States in a world at war and demanded that more vigorous and definite action be taken at once to strengthen the national defense. As a matter of record, it may be pointed out that, as early as January, 1940, in an interview with the press at Portland, Maine, he came out unequivocally in favor of a Navy capable of defending both American coasts. This remark, made more or less incidentally in a discussion of other matters, attracted little attention in the East, but it was played up in the newspapers of the Pacific Coast, where the demand for a two-ocean Navy had been strong and persistent. In Washington, spokesmen for the administration said that Dewey did not know what he was talking about, that he was essentially an ignoramus, and that a two-ocean Navy was out of the question.

It is of some historical interest to note that shortly after Mr. Dewey's declaration in favor of a two-ocean Navy, President Roosevelt went on record in one of his press conferences as ridiculing such an idea. He was quoted as saying that if the theory of a two-ocean American Navy ever had any merit that theory became outmoded with the acquisition of California in 1847. Such a conception of the nation's floating defenses was "just plain dumb," he said.

Two months later Mr. Roosevelt asked Congress for a two-ocean Navy.

The last speech of the Dewey preconvention campaign was a radio address which bore the adequately blunt title "Roosevelt Must Go." Although these speeches contained many passages of straight factual exposition, they were fighting speeches. Indeed, some of the more timorous Republicans thought he may have "gone too far" in his attacks.

This long speaking campaign helped Mr. Dewey in many ways: He came to have a much more accurate "feel" of the country, sympathy for and understanding of what the people were thinking about. He made many friends. He impressed the country with his assured platform manner, his well-modulated voice, and the logical train of his thought. People realized that here was a capable campaigner.

Historical note: Harold L. Ickes, Secretary of the Interior, who at that time had achieved considerable fame as a coiner of epithets, derisive phrases, puns, and somewhat rump-sprung similes, came up with the observation that Dewey had "thrown his diaper into the ring," to call him a "Clamor Boy," to describe him as a "photogenic, radiogenic Charlie McCarthy," and to allege that "the voice may be the voice of Dewey but the hand is the hand of Mark Hanna." This allusion to the long, ghostly fingers of the late Mr. Hanna was provoked by the activities of Mrs. Simms on Mr. Dewey's behalf. That spring of 1940 was one of Mr. Ickes's best seasons. His curmudgeonly wisecracks were greatly admired, not alone by Mr. Ickes himself but in most smart word-painting circles. After 1940 he seemed to become quieter and, more's the pity, not quite so funny.

For the 1940 Republican National Convention the Dewey forces opened their headquarters in the Hotel Walton in Philadelphia, the same hotel where William McKinley once held forth when he was nominated for the Presidency. Senator Robert A. Taft opened his headquarters at the Benjamin Franklin Hotel. Frank E. Gannett, the upstate New York publisher, who was having his own mild boom for President, also was at the Benjamin Franklin; Mr. Gannett had obtained a troupe of elephants from the estate of Pierre Bernard, a noted metaphysician who once was known as "Oom the Omnipotent" and "The Loving Guru of the Tantriks." There was a boom on for Wendell L. Willkie also, but at the beginning no one paid a great deal of attention to him. The Taft and Dewey campaigns had been carried on by skilled politicians; the forces of both men were inclined to look upon the Willkie boosters as a bunch of zealots and amateurs.

Mr. Dewey knew he was in the lead. He made himself available to visitors. He was optimistic but made no sweeping claims. He understood thoroughly that his great weakness lay in the delegation from his own state. The coolness between him and Kenneth Simpson had increased; Rolland Marvin, of Syracuse, was not enthusiastic about Dewey. Other delegates were wavering and looking upon Willkie with increasing favor.

John Lord O'Brian of Buffalo placed Mr. Dewey before the convention in the Municipal Auditorium in a long speech in which he reviewed Dewey's life, his career as prosecutor, and his qualifications as a leader. Mr. O'Brian said:

"There is no sectional or class cleavage in the support given him throughout the nation. He is strong in the agricultural West and strong in the industrial East. Here is the man who can make us a united nation.

"As President, he will call to our aid the ablest advisers in the country. There will be no blacklist; no palace guard to exclude patriotic businessmen or labor officials, or any other right-minded citizens able to contribute to the welfare of the country. There will be no more demoralization in government caused by periodic purges of personal grudges. No past associations will hamper this man's single-minded service to his country. The resourcefulness and freshness of approach that have characterized his past work are the best proof that he will be able to bring into harmony the conflicting interests in our economic life. From him those subversive forces which even now are operating about us will receive no aid or comfort. On election night the fellow-travelers will be outward bound."

On the first ballot the vote was: Dewey, 360; Taft, 189; Willkie, 105. Dewey waited at the Walton with Mrs. Simms, John Foster Dulles, Roger W. Straus, and Paul E. Lockwood. The first ballot showed about what they had expected. Mr. Dewey said:

"The results are great and I am greatly pleased. I expect a gain on the second ballot."

But instead of gaining the Dewey strength quickly began

to crumble, while both Taft and Willkie went ahead. It was impossible for the Dewey managers to hold their delegates in line. On the fifth ballot the vote was: Dewey, 57; Taft, 377; Willkie, 429. While the galleries were screaming with an almost evangelical fervor, "We want Willkie!" the shaggy man from New York and Indiana was nominated on the sixth ballot. Dewey immediately sent a telegram to Willkie:

"I congratulate you on your nomination as the Republican candidate for President and I pledge you my full support in the fight ahead."

Dewey had tasted disappointment at Philadelphia, yes, but he came out of the campaign with vastly increased prestige. His little circle of close friends, who had stood with him during the long months of campaigning, seemed more depressed than Dewey at the outcome.

Keeping his promise to Willkie, Dewey with all good will threw himself into the fight ahead. Unquestionably much of the large Willkie vote in 1940 can be attributed not only to Dewey's speeches in Willkie's behalf but to the groundwork laid by Dewey in defining the issues in his preconvention speeches throughout the country. Moreover, the country came to understand that here, win or lose, was a consistent battler who was in the fight to stay.

Meanwhile, Dewey took his defeat in good humor, remarking, "I led on the wrong three ballots out of six."

XII

INTERLUDE

THOMAS E. DEWEY was sitting in his office—the office of the District Attorney of New York County—one spring day in 1941, months before Pearl Harbor, when a three-man delegation came to see him on an errand that was to have a tremendous effect upon the comfort and relaxation of the hundreds of thousands of men who at that time were being taken into the armed services. The committee represented the various welfare groups which had decided in a general way upon a plan for the United Service Organizations—a great, all-embracing group which should represent them all.

It was explained that the plan was to organize, finance, and then administer the job of providing for the leisure time of the servicemen. By this unity of effort, it was pointed out, they hoped to avoid the conflicts, criticisms, and dissatisfactions which arose in the First World War when numerous organizations, with the best intentions in the world, sought to do the job separately. It was recalled that separate drives for funds in 1917 had duplicated effort and annoyed the public. It was true, of course, that some organizations were praised highly for their part in that war, but others received blame for matters which usually, in the very nature of things, were more or less unavoidable under the setup.

The delegation asked Mr. Dewey whether he would accept the chairmanship of the first national campaign committee of the United Service Organizations in a drive for

$10,500,000, to be conducted all over the country. Dewey sought more information and was told that the Federal government had allocated $15,000,000 to put up 365 buildings near but not on military reservations. The USO idea had the full approval of the national administration and the Army and Navy Departments. The Federal government would provide the buildings; the money raised by the USO would be used to staff and operate them.

The main objective of the USO, Mr. Dewey was told, was to provide "off-reservation" recreation centers for men in the services. On the reservations the services themselves would handle the task—providing entertainment, selling cigarettes, or assigning chaplains for religious services. Dewey accepted the chairmanship. The formal announcement was made at a meeting in the Empire State Building in the presence of W. Spencer Robertson, chairman of the national board of the YMCA; Francis P. Matthews, chairman of the National Catholic Community Service; Edward J. Parker, national secretary of the Salvation Army; Frank L. Weil, president of the Jewish Welfare Board; Randall J. LeBoeuf, Jr., president of the National Travelers Aid Association, and Mrs. Henry J. Ingraham, president of the National Board of the YWCA. Mr. Dewey said:

"All shades of opinion can unite in this truly American effort. It is solely an effort to provide decently for our own boys. The President and the responsible officers of the Army and Navy strongly indorse this effort and urge its support.

"The appeal is a major challenge to the whole people. If the government should be compelled to provide these funds the result would be government control of the religious activities and the private lives of the youth of America. To that all Americans are unalterably opposed."

Mr. Dewey recognized that before any actual drive for funds could be undertaken, the USO idea must be built up favorably in the public mind. Into this task he put six strenuous weeks. He faced two immediate tasks: (1) to dramatize, publicize, and "sell" USO to the people, and (2) to reconcile and blend into a common-sense, workable plan the numerous and sometimes conflicting ideas of the various organizations as to how the money should be collected and spent. And what, after all, was best for soldiers, sailors, and marines in the way of recreation and leisure pursuits? What did the men themselves think?

"Let's ask them," said Dewey.

For six weeks Dewey inspected Army camps and naval bases as well as the near-by communities and sites in all sections of the country. In these trips he and his companions covered 41,000 miles. With him on his first swing were Walter Hoving, president of the USO and the dynamic, public-spirited head of the New York department store of Lord & Taylor; Marshall Field, publisher of the *Chicago Sun,* and Paul E. Lockwood, at that time the Executive Assistant District Attorney. On this first trip they visited the Chesapeake Bay area, including Fortress Monroe, the Norfolk Navy Base, and several camps.

On this, as well as on subsequent trips, Mr. Dewey ruled out fanfare. He talked with generals, with high Navy officers, with mayors, and with many officials and leading citizens of communities near the service camps but most of all with the privates and the sailors. His main objective in all his conversations was to learn the attitude of the men in the ranks. What were their ideas on what USO could do for them? Dewey and his party slept in tents, took morning showers with the men, and out of all their talks and experiences gained what they believed to be an accurate understanding of what the men wanted.

On the second trip Mr. Dewey, using the airplane of General George C. Marshall, Chief of Staff, covered service reservations in most of the territory east of the Mississippi. On the third swing, he covered the West Coast, starting out with a rally in the American Legion Bowl in Hollywood.

After a brief check-up swing through the camps of the Northeast, Mr. Dewey ended the educational phase of the campaign with a national rally in Madison Square Garden in New York. He did not do things in quite the way that the usual high-powered publicity experts performed; instead, he kept speech-making to a minimum. Madison Square Garden, the site of many a prize fight, the circus, and political rallies, was turned into an enormous USO center. Many headliners from the stage and screen were present, and some of America's best known bands played. It was Dewey's idea that this Garden show should reflect—in its liveliness and friendly spirit—something of what USO hoped to do in a smaller way in the neighborhood of every spot where men were in training.

The audience was made up of fathers and mothers of servicemen. They had been especially invited for the occasion. Dewey told them that he had seen a lot of their boys and they were looking fine. "I have never seen an American boy who didn't want to go to town once in a while," he said. "If he didn't, he wouldn't be an American boy."

Dewey worked hard in laying the foundations for the great USO campaign. He had plenty of help. The fundamental good sense back of the idea soon made its appeal to everybody. Many thousands of volunteers in the big cities and the small towns as well—wherever servicemen were likely to visit in their off time—came forward and joined the drive for funds. By the time the actual drive for money started, Dewey and his assistants, aided by friendly publicity from many sources, had impressed upon the country the wisdom of the USO idea. The first drive had set $10,500,000 as its goal; the collection amounted to $16,000,000.

The success of this undertaking was due primarily to the generous instincts of the American people, who were quick to see the advantages of the USO program. The initial driving force, as well as the enthusiasm necessary to such enterprises, was supplied by Dewey. He was undoubtedly the right man in the right spot at the right time.

In February, 1942, when Dewey was back in private practice (he had opened an office at 20 Exchange Place) he was again called upon to aid in a fund-raising campaign, this time for the Navy Relief Society, which sought quickly to raise a national fund of $5,000,000. Here was something less spectacular than the USO campaign, and requiring less energy, but the cause appealed to Dewey—partly, perhaps, because of his family relationship, distant though it was, with Admiral George Dewey.

The Navy Relief Society is one of the most admirable of all such organizations. It tides the families of Navy men over periods when the need is greatest and when the distress otherwise might be tragic. Dewey accepted the chairmanship for the Third Naval District, embracing New York, Connecticut, and northern New Jersey. The campaign started with a dinner at the Waldorf Astoria. Dewey soon had whipped together an organization that made a strong appeal throughout the area under his jurisdiction. One of the high lights of the campaign was on April 15, when Dewey and Mayor La Guardia spoke at a large open-air meeting at City Hall Plaza. The drive was entirely successful.

Notwithstanding the fact that he was out of public office in 1942, that was one of the busiest years of his career. As soon as he hung out his shingle at 20 Exchange Place, he was engaged as counsel in a wide variety of civil cases—civil cases for the man who for a decade had been wholly absorbed in the administration of the criminal law. Within a few months it had become plain that his practice was established and lucrative. He soon realized, however, that he had become a public figure, a leading citizen, and as such he was sought on the boards of hospitals and charitable organizations, and as a speaker at many affairs of a civic or philanthropic nature. As he demonstrated by taking over the Navy Relief Society Drive, he was always ready, often when his burgeoning law practice would hardly permit, to throw himself wholeheartedly into any cause that he believed to be for the good of his own community or of the nation.

But 1942, the year of the Governorship campaign, turned out to be only an interlude, a breathing spell, between one type of public service and another. Mr. Dewey has always had the knack of keeping busy.

XIII

LANDSLIDE

THOMAS E. DEWEY, upon leaving the District Attorney's office on the last day of 1941, at the end of his distinguished four-year term, was almost immediately put forward as the next Republican candidate for Governor of New York. His brilliant showing against Governor Herbert H. Lehman in 1938 had made it certain that he could have his party's nomination again if he would take it.

The Dewey boom for Governor began to take form in the latter part of January, 1942. Bruce Barton, the trenchant writer of books and advertising, and former Representative from the Seventeenth Congressional District in New York, arose at a dinner of the New York Young Republican Club in the National Republican Club in West Fortieth Street and said, "It is a great privilege to be sitting beside the next Governor of New York."

Mr. Barton happened to be sitting next to Thomas E. Dewey. His remarks brought great applause. In his own speech on this occasion, Mr. Dewey advocated the vigorous prosecution of the war, saying that "there is not a single Republican who wouldn't offer his entire time and service to whatever job the President might assign him." At the same time he said the Republican Party should "fight public waste and unsound measures with vigor," that incompetents in office should be removed, and that multifarious agencies of the national administration should be consolidated. In the months following, it became apparent that Republicans of virtually all shades of thought, even those who had opposed his Presidential ambitions at Philadelphia, were united behind him for Governor.

The Republican State Convention, meeting at Saratoga in August, in the same hall where Dewey had been first nominated for Governor in 1938, again selected Dewey to lead the party. Kenneth F. McAffer of Albany spoke for less than a minute in announcing his intention to put Mr. Dewey's name in nomination, and then said he would let motion pictures tell the story. For fifteen minutes the delegates and visitors sat in the darkness and watched a picture giving the high lights of Dewey's public career—the "Lucky" Luciano conviction, the trial of James J. Hines, and other episodes of a busy life. The film was accompanied by soundtrack commentary. After the seconding speeches, Mr. Dewey was nominated by acclamation.

A strong state ticket was named with him: Thomas W. Wallace, District Attorney of Schenectady County, for Lieutenant Governor; Nathaniel L. Goldstein, of Brooklyn, for State Attorney General; Frank C. Moore, of Kenmore, for Comptroller. The platform, in the writing of which Mr. Dewey had a guiding hand, pledged the party to fight the war to complete victory, a just and lasting peace, and to support the President in all measures to win the war. At the same time it criticized "management of the war effort on the home front—the blundering, the inefficiency, and the inconsistency in policies."

It was on this occasion that Mr. Dewey made his much-discussed announcement of his intention not to seek higher office while serving as Governor of New York. His words were:

"Neither you nor I are here concerned with 1944. This convention and the Republican campaign are concerned only with the winning of the war and with good government for the people of the State of New York for the next four years. *For my part,* let me say right now that I shall devote the next four years exclusively to the service of the people of New York State."

Herbert Brownell, Jr., a young New York lawyer who had served several years in the Assembly, was selected as campaign manager. He did a good job of it; his claims for Mr. Dewey were surprisingly accurate, though slightly on the conservative side. The campaign, as Robert Moses, the learned, phrase-making Park Commissioner of New York City, said at the time, "had its humors." Hamilton Fish, the isolationist Congressman, came out for Dewey; Dewey repudiated him in a speech in Fish's own district. Mrs. Helen Simpson, the widow of Kenneth Simpson, the Republican leader who had broken with Dewey before the Philadelphia convention in 1940, issued a statement in June attacking Dewey on several grounds, saying that he and his political advisers had succeeded in turning the Republican Party in New York State into the most rigid disciplinary and proprietary political machine the State of New York had seen since the days of Tom Platt.

The position of Mr. Dewey in the 1942 race was greatly improved by the rift between the adherents of the Washington administration and the wing led by James A. Farley, then chairman of the New York State Democratic Committee. Mr. Farley insisted that the Democratic nomination be given to John J. Bennett, the State Attorney General, who had a good record but who was not a particularly stirring candidate. Many of the New Dealers openly snubbed the Bennett candidacy. To complicate matters further, the American Labor Party put up Dean Alfange, who was supported by many influential people. Mayor La Guardia said that although Dewey, Bennett, and Alfange were all "able, competent men," he was going to support Alfange.

As for Wendell Willkie, he was busy making plans for his famous "One World" tour at the time Dewey was nominated for Governor. He declined to discuss the state campaign at that time, although it was known that he was not one of Mr. Dewey's most rapturous admirers. There never was any particular bitterness between the two men; they simply never seemed to hit it off together. Just before the election, Mr. Willkie, having returned from his world tour, issued a statement giving his views on the war leadership and other topics, adding:

"And I, of course, expect to vote the Republican state ticket, anticipating from the state platform that Mr. Dewey and his fellow candidates will give New York a liberal government."

The 1942 campaign, though it had its interesting points, was much less exciting than the one in 1938. Mr. Dewey reiterated many of his familiar charges against the Democratic Party in the state, amplifying his theory that its good men were merely the respectable façade of a structure that was unsound at the core. He was particularly effective in assailing what he termed the lethargy of the Democratic administration. He also paid much attention to the problems of the farmers of the state. Among other things he promised assistance in obtaining a larger share of farm machinery than was at that time allotted to New York, and to do all he could to put an end to the trend toward breaking up dairy herds and abandoning potentially productive farms. Discussing Dewey and the farmers, the *New York Herald Tribune* said:

"We of the metropolitan district visualize New York so exclusively in terms of the city and of the near-by suburban counties on Long Island and along the Hudson that we forget that New York for years has ranked sixth or seventh among the forty-eight states in the cash value of its farm crops. To have in Albany as Governor a man who knows farm life, understands the farmers' problems and is determined to fight to help the farmers would obviously be a distinct advantage to the state and nation. New York is one of the pivotal states in the nation's farm production program and one in which the farmers have long been most neglected. The benefits showered—mostly for political purposes—on the farmers of Middle Western and Southern states, benefits that bore rich dividends in votes for the New Deal in the last decade, have not been as lavishly handed out in New York."

In closing his campaign at a rally in the Bronx, Mr. Dewey reviewed his campaign, summed up the issues as he saw them, and then said:

"Throughout the campaign I have offered programs to deal with the tremendous problems which will confront the next state administration in making New York the vital factor it should be in the war effort. I have repeatedly said the war is not a political issue. The preservation of our country must never be the subject of debate between Americans. But I have also said repeatedly that the part of New York State and its 13,000,000 people in this war is definitely an issue. That part can be reactionary, supine, and listless or it can be vigorous, alert, and progressive. We can lie down and join our opponents, saying: Let Washington do it. Or we can see that we do our share. I know that every citizen of New York wants to do his share. America expects the state of New York to do its full share."

A great many persons who ordinarily voted the Democratic ticket swung to Dewey in 1942. The state, it appeared, was growing tired of a succession of Democratic Governors who had spanned two whole decades. There was a widespread feeling that it was a "Dewey year." Many men of rather pronounced "liberal" views swung to Dewey. An important letter from Dr. Alvin Johnson, director of the New School for Social Research, was printed in the *New York Times*. After saying that Mr. Dewey was "his own man," Dr. Johnson, a Democrat, wrote:

"In time of crisis it is of paramount importance that the chief executive of a state should be a man of flexible mind.

That Dewey has a flexible mind is recognized on every hand. Indeed, this characteristic is sometimes brought against him as a reproach. 'We do not know where he stands,' it is said.

"This we know, that Dewey sees in individual initiative the mainspring of progress; that he regards as imperative political objectives a rising standard of living, the increasing participation of organized labor in industrial life, the rehabilitation of agriculture, a judicious development of international economic relations, the unequivocal assumption by the nation of a share in the responsibility for the maintenance of world peace. By what concrete measures these objectives shall be realized Dewey does not pretend to know at the present time; nor does anyone know. Principles can be established in advance; their application must depend on the course of events, faced with open mind.

"It is charged that Dewey looks beyond the Governorship to national leadership. It is to be hoped that this is true. The American form of government needs two strong, vigorously led parties. Today the Republican Party is weak. As in the First World War, it is characterized by negativism and reaction. Dewey is a progressive who looks boldly to the future. Insofar as his election to the Governorship of New York places him in a position of national leadership in his party, it offers a promise that in the trying postwar period the Republican Party will assume its proper place in working out the policies under which we may live prosperously and in peace."

This letter, coming from such a respected source, made a profound impression in many quarters. Meanwhile Dewey was being attacked freely by his opponents. Bennett made a busy campaign, but he was not especially effective. Henry Epstein, the Democratic nominee for State Attorney General, devoted most of his own campaign to attacking Dewey. He called Dewey a "straddler" and quoted many excerpts from statements and speeches to prove that Dewey had changed his mind on various issues, particularly on foreign affairs. Mr. Epstein also alluded to Herbert Hoover as Dewey's "fairy godfather in politics." Mr. Epstein, to this day, never misses an opportunity to make a speech attacking Dewey for something or other; it has grown to be a hobby with him. Governor Lehman also came out in support of Bennett and tried to cast doubts on Dewey's grasp of state affairs as well as his progressiveness. "Novice" was one of the epithets. Alfred E. Smith came out for Bennett, but in speaking for his candidate he was careful not to attack Dewey, for whom he has always had a high regard. He did say that a victory for Dewey would result "in a scramble for patronage and favor that will turn the state government upside down at a very critical time in our history." Owen D. Young, whose words probably carried some authority, made a speech arguing that Dewey had the "prosecutor's mind" rather than the judicial temperament required of a great executive.

Mr. Farley made his first great mistake in forcing the nomination of Mr. Bennett upon the reluctant Democrats; it is probable that a speech he delivered, making preposterous insinuations against Mr. Dewey, was an equally serious error. In any event, although he kept up a smiling exterior and pretended to believe that his man Bennett would win, he was smart enough politician to know that Dewey was showing tremendous strength. Not even a hard-won statement from President Roosevelt that he felt Bennett was the "best qualified" of the three candidates could do much to help the cause of Farley and Bennett.

Soon after the returns began coming in on election night, November 3, 1942, it was clear that Dewey had been swept into office. Herbert Brownell had predicted that he would win by 600,000 votes—a figure believed at the time to be unduly optimistic, the conventional hyperbolic claim of a campaign manager. The figures showed that Dewey had a plurality of 647,628 votes. His total vote was 2,147,702. Bennett's was 1,500,074; Alfange's, 403,552. Dewey carried Queens and Richmond Counties, in New York City; Bennett's plurality in the heavily Democratic city as a whole was only 85,076. Dewey carried the entire Republican state ticket into office with him, giving him the "team" he had asked for, and the Legislature, in addition, was overwhelmingly Republican.

In his quarters at the Hotel Roosevelt in New York, Mr. Dewey received the news of his victory happily, but he indulged in no celebration such as had been customary for winning candidates in peacetime elections. Asked "How does it feel to be elected?" he said, "Being Governor is pretty sober business in these times." Then he gave out this statement:

"A great responsibility has been placed upon me today by the people of the State of New York. I am deeply grateful for the honor. I shall do everything within my power to be worthy of the trust.

"This election has one simple meaning. It means that we, of the Empire State, want to put every ounce of our energies and of our resources wholly into the national war effort.

"The fact that one party lost and the other party won is not important. We are not here tonight to celebrate a party victory. We are all of us interested in only one victory—total, uncompromising, crushing victory over our country's enemies.

"If this election has any meaning, it is that the American people are pledged with all their hearts and souls to that end and to that end wholly.

"Today we have made a great new affirmation of our faith in freedom, in the ultimate triumph of justice and in the ultimate triumph of free men under the God of all of us.

"We have sent a stunning message to our enemies. We have shown to all the world that we—even in the midst of total war—can hold a free election under the American two-party system—that even in the midst of total war we can make changes necessary to strengthen our government. We have shown once more that the system of free government for which we are fighting is a living, vital thing, and that we care deeply for it.

"Let every man and woman now put aside all rivalries. We are all Americans together. The only task before us is to redouble our efforts in the winning of the war. In that cause we all belong to one great opposition party—the party of uncompromising opposition to Hitler, his allies, and all the hateful things they stand for. In all things needed for the winning of this war we are united in unswerving loyalty to our Commander in Chief. Let us make this clear to all the world: We in America are solidly united. Shoulder to shoulder we shall with every resource at our command carry on this fight to total and lasting victory."

In an exceedingly friendly editorial the *New York Times,* a Democratic paper which had supported Mr. Dewey's Democratic opponent, said that the election of Mr. Dewey meant that "the people of New York have not chosen to write Finis to the fine record of progressive social legislation which has been written at Albany under the leadership of Alfred E. Smith, Franklin D. Roosevelt, and Herbert Lehman." It was pointed out that Mr. Dewey and his colleagues had thoroughly renounced "the old Republican position of unfailing opposition to all progressive measures." The editorial went on to say that the result "by no hook or crook" could be interpreted as a "repudiation" of the government's war policy or as evidence of a division of American opinion on the war issue. Then the *Times* said:

"To the Governor-elect this newspaper offers its best wishes. We hope that his administration will be successful in every way. We know that we do not need to tell him that he will have our support in every step he takes to bring the resources of this state completely into the war and to assure as best he can the safety and the health and the happiness of the people of New York."

The election out of the way, Governor-elect Dewey immediately buckled down to a study of state problems. He said he planned no political appointments on the spoils system basis; he sent out thanks to the thousands who had worked for the Republican cause. As to appointments, he said:

"I have not one single person in mind for a state position at this moment, to say nothing of any commitment to any man or woman alive. Every appointment will be considered carefully and with all the deliberation necessary, and it may take months to bring the best service possible to the state."

Back in Owosso the people who remembered Tom Dewey as a boy were happy over the result. Earl Putnam, on whose farm young Dewey had worked that summer twenty-four years before, said, "Tom has proved his caliber in public life just as he proved it by doing a man's work on our farm."

XIV

THE NEW BROOM

THOMAS E. DEWEY took the oath of office as Governor of New York on the last day of December, 1942, at a private ceremony at the Executive Mansion. The oath was administered by that same Justice Philip J. McCook of "the Fighting McCooks" who had presided over the special grand jury when the young prosecutor was making his first moves against the New York rackets. It was said that in those early days Justice McCook had wondered whether Dewey was not, to put it mildly, somewhat immature; whatever that feeling may have been, it was replaced now by something quite different. The men were deep, warm, and lasting friends. Each admired and respected the other. The ceremony at the Mansion was a proud moment for both.

The next day, January 1, 1943, the official inaugural ceremonies were held, but on a much smaller scale than usual. At the official swearing-in ceremony, Judge Irving Lehman, Chief Judge of the New York Court of Appeals, administered the oath.

When Dewey said that he had made no commitments as to appointments, he was telling the truth. If he had any individual in mind for any state office, not even his closest advisers, men who had worked with him day and night, could have named that person. Those who knew Dewey best were confident that when the time came he would gather able men about him. True, the Republican politicians were hungry for patronage after twenty years of living on husks and hope long deferred. Dewey took his time.

There was, in fact, no general exodus of Democratic office-holders; a few of them are still in office. "The sure-footed Mr. Dewey," as the *New York Herald Tribune* once called him in an editorial, made no move until he was convinced he was right, but then he moved swiftly. He had mentioned "dry rot" in his campaign speeches. The retort to this charge was that the Democratic administrations of Smith, Roosevelt, and Lehman had given the state a new high level of competent administration. Dewey, admitting that these administrations were not without merit, still insisted that the state's functions were being crippled by inertia—that slowing down, that officeholders' fatigue, that tired outlook which seems to be the occupational disease of so many political appointees of whatever party.

From his viewpoint, the state's governmental machinery was somewhat like a beautiful and essentially well-made old clock that had been allowed to become dusty, corroded in spots, and not as efficient as it should be. Far from shouting the traditional blanket indictment of "Throw the rascals out," he went ahead planning certain changes designed to make the machinery in hand work better. To do this, he felt after study, it would be necessary to make some changes. He made these changes with quick decision when he felt the time had come.

As a rough generalization, it may be said that most of the men in the key positions around Governor Dewey are about his own age—with a variation of not more than ten years in either direction. There are, to be sure, exceptions. He appointed some men who were strangers to him, but he knew their records and liked their personalities. He was anything but a stranger to many of the men he brought into important posts. These men differ widely, but they have a few things in common: they are clean, they are vigorous, they are intelligent, and they have complete faith in what Thomas E. Dewey has been trying to do in public life.

For example, there is Paul E. Lockwood, secretary to the Governor, who has been close to him since the racket-busting days. When Dewey announced that he was not going to run for reelection as District Attorney, Lockwood was one of those mentioned as his successor. Starting his career as a reporter on the *Brooklyn Eagle,* Lockwood left journalism after a few years to study law at Columbia. He is a level-headed lawyer; he is also an excellent executive and has a thorough knowledge of the ins and outs of politics. His acquaintance in New York State and through the country is enormous. He is a big chap—about 240 pounds and 6 feet 3 inches tall. He has the trained boxer's knack of preventing people from running over him; that is to say, he can be an amiable fellow, but no one is going to batter down his defenses. Moreover, he has the priceless gift of being able to keep his shirt on in all sorts of stormy political weather.

As his executive assistant, soon after he took office, Governor Dewey appointed James C. Hagerty, a political writer on the *New York Times,* a son of that revered, veteran *Times* man, James A. Hagerty. Among many other duties, Hagerty is charged with seeing that the news regarding the Governor's office and the principal state departments is available to the press. But Hagerty is by no means simply a Dewey press agent; most of the time he has been occupied by state business which might or might not make news.

A few of the other people in the Dewey regime at Albany:

One of the first advisers to the Governor back in the days when he was first being boomed for President was Elliott V. Bell, a short, unobtrusive scholar with wavy hair. Bell had been a financial writer for the *New York Herald Tribune* and later for the *Times.* He is respected not only in Wall Street but in more academic circles for his knowledge of economics and finance. Dewey made him State Superintendent of Banking. Bell has recently become a neighbor of Dewey's at Pawling and has been the Governor's close friend for nearly twenty years.

Another man who, Dewey was sure, understood finance was John E. Burton, a lean, scholarly student of government who was born in Ohio thirty-six years ago, reared there, and educated at Hiram College. Burton has been a Dewey adviser off and on for years. Dewey made him Director of the Budget, where his skill in research and passionate interest in effective, liberal, but sound government can have free play. Burton is also chairman of the Temporary State Commission for Post-war Public Works Planning.

Dewey named Rollin Browne, a well-known lawyer and tax expert of New York City, as President of the State Tax Commission. Here was an appointment entirely devoid of either personal or political significance. Dewey did not know Mr. Browne, but after two months of investigation, decided he was the best man in New York for the job and talked him into leaving a profitable practice and joining the Albany cabinet. Mr. Browne was born in Talladega, Alabama. Dewey never has seemed to care where a man was born.

Edward Corsi, who had served as Commissioner of Immigration and Naturalization at Ellis Island and as an official of the New York City Department of Public Welfare, was appointed State Industrial Commissioner and assigned to cleaning up the tangled affairs left by previous administrations in the field of workmen's compensation. Mr. Corsi, known as a hard worker and a man with a social conscience, was born in Italy and came to this country when he was ten years old.

Dewey was delighted to reappoint John A. Lyons, who in 1939 had succeeded Edward P. Mulrooney as State Commissioner of Correction. Long recognized as one of the ablest officials in the New York Police Department, Mr. Lyons first became associated with Dewey back in 1931 in investigations in cooperation with the Federal government. In 1935 Lyons was an inspector of police, and Dewey picked him to head a special squad of carefully selected young policemen. Lyons, white-haired and calm, has always had Dewey's respect and confidence.

Another reappointment was that of Dr. Edward S. Godfrey, Jr., as State Commissioner of Health. Dr. Godfrey, who was born at Fort Yates, North Dakota, has had wide experience as a public health administrator and has written many articles on medical problems. His standing in the field of public health is beyond question.

For Chairman of the New York State Liquor Authority, Dewey picked John Francis O'Connell, who had served with him as chief investigator in the District Attorney's office. Mr. O'Connell had also performed distinguished service in many parts of the country as a member of the Federal Bureau of Investigation. In his time he has handled the cases of kidnappers, fraudulent bankrupts, gangsters, tax evaders, and many other types of unlovely miscreants. There is no "side" to Mr. O'Connell. He is a slim, quiet man who, in a crowd, would hardly be noticed; he has no more "front" than an ordinary bank teller. But he knows his business. As head of the Liquor Authority, he is in a position where it is exceedingly important to keep an eye on the ambitions and machinations of certain characters, both underworld and outwardly respectable, who fancy they can make money quickly in the illicit conduct of the liquor business. Mr. O'Connell understands these wise boys.

Dewey wanted a new State Superintendent of Public Works. He had heard of Charles H. Sells, who had for some years been Commissioner of Public Works in Westchester County and who was largely responsible for the magnificent improvements in that area. But he had never met Mr. Sells. It so happened that Mr. Sells had just returned to this country from Iran, where he had passed thirteen months in charge of building military supply lines into Russia—a $16,-000,000 Lend-Lease project involving the construction of roads, docks, camps, bridges, and barges. From that assignment he had gone to Brazil to work on airport projects. Dewey located Mr. Sells in Florida, induced him to fly to Albany for a conference, and was instantly impressed by the man's personality. He talked Mr. Sells, one of the world's ablest engineers, into taking the state job at $12,000 a year.

Another appointment, one that appeared to please even the most rabid of the Dewey critics, was that of Robert T. Lansdale as State Commissioner of Social Welfare. Mr. Lansdale, educated at Oberlin College and the University of Michigan, had been an assistant to the United States Commissioner of Indian Affairs. He had served in Washington on unemployment relief, he had made a relief survey for Governor Lehman, and he had been a teacher in the New York School of Social Work. He is what is described as a "middle of the road" man in social welfare work. He has been busy on postwar planning. Largely through his efforts, also, the sum of $103,350 was allocated from the State Emergency Fund to provide facilities for boys committed for juvenile delinquency to the State Training School at Warwick. He is aggressive, independent, without political ties— and still seems to be satisfactory to the adherents of different schools of thought in social work.

The State Department of Commerce, newly created, has grown rapidly under Dewey. The importance of this department may be judged by those who had been reading the various conflicting reports on the position of the City and State of New York in the nation's economy. The job of the present Commissioner, M. P. Catherwood, and the deputy commissioner and director of state publicity, Harold Keller, is to gather the facts, to help manufacturers who want to operate in New York, and to make things easier for industry. Many new firms have been brought into the state; the value of war contracts has increased. It seems fairly clear that New York is not dying and that its state government is doing something to create business opportunity and more jobs for its people.

The foregoing names—a few out of a great many—may give an idea of the sort of men the Governor prefers to appoint to office. They may be men who have worked with him for years, as in the case of Charles D. Breitel, the Governor's brilliant and remarkably able counsel, or they may be executives of whose work he has heard favorably. They may be utter strangers. Either way, Dewey surrounded himself with the best, a feat not always easy in wartime.

The wartime situation, however, did make it possible for Governor Dewey to obtain the full-time services of Lieutenant General Hugh A. Drum as Commander of the New York Guard. This veteran military man, who saw service as far back as the Spanish-American War, had been commanding general of the Eastern Defense Command of the First Army, with headquarters in New York. Knowing he was to reach retirement age soon, Governor Dewey prevailed upon him to take over the Guard, a stroke that was widely praised. Besides being commander of the State Guard, General Drum is chairman of the New York State Veterans' Commission.

As a going financial concern, the State of New York is today in a better position than at any time in its history—a fact for which no particular individual can claim credit. As the Governor pointed out in his report to the people in April, 1944, the state on the first of that month (the beginning of the new fiscal year) had a surplus of $163,000,000. The surplus was approaching that figure when the Legislature met. The money had piled up, as the Governor said, "as a result of abnormal wartime conditions and of good state housekeeping." In his report the Governor said:

"There were many suggestions of pleasant and useful ways in which we might spend it. But it seemed to me, and to the

Republican members of the Legislature, that this money was not really ours to spend. Rather, it was a fund to be held in trust for the million young men and women of our state who are in the armed forces, for the millions of war workers who, when hostilities end, will be changing over to peacetime jobs. When that time comes, a great responsibility will fall upon the state, which it must be ready to meet without delay—to help industry convert itself to peace production and to contribute its own part through immediate launching of needed and much deferred public works.

"Accordingly, in my opening message to the Legislature—to forestall raids which were later vigorously attempted by pressure groups on this wartime surplus—I proposed to create a Post-war Reconstruction Fund and to lock up in it, the entire surplus. This was done, as Chapter 1 of the Laws of 1944.

"Our Post-war Planning Commission has been working hard to prepare for the day of reconversion for peace. Blueprints are now being drawn for many new housing projects. Plans are being made for urgently needed additions to our overcrowded state hospitals. Under a law passed this year we are now already at work, preparing to purchase rights of way for a great arterial highway system.

"When the day of reconversion comes, New York State will approach it, not merely with blueprints and bond issues to create new debts; we shall have, ready for instant use, a minimum of $163,000,000 cold cash. Moreover, the State Department of Commerce is working intensively with business, big and small, all over the state, for the new industries and quick change-overs, which will provide the great bulk of opportunity and employment for our people."

The Governor's new taxation experts put into effect a simplified form for the making out of state income tax returns. Because of the state surplus, a 25 per cent reduction in the fixed amount of income taxes was kept in effect. In addition, under Dewey it became possible to pay the state tax in four installments, and to make deductions for medical expenses, life insurance premiums, and children over eighteen in school.

Thomas E. Dewey has been what may fairly be known as "a strong governor." Most observers, even those who might naturally be inclined to be critical, have agreed that he also has been "a good governor." His record has been made somewhat easier of accomplishment because of the fact that the Legislature under him was Republican. The Legislature, in both 1943 and 1944, approved his recommendations. To say that he "steamrollered" the Legislature, or "had them under his thumb," or "bossed" them, seems, however, to be an unjustified straining of terms. He did not get his recommended legislation through by nodding his head, or expressing a whim, or pushing a special set of buttons, or performing any acts of hypnotism. Night after night he sat in the Executive Mansion, or in his office at the State Capitol, conferring with legislative leaders, ironing out differences on the form of certain bills, and bringing different groups into harmony.

There was, to be sure, one bitter fight—the one over reapportionment, the bugbear of politicians everywhere. The legislative districts of New York had not been revised for twenty-six years, though the Constitution requires decennial apportionment. Shifts of population had thrown many districts far out of line. In his 1942 campaign Dewey promised reapportionment. When he took office, a bill was introduced, with his backing, which increased the Senate membership from 51 to 56 and revised Assembly lines so as to shift eight seats, mostly held by Republicans, to New York city areas. Vague attacks were made by frightened members on the constitutionality of the bill. One Republican, Assemblyman William M. Stuart, of Steuben County, denounced the bill as "suicide" for his party.

The Governor, however, had one unassailable argument

on his side. That was the argument of public interest. When the showdown came, it was clear that neither party could afford to vote against the reapportionment bill, imperfect though it may have been in some respects. The bill was passed and was later held to be constitutional. Here was one of Dewey's most important and clear-cut victories as an executive who was determined to keep his campaign promises on a matter of paramount concern to the state.

Another squabble, which for a short time appeared to have serious possibilities, occurred toward the end of the 1944 Legislature over a bill that concentrated in the New York City Superintendent of Schools powers which previously he had shared with a board of associate superintendents. Most of the influential newspapers of New York City were in favor of the bill. It was argued that it would make for better school administration and eliminate a situation under which the Superintendent was subject to the whims of those under him. The Democrats, however, held that the bill was a step toward giving Mayor La Guardia even more control over the school system than he already had—and that, they felt, was too much. A great many Republicans sided with the Democrats, although they admitted privately that the bill was good, and the measure was defeated in an Assembly vote. The bill was tabled. Then Dewey was supposed to have "put on pressure." In fact, he conferred at length with the five leaders of both houses. All agreed that the bill was good and decidedly in the public interest. The only real opposition was from a lobby that deserved a licking. On reconsideration, just before adjournment, the bill was passed. Legislators behave strangely in the last gray hours before adjournment; one Republican is said to have voted for the bill while hiding under a desk, and another while holding his fingers to his nose. Whatever their impious attitudes, the bill passed—and respectable commentators agreed that it was a sound piece of legislation.

Thus the Governor, administering the affairs of the state with a hand of extraordinary firmness, not only carried out his campaign pledges but devised means of meeting new conditions as they arose. In the main, he received excellent cooperation; for his part, he showed once more that he could cooperate with others. In revitalizing the state departments, cleaning out unsavory situations which came to light, and giving due recognition to important elements among the people, in "humanizing" taxes, and in preparing for the state's future needs, he did all that most of his well-wishers had expected of him—and in some instances a great deal more.

He handled still another situation firmly but contrary to the wishes of many of his advisers; this involved that notorious chunk of emery dust in the engine of democracy, otherwise Thomas A. Aurelio. If this affair proved anything, it proved that there has not yet been found a perfect method of selecting judges. The Governor's own statement explains the entire matter. It follows:

"I have been asked to invoke the power vested in me by the Constitution to convene the Legislature into Extraordinary Session to enact a law designed to permit the withdrawal of the nomination of City Magistrate Thomas A. Aurelio for Justice of the Supreme Court in the First Judicial District.

"On August 23, 1943, the Democratic Judicial Convention of the First Judicial District, comprising the counties of the Bronx and New York in the City of New York, nominated Magistrate Aurelio as one of their candidates for Justice of the Supreme Court in that District. On the following day the Republican Judicial Convention for that District made a similar nomination of Magistrate Aurelio.

"Four days later Frank S. Hogan, District Attorney of New York County, publicly disclosed that on the morning after Magistrate Aurelio received the Democratic nomination, he telephoned to one Frank Costello on Costello's private, unlisted telephone. The conversation, in part, was as follows:

"Aurelio: 'Good morning, Francesco, how are you and thanks for everything.'

"Costello: 'Congratulations! It went over perfect. When I tell you something is in the bag you can rest assured.'

"Aurelio: 'It was perfect. . . . Right now I want to assure you of my loyalty for all you have done. It's undying.'

"Costello: 'I know. I'll see you soon.'

"This conversation Magistrate Aurelio subsequently admitted.

"Costello is a leading underworld character with a criminal record. He has been widely publicized over a period of years as the principal operator of slot machines throughout the United States and as the backer of gambling and other criminal enterprises.

"Following the revelation that the Democratic nomination of Aurelio had been procured by Costello, the Committee on Vacancies of both the Republican and Democratic Parties declared the nomination vacant and attempted to nominate other candidates for the office. Magistrate Aurelio then appealed to the Courts, which upheld his legal right to remain on the ballot.

"I am satisfied that Magistrate Aurelio's indebtedness to Costello for his nomination has rendered him unfit to hold any public office, let alone the high judicial office he seeks.

"I am keenly aware of the effects of such demoralizing influences upon the administration of justice. On too many occasions criminals have benefited by apparently unsupportable judicial decisions, from which there was no appeal.

"Nevertheless, through the years, the American system of justice under law has been vindicated through the democratic process. Of infinitely greater importance than the defeat of any candidate is the maintenance of the fundamentals of our system of government by which the right of the people to select and elect public officers shall be preserved inviolate.

"The Courts of our State, including the Court of Appeals, have unanimously held that this candidate, ignoble as he may be, was lawfully nominated beyond recall. I am now asked to convene an Extraordinary Session of the Legislature and recommend the enactment of special legislation to cover this case. The legislation which is sought is not of a general character. It is not even suggested that a measure either permanent in character or state-wide in scope would be desirable. It is designed solely to prevent one individual from being a candidate for judicial office.

"If this were to be done in this case, it would be in many others. It would amount to legislative review of party nominations. It would permit the party in control of the Legislature to pass special laws against the candidacy of any individual whom it disliked or feared.

"Moreover, if a law can be passed permitting parties to withdraw their nominations and name new candidates within a few weeks of election, then a law can be passed substituting new candidates the very day before election. Thus, whenever, in the process of an election campaign, a candidate becomes undesirable or falls from favor, a new nomination could be made at any time up to election day.

"The right to vote can easily be dissipated by rendering it impossible for the voter to act intelligently and with knowledge. Similarly, the right to vote can be dissipated by uncertainty and lack of stability in the governing rules and law. It must never be forgotten that under our theory of government the ultimate object is a free choice by the people. Therein lies the surest protection against the election of unfit officials. The choice should always be that of a good official. But it is fundamental that the people have the choice.

"Legislation aimed at a single individual perilously resembles a bill of attainder. Abolition of all bills of attainder was one of the purposes for which we fought the War of the Revolution and they are twice prohibited by the Constitution of the United States.

"Throughout our history no remedy such as that now suggested has ever been attempted. We must not permit the painful incident of the moment to lead us into a course which would destroy the fundamental principles of our form of government. The legislative power may not be invoked to destroy the fiber of free elections by a free people in a constitutional republic.

"The remedy is not in special laws to be passed by the Legislature. The remedy lies with the people at the polls.

"I have concluded that no Extraordinary Session of the Legislature should be convened."

Unexpectedly, in the fall of 1943 the Republicans were forced to put up a candidate for Lieutenant Governor. Thomas W. Wallace, who had been swept into office in the Dewey landslide of 1942, died, and the Court of Appeals ruled that an election was necessary to name his successor. Many Republicans doubted that they could carry the state for this one office. Joe R. Hanley, majority leader of the State Senate, who had automatically succeeded to the Lieutenant Governorship upon the death of Mr. Wallace, was selected by the Republicans; General William N. Haskell, an able man, long head of the New York National Guard, was the Democratic candidate. Governor Dewey spoke twice for Hanley, urging that the voters continue the "team" intact at Albany. It was argued, by others, that if Mr. Dewey should be nominated and elected President in 1944, Senator Hanley would be well equipped to carry on the Dewey policies in New York State. Mr. Hanley was elected by 350,000 votes.

In his first seventeen months in the office of Governor, Mr. Dewey made only three trips outside the state—to the

Governors Conference at Columbus in June, 1943, where he spoke principally on the farm situation; to the Mackinac Republican conference, where he made his statement favoring continuing close cooperation for peace between Great Britain and the United States and expressed the hope that Russia and China would join in; and to the 1944 Governors Conference held at Hershey, Pennsylvania. Many times in the course of these seventeen months he was reminded of his declaration of intention to serve out his full term as Governor. He never altered that declaration; he scrupulously avoided even the appearance of being a candidate for the Republican nomination for President.

At the Hershey conference, Dewey was a pleasant visitor. At that time he was far in the lead for the Republican nomination, but he declined to discuss the situation. Among the newspapermen at the conference was Lowell Mellett, who had gone back into journalism after a long association with President Roosevelt. Mellett assigned himself to explain Governor Dewey's popularity, and posed many tentative answers, none of which seemed to satisfy him. Was it "youth"? "Controlled swagger"? All-round competence? Mellett was unable to settle on any particular reason and finally confessed his "bafflement." He could, in essence, only report that the other assembled governors were asking, "What's he got that I haven't got?"

Mr. Mellett's bewilderment, even so, is understandable. A great many persons have tried to put their fingers on the precise reasons for the Dewey popularity not only among the shrewd, vote-counting politicians, but among the ordinary inarticulate voters as well. Actually there are many reasons.

Dewey is personable. To say that he lacks some of the appealing human juices of an Al Smith, that he has none of the strange mesmerizing voice of a Bryan, that he is innocent of the curious saucy charm of a Jimmy Walker, that he is no rabble-rouser like Huey Long, that he is devoid of the august impressiveness of a Charles Evans Hughes—all this is to say approximately nothing. Dewey is what he is: extraordinarily alert, friendly, quick with his sympathies and his understanding. He is a rare combination of cool competence and plain humanity. Just as there is nothing aloof about him, so is there nothing of the specious friendliness and claptrap of the demagogue. He talks neither the language of the stuffed shirts nor that of the bleeding hearts.

Two of the battered ornaments of political language are that So-and-So "humanized government," and "brought the government closer to the people." Such clichés, mouthed by many a campaigner, rarely mean much of anything; in Dewey's case, his closest associates argue that, through his work in almost fourteen years of public life, the fine old phrases have come to life. Throughout his performances in public office he has time and again reminded the men about him that they were there for the service of the public. He has been the consistent foe of buck-passing. Any complaint, however small, has received attention—or Dewey would want to know the reason why.

Is it a farmer from up in Columbia County who is having trouble with his pigs and who has journeyed to Albany to try to find out what to do? Dewey is no pig expert, but he has impressed upon his departments that the gentleman from Columbia County must be taken care of. Is it a group of kosher meat dealers from the Catskills who are alarmed over a ruling of the Office of Price Administration which might easily wreck their business? Dewey is no authority on the kosher market, and as Governor the rulings of the OPA are outside his province. Nevertheless, in the case of the distraught men from the Catskills, he did something about it. These instances could be multiplied by the scores. They add up to "bringing the government closer to the people." As one blunt commissioner said to some of his friends, "The idea is that we are trying to conduct this administration just as if we were all going to be up for reelection next week."

And there is something else, the importance of which may be assessed for what it is worth. It has to do with ordinary honesty—or, better, what used to be known as "honest graft." A story: One afternoon, a few days before the Republican Convention met in Chicago, a tight-lipped little man approached a friend of Dewey's on the station platform at Albany. This man, a Democrat from the East Side of New York, had been an errand boy, handy man, and adviser for politicians for upwards of thirty years, and had observed political practices—practices which can be appallingly snide and cheap—from the inside.

"I hope your man gets the nomination," said the little man to the Dewey friend. "Then I hope to God he's elected President. Anything to get him out of Albany. Then maybe a man can pick up a little change around here again."

The philosophy of the political buccaneer is wholly alien to Thomas E. Dewey.

WARDS OF THE STATE

CREEDMOOR is a vast establishment situated in what is known as Queens Village, in the County of Queens, which lies within the confines of New York City. It is part of the New York state hospital system which comprises eighteen mental hospitals, six schools, and two institutes. These places care for more than 100,000 patients, who constitute a claim upon both the pocketbook and the conscience of the people of the state.

Thomas E. Dewey, who had many ways of learning what was going on behind the impressive fronts of New York institutions, understood perfectly well that something was wrong with the mental hospital situation. He had many of the facts about Creedmoor when he was running for Governor in 1942; he did not make an issue of them for the simple reason that he hesitated to alarm the relatives of the patients.

A crime was being committed at Creedmoor, a crime of the sort which the public seems to care little about until the shocking details are dragged into the light. Here was filth, maladministration, and a seemingly wanton disregard for the most elementary rules of sense and decency. Creedmoor would have fascinated Charles Dickens. Its size would have astonished him; what went on inside would have repelled him. And yet Creedmoor was, and is, a relatively modern institution. Its trouble was that it was rotten with amoebic dysentery.

The hospital officials knew about the amoebic dysentery.

149

Polite suggestions had been made from time to time that it be cleaned up. A few deaths had been reported. Then, in the early part of 1943, conditions seemed to grow worse. Alarmed by the rumors he had heard, Seymour Halpern, a State Senator, visited the hospital on Sunday, March 7, without making his identity known. He spent three hours there. What he found makes unpleasant reading. He was struck at first, in one of the violent wards, by the horrifying obnoxious odor that comes from places where amoebic dysentery patients are gathered.

Senator Halpern went on. It was bad enough in Building S, where half-dressed patients went around wearing dirty cotton slacks. In Building P he found "mice waste" on dishes that were about to be used by patients. He found here, also, that patients were using beds occupied until recently by dysentery cases, and which had not been sterilized. In bringing this matter to the attention of Governor Dewey, Senator Halpern said:

"The plight of the patients in this institution is pitiful. The disheartened employees go about their daily work in constant fear of contracting disease. Many of them are afraid to eat in the assigned dining halls. Instead they go off the grounds to buy their own meals."

Governor Dewey, acting under the broad powers of the Moreland Act, immediately got in touch with a lawyer whom he trusted, Archie O. Dawson of New York City, and commissioned him to get busy at once. Mr. Dawson swung into action. He was able to report the results of a preliminary investigation at the end of a few days. He had found that the disease had been prevalent at Creedmoor since 1940 and that "so far in 1943 there have been 81 cases." Forty-two of these were active cases, thirty-nine "carrier" cases. Food handlers were infected. Milk cans stood in a lavatory used by employees. Mr. Dawson was so astonished that he told the

Governor that "these conditions should not be allowed to continue even for another day."

Governor Dewey agreed. He directed, the same night he received Dawson's first report, that Dr. Edward S. Godfrey, State Commissioner of Health, should go to Creedmoor at once, accompanied by Dr. James E. Perkins, director of the division of communicable diseases, along with whatever administrative personnel might be necessary. The epidemic was cleaned up, but Mr. Dawson continued gathering evidence for his final report to the Governor, which was soon completed.

Acknowledging the report, Governor Dewey said that he hoped "shortly" to be able to announce the appointment of a Commissioner of Mental Hygiene "of distinguished qualifications." It was clear enough that Dr. William J. Tiffany, who had held the office for many years, was on the way out largely because of the Creedmoor trouble. But the Governor went further. He announced the enlargement of the Moreland Act Commission to study the entire mental hospital system of the state, and to suggest methods of improving administration and the treatment of patients. He said:

"Patients and their families are entitled to know that they are entering hospitals of hope for cure and not a bastille of despair. Custodial concepts must give way to a major effort to cure."

Archie Dawson promised to continue on the enlarged commission. Appointed to serve with him were Lee B. Mailler, of Cornwall, an Assemblyman and superintendent of Cornwall Hospital; Dr. Peter Irving, of New York City, secretary of the Medical Society of the State of New York; Dr. Fraser Mooney, of Kenmore, superintendent of the Buffalo Hospital and vice-president of the American College of Hospital Administration; and Charles Roswell, of Springfield, Long Island, assistant director of the United Hospital Fund and an expert on hospital accounting.

While this commission was at work, Governor Dewey, on June 3, 1943, announced the appointment as Commissioner of the Department of Mental Hygiene of Dr. Frederick Mc-Curdy, professor of hospital administration at Columbia University and director of the Vanderbilt Clinic of the Columbia-Presbyterian Medical Center. He succeeded Dr. H. Beckett Lang, who had been acting commissioner following the rather precipitate resignation of Dr. Tiffany following the Creedmoor incident. It had been necessary for the Legislature to remove certain restrictions in order that Dr. Mc-Curdy could take the post; there was no difficulty about this, as he was the man the Governor wanted, and his abilities were above question. With Dr. McCurdy at the helm the Governor felt sure that there would be a new and enlightened administration of the mental hospitals—institutions which, by the way, cost the State of New York $45,000,000 every year.

Mr. Dawson and his committee did a thorough job of investigation. They found things almost as astonishing as the early discoveries at Creedmoor. And yet they also found that many of the institutions were in capable hands and were among the best establishments of their type in the country. Moreover, the war had increased their problems by draining off some of the better members of the staffs.

Many specific instances of laxity, and worse, were cited. The commissioners said that "over the years a slowly creeping paralysis of bureaucratic initiative and lack of effective organization and direction from the top had been crippling the department at the very time when its responsibilities were increasing." This had resulted, said the report, in the mental hygiene hospitals becoming "principally custodial institutions rather than hospitals in the true sense of the word."

The commission found that shock therapy, in which New York had pioneered, was being neglected in many hospitals.

It found that the incidence of tuberculosis reflected a lack
of medical care. It recommended a complete overhauling of
the diet of the patients. It reported that the Craig Colony
for Epileptics housed conditions which it was believed could
never have existed in a civilized community. It found that
many aged persons, suffering solely from those symptoms resulting from their great age, had been admitted to the hospitals and were "not in need of mental hospital care." It
warned against letting the hospitals become "old folks'
homes" rather than the primarily curative institutions for
which they were intended.

The distinguished members of the commission had chosen
as their director in making the survey Dr. Christopher G.
Parnall, medical director of the Rochester General Hospital.
Many other experts were also called in. The study was thorough; the report was as devastating as it was constructive.
It was found that the men in charge of certain of the institutions lived rather too well while their patients existed in
the most unspeakable squalor. In some instances, where adequate equipment for occupational therapy was available
(especially the opportunity to do work in the gardens), the
patients were permitted to remain in hopeless idleness.

A relatively small part of the conditions uncovered by
Mr. Dawson's commission will require special legislation for
eradication or improvement. Most of the recommendations
have either been put into effect already or will be effective
as soon as it is physically possible to do so.

Here, again, the problem was first of all one of administration. So far as plant and personnel were concerned, as the
commission was careful to point out, New York State has
long held a high place in its care of mental patients. The
deficiencies in the mental hospital system were precisely the
sort of thing Dewey had in mind when, in his campaigns for
Governor, he went up and down the state denouncing "dry
rot." The disclosures at Creedmoor and at the other institu-

tions served to confirm his charges in a convincing, though highly unpleasant, fashion.

The system, of course, still has its imperfections, but at least it is functioning with a refreshing absence of the lethargy which made the Creedmoor tragedy possible.

WORKMEN'S COMPENSATION

Q. How long have you been hard of hearing? A. How long have I been what?

Q. Hard of hearing. A. How long have I been what?

Q. (*coming close to witness and shouting*). How long have you been hard of hearing? A. What?

Q. How long have you been hard of hearing? A. How long have I been what? I don't hear.

Q. How long have you been hard of hearing? A. Oh, out there?

Q. How long have you been hard of hearing? A. You speak too loud. You are speaking too loud.

Q. How long have you been hard of hearing? A. How long have I been what?

Q. How long has your hearing been bad? A. Oh. One ear has been deaf for 25 years. Oh, it is more than that; 30 years, and the other one about 15 years.

The foregoing colloquy may sound odd, but it is not really funny. It is a transcript of an examination by William F. Bleakley and Herman T. Stichman, Moreland Act Commissioners, of an unfortunate gentleman they had called before them in their inquiry into the administration of the Workmen's Compensation Laws in the State of New York. The somewhat less than acute hearing powers of the witness had been well known to his superiors for a long time, and still he was permitted for several years to continue serving as a referee in compensation cases. One of his superiors, indeed, defended him by saying, "I am not sure but what a physical handicap of that sort keeps his record from becoming too cluttered with nonessentials." A novel theory of jurisprudence.

The State of New York has provided workmen's compensation for more than thirty years. The purpose of the law was to provide the injured workman and his family with financial support and the workman with medical care while he was incapacitated. Almost all admit that the law was well planned and progressive. As Governor Dewey said in a report to the Legislature on March 6, 1944:

"It has been the state's misfortune, however, to see the fine purposes of this legislation defeated by bad administration. Callous mishandling of cases and corrupt practices under this law by various groups of persons deprived workers in this state for many years of the benefits to which they were entitled and which they sorely needed."

In both his campaigns for Governor, Mr. Dewey referred to the workmen's compensation mess—for he knew that was what it was. A short time before his term was up at the end of 1942, Governor Herbert H. Lehman appointed William F. Bleakley, a Republican, of Westchester County, as Moreland Act Commissioner to look into the situation. As soon as he took office in 1943, Mr. Dewey reappointed Mr. Bleakley and appointed Herman T. Stichman, a New York lawyer of high standing as a capable investigator and a former Dewey assistant, to serve as Moreland Act Commissioner with him. The two commissioners uncovered a situation that may well serve as a model for what can happen when bureaucracy is allowed to run wild. Their hearings covered many months and wandering into many surprising bypaths; the case of the deaf referee was only one that caused them to repeat the famous question propounded by the late Ambrose

Bierce, "Can such things be?" The answer, they found, was yes.

Previously, so strange are such things during regimes that are ostentatious concerning their "social consciousness," Miss Frieda Miller, the State Industrial Commissioner under Lehman, had been requested to investigate her own administration. She appointed one of her own deputies for the job, and there was assigned to him as investigator a former bootlegger. Miss Miller's investigation of herself failed to get very far.

The team of Bleakley and Stichman, however, were horses of a different color. They examined 1,000 witnesses under oath at private hearings, and 251 witnesses at thirty-nine public hearings; more than 5,700 pages of testimony were taken. They had a staff of lawyers, accountants, and police officers to assist them. They found, as the principal items, that "a lethargic leadership" had for years thwarted the purposes of the compensation law, that the administration had been "detrimental" to the well-being of more than 5,000,000 workers, and that "it has also prevented honest disbursement of a substantial part of the more than $56,000,000 estimated to have been expended under the law for compensation and medical expenses during 1942 alone."

Bleakley and Stichman named four groups as being responsible for the conditions found: (1) lethargic leaders at the Department of Labor; (2) employers and insurance carriers; (3) so-called "licensed representatives," and certain lawyers, specializing in compensation cases; (4) physicians specializing in the same field.

The commissioners said bluntly that the "undesirable activities" of some of these physicians had seemingly been tolerated by certain medical societies. The whole system was so administered as to rook the injured workman for the benefit of various parties. Delays in settling claims were so great that an injured man might, and often did, have to undergo a long period of hardship before getting his compensation. A few laymen and a few lawyers were shown to have built up a virtual monopoly in the handling of claims. In parts of the state, it was shown, injured workers were compelled to accept representatives not of their own choosing. Officials were guilty of selecting incompetent personnel whose good will was often for sale. Fee-splitting among physicians and surgeons, as well as kickback schemes, was prevalent.

In presenting the report to the Legislature, and in suggesting certain legislation, Governor Dewey said:

"To permit these conditions to exist for one day would be an injustice. To permit them to continue these many years was inexcusable. I am determined that the administrative deficiencies which have not already been cured shall be promptly remedied."

Some new laws were passed; under some of them a crooked physician may now be sent to jail instead of being merely reprimanded. The new State Industrial Commissioner, Edward Corsi, immediately began the tedious job of cleaning up the department and meting out punishment. He still has a long, difficult task ahead. In Brooklyn alone, on one day, Mr. Corsi announced that 272 doctors had been penalized for receiving kickbacks in compensation cases; this action came after a private inquiry by the Medical Society of Kings County. He revoked, in the case of nine doctors, licenses to practice in the compensation field. As a result of Mr. Corsi's discoveries, he directed the various medical societies to get busy and "clean their own house." Said the *New York World-Telegram:*

"The whole situation is one to shock into a new sense of responsibility medical societies that have waited for outside probes to force them to note and act against violation of medical ethics so widespread and so flagrant. It should be a salutary lesson to them."

It was not an enjoyable duty for Mr. Corsi either. He regretted he had had to take action against physicians "many of whom, through long years of service, have earned positions of respect and confidence in their community."

"But this," he said, "is an instance wherein the protection of the public welfare far transcends personal preference, one that men privileged to be part of such a noble profession as medicine should never have permitted to exist."

Very well. But who was responsible for that celebrated "lethargy" at the top? It so happened that Elmer F. Andrews was State Industrial Commissioner from the start of the Lehman administration in 1933 until 1938; Miss Frieda S. Miller succeeded him and held office from 1938 to the last day of 1942, the day before Mr. Dewey moved into the Governor's office. The testimony before Bleakley and Stichman showed clearly enough that they knew what was going on—most of it, anyhow. It was also shown that, in the matter of appointments and salary increases, both Mr. Andrews and Miss Miller were in frequent correspondence with Bert Stand, the secretary of Tammany Hall, who used to be known in prize-fight circles as "Bashful Bertie." The report showed that referees and doctors admitted receiving gift certificates and merchandise from those having business before them—gifts including turkeys, boxes of cigars, razors, liquor, and assorted delicacies. Said Bleakley and Stichman:

"The responsibility for this cash and 'gift' giving, which we regard as nothing more than a sly attempt to buy favoritism, and for all its evil results, we attribute directly to Commissioners Frieda Miller and Elmer Andrews."

Miss Miller and Mr. Andrews, at last reports, were still in high favor with the Washington administration.

Here again it was shown by two of the most respected and competent investigators in the state that the campaign charges made by Dewey in his campaigns for Governor were based on solid and sordid facts—and that not all the protestations of high purpose, or all the countercharges of "ignorance" and "misinformation" counted for much in the face of the damning evidence.

In certain instances, in the case of certain officials, there are penalties for various offenses classified as malfeasance, misfeasance, and nonfeasance. Such charges are hard to prove, but the well-known feasance triplets have figured in the courts many times, and juries have been known to convict. It would appear, however, that the crime of the Little New Deal in New York was really nothing more than "lethargy"—a rather prime degree of lethargy, to be sure— which apparently can be convicted nowhere except at the polls.

Whatever the whole truth about the original blame for the hideous goat's nest which the idealistic Democratic administration left behind in the field of workmen's compensation, some friends of the workingman will probably be pleased to know that compensation in cases of injury is coming along promptly now and that the parasites are fattening upon him no longer.

XVII

NEW YORK'S FARMERS

FEW of New York's governors in the last few decades have been distinguished by their preoccupation with the soil or with the problems of the farmer. To say this is not to imply that they were unaware of the importance of the farmers of the state, socially, economically, and politically. Even Al Smith, so thoroughly a child of the sidewalks of the big city, took an interest in the farms; indeed, it was always a stirring sight when Governor Smith appeared every year at the State Fair at Syracuse and had his picture taken with the Guernseys and the Holsteins, the Poland Chinas and the Chester Whites, the Dorsets and the Shropshires.

But Mr. Dewey, when he took office at Albany, brought with him more of a farm background than most Governors. He had known something of farming at first hand in Michigan; he had made his own farm at Pawling a going concern; he had made many friends among the farmers and the farm leaders of the state, and he had a quick sympathy for their manifold problems. No one would attempt to set up Mr. Dewey as a horny-handed dirt farmer; he isn't. But he did know what farming was about.

It is from among the farmers scattered throughout the state's rich and wonderfully diversified countryside that the Republican Party has always depended for the backbone of its support. They voted for Dewey in droves. At the same time, many of them raised the question whether a city lawyer, no matter how sincere his intentions might be, could quickly understand the problems of the farmer and give them the attention they deserved. Soon after taking office, Governor Dewey began receiving delegations of farmers—serious, worried, substantial gentlemen, who, in addition to their ever-present tribulations, were now confronted with the vexatious complications of wartime. They were expected to produce more than ever before. The unanswered question was—How, and with what?

In these first conferences the Governor listened carefully; he asked questions in order to bring out all the aspects of the many-sided picture. The farmers found him friendly, cooperative, but unwilling to be rushed into immediate decisions. They soon found that he could get things done, and get them done largely by giving the organizing brains among the farmers themselves a chance to see what they could do. Little about the farm program was spectacular, none of it revolutionary; the gains, however, have been steady, positive, and cumulative.

Of the grave problems first presented to the Governor, the first was the farm labor situation. New York farmers were in the same plight as others; their help had been drained away into the war services and the war industries. First, in February, 1943, he appointed T. N. Hurd as Farm Manpower Director. Mr. Hurd, a hard-working man who knew his field, had all the state agencies behind him, as well as the various independent organizations. One of the results was that an army of 111,000 volunteers, recruited from among high-school students, vacationists, soldiers, and prisoners of war, pitched in to help harvest the 1943 crops. There was little loss.

Soon after setting Mr. Hurd's organization in motion, the Governor created the New York State Emergency Food Commission to meet the problems arising from the war. H. E. Babcock was head of this commission. Serving with him were Carl E. Ladd, the late dean of the New York State

College of Agriculture, as executive director; Austin W. Carpenter, president of the Eastern Federation of Feed Merchants; C. Chester DuMond, president of the Farm Bureau Federation and chairman of the New York Farm Conference Board, later to become the new Commissioner of Agriculture and Markets; Dr. L. A. Maynard, director of the school of nutrition at Cornell University; Joseph F. McAllister, feed merchant; Lloyd R. Simons, director of extension of the state colleges of agriculture and home economics; Henry H. Rathbun, leader of the Dairymen's Cooperative League; Harold Stanley, secretary of the New York State Grange, and Mr. Hurd, the man-power director.

One of the first problems was how to obtain sufficient gasoline to keep the farm tractors running. The commission learned exactly where shortages existed and then presented the facts to the Office of Petroleum Administration in Washington. As a result, very few tractors were idle during the critical periods in the crop seasons of 1943. Moreover, the commission anticipated the shortage in containers for farm products and immediately prevailed upon local mills to start turning out baskets, crates, and boxes. The commission encouraged the salvage campaign to save the used containers and assisted in obtaining priorities for replacement equipment for container manufacturers. Although Governor Dewey in a general way kept hands off, he was constantly in touch with what was going on.

The commission also worked out a nutrition program that started on the farms and in the tens of thousands of victory gardens and proceeded all the way through the food-preservation stage to meal planning and school and factory lunches. The Governor, like almost every other student of nutrition, has often had a good word for the soy-bean.

A near crisis arose in the attempts to obtain feed for animals and poultry. For a time it appeared that the animal population would have to be reduced; dairymen and poultry raisers were down to the bottom of the barrel many times, and some of them lost money because of lowered production and substitute feed that cost more than the usual rations. This situation was eased when high-moisture corn in the Middle West had to be moved to market. In all these serious times, the Emergency Food Commission, which was in full possession of the facts, sounded warnings when necessary.

The Governor himself, in his speech at the conference of governors at Columbus, Ohio, on June 21, 1943, told of the New York farm problem and outlined what had been done to meet it. Incidentally, he made what at the time appeared to be a possible political error when he said that the New York farmers must have feed, and suggested that the Middle West farmers cut down the pig production and ship their corn to New York. If they did not do this, he warned, it would be necessary to import more feed from Canada, a circumstance that might in the future result in the loss by the corn states of their most profitable market—the East. Perhaps it was a politically injudicious remark. Certainly it was one that took courage; but in any event, it was the truth. In the Columbus speech, also, the Governor described what he believed the states should do to meet the food emergency. He said:

"Our conclusions in New York have been fairly simple and direct. Because the national government would not or could not see or understand as a whole the problem of feeding our people, we moved in to meet it ourselves.

"Because the national government still cannot or will not understand the food problem in America, the war governors of the United States, who are close to their people, can and will do the job.

"In so doing, I am sure that none of us will suffer from the misconception that either the national government or we as governors can ourselves meet the need. What we can do is to use the great reservoir of ability, character, and courage among our people. We can release that ability to serve the needs of the nation."

The Governor also made a good impression upon farm leaders by his support of the research programs of the college and experiment stations, in the allotment of funds for continuing research projects and in making possible expansion in the fields of the freezing and dehydration of foods. He approved legislation allowing exchanges of livestock between institutions to promote the more efficient use of state lands. The State of New York, by the way, is the largest farm operator within its own boundaries. It farms more than 32,000 acres on forty-seven state institution farms. The Governor sought to have these lands operated, not as a unit, but in a well-integrated system—under which, for example, an overproduction of potatoes in one place could be used to relieve a shortage in another spot.

Naturally enough, for weeks after the Governor assumed office, he was subject to pressure from the friends of various farmer-politicians who sought the office of Commissioner of Agriculture and Markets. Finally, in May, he chose C. Chester DuMond, a successful farmer who as far as is known never had any particular political affiliations or nursed any political ambitions. The Dewey record of appointments in the agricultural and marketing field has generally been approved by the more farsighted farm leaders of the state—an excellent group of men who are vastly more interested in the future of farming than in the future of any political party or any political figure.

For 1944, the program, with a few necessary minor adjustments here and there to keep up with changing conditions, is going through without a hitch. Perhaps because the entire program was conceived in no great haste, revisions have been so few as to be unimportant. The goals, along a broad front, have been kept clearly in mind, and the gains have

been there for all to see. Not the least important aspect of
the Governor's program is its insistence on making at least
some tentative plans for the agriculture of the future. No
detailed blueprint has been drawn, and such a scheme may
never be feasible because of the constantly changing technological picture. At the same time, the Governor and his advisers have foreseen that, largely by taking advantage of
the wide variety of new and improved techniques, the
farmer may in some degree be spared the nightmare of
alternating bumper crops and lean years. As one farm expert, in discussing the neglect of the basic principle of the
full larder, said:

"Governor Dewey is among the first in high public office
to take off his coat and tackle problems arising from this
neglect. The farmers of New York State have backed him
magnificently in this. Their underpaid overtime labor and
favorable weather have so far kept the larder full. Improvement of the larder itself by way of the quick-freeze unit is
the next logical step."

The Governor and his farm administrators obviously have
demonstrated that, so far at least in an unpredictable world,
they know what they are doing. Their correlation of all the
facts was admirable; their summation of what was needed
was explicit; their methods of achieving their objects were
direct and effective. The farm problem is no more "solved,"
it may be, in the State of New York than it was in another
land back in the time of Joseph and Abraham, who also
had ideas on agriculture. But at least a program is moving
along lines which, at the moment, have won wide approval.
The "city lawyer" has already shown that he knows a lot
about growing things—and what to do with them after they
are grown.

XVIII

THE STATE POLICE

ONE of the common outcries of the traditional prosecutor, or the traditional reformer, is that the police are crooked—and sometimes they are. At times, however, reform movements have proceeded upon the quite fallacious assumption that a 100 per cent honest police force will of itself cure most of the community's problems.

Thomas E. Dewey, as prosecutor and governor, has never been a cop-baiter. With full understanding of the imperfections of the police, he has always worked on the assumption that most policemen, if allowed to follow their natural bent under competent officers, would much prefer to be straight than otherwise. The times when he has been disappointed have been very few indeed.

It is still remembered how the New York police attending a Holy Name breakfast one Sunday morning rose spontaneously and cheered when a speaker happened to mention the name of Dewey. This was at a time when Dewey was in the thick of his racket-busting activities—a time when some police were under suspicion. It is probable that most New York policemen are Democrats; nevertheless, the majority of them have always seemed to feel that Dewey was O.K. because he was on the level.

Long before Dewey became Governor there were whispers that the New York State Police were not all they should be. At no time did these whispers suggest anything approaching

167

a major scandal; indeed, there was no major scandal. Inertia, yes.

The members of the New York State Police, taking them by and large, are superior men, and the force has a splendid tradition. Though hardly so fabled as the Northwest Mounted Police or the Texas Rangers, the state troopers of New York, man for man, would stack up pretty well beside those other two groups of straight-shooting man hunters.

Indeed, a few years ago, the good gray New England farmer and writer, Frederic F. Van de Water, became so engrossed in the traditions, the routine and the adventures of the New York State Police that he decided they deserved a place in literature. He wrote a series of stories about them—pretty good stories, too. The police appreciated all this. It was about time somebody noticed these upstanding fellows. They had helped solve kidnapings, out-of-the-way murders, and robberies without end.

These police watch the highways. They look in on strange, secluded mountain resorts where fugitives may be hiding, or where some sort of deviltry may be cooking. They seek out the private burial grounds of the mobsters. They cover a vast territory, from Long Island to the Canadian border. They have performed an astonishing list of daring deeds— from shooting a locoed Guernsey bull that had killed two farmers on Long Island to intercepting a prison break at Sing Sing.

The citizens of New York State who have had occasion to deal with these guardians of the law will generally agree as to their courtesy, their good humor and their all-round competence. They are strikingly handsome as a group, and their intelligence rating is high. They are fine horsemen. They know all they are supposed to know about modern crime detection. And, so far as this may be said of any group of men, they are without fear.

And yet, when Dewey became governor, it soon became

obvious that a certain amount of laxity—probably a form of the well-known "dry rot"—had been allowed to creep into the State Police. A few of the older officials had been allowed to stay in service long after their days of usefulness had passed. Reports were received of strange goings-on in the various barracks scattered over the state. It was even alleged that some of them looked the other way when certain mild forms of criminality were under way. Others had been stationed too long in one spot. They were taking things easy.

As these stories became more definite, Governor Dewey, in July, 1943, decided to look into the organization. He directed the State Attorney General, Nathaniel L. Goldstein, to conduct a sweeping investigation into allegations of systematic bribery by truck fleet owners of "one or more members of the State Police." The inquiry extended into Ulster, Sullivan, Chenango, Montgomery, Washington, Dutchess, Orange, Westchester, Madison, Schenectady, Rensselaer, Schoharie and Columbia Counties.

The allegations of bribery, when investigated, turned out to have more than a grain of truth in them. The Governor, whose admiration and friendship for the police have always been strong, directed the Attorney General to "root out and convict" not only the state troopers involved but also the truck owners who might have been guilty of bribery.

"There is nothing so disreputable," said the Governor, "as a man who, for his own benefit, will bribe a public officer."

The Attorney General appointed Edward W. Scully, a former Assistant District Attorney of New York County and then associated with a New York law firm, to be a special assistant in charge of the inquiry. Mr. Scully worked with John Powers, an Assistant Attorney General.

On the same day that the Governor announced the opening of the investigation, one trooper, a sergeant, was arrested on the charge of having accepted a bribe of $600 from the owner of a trucking company. It developed that the bribery had to do with the workings of a gadget known as the Load-O-Meter Truck, which has special devices for weighing heavy vehicles. Alas, it was not foolproof or entirely proof against crookedness. In the hands of an honest trooper, it could give an accurate weighing of an overweight truck; in other hands it could indicate that the truckload was within the law.

The situation in the state police force was cleaned up quietly; at no time did it have the makings of a major scandal. Several officers were allowed to resign, for a variety of reasons. Others were transferred to posts where their talents might show to better advantage.

One of the officers had made the mistake of allowing his photograph to be taken, in a pose indicating friendship, with a notorious hoodlum, a former member of the old Dutch Schultz gang.

Another officer had a much more amiable weakness, but a weakness nevertheless: He was extraordinarily fond of locomotives. This did not mean that he was a bad man; indeed, such splendid citizens as Vincent Astor, the millionaire New Dealer; the late William Gillette, the actor who played the part of Sherlock Holmes for so many years; and Lucius Beebe, the dude journalist, all belong in any list of authentic admirers of the railroad locomotive.

This particular officer of the State Police, however, went a bit far. He wangled an old locomotive from the New York Central, built his own branch railroad line to the rear of the police barracks, and proceeded to satisfy what apparently had been the ambition of a lifetime. Instead of devoting himself assiduously to his police duties, this gentleman, when he got the chance, would change into the noble habiliments of a locomotive engineer. Then he would get up steam in his engine, and, with a great tootling and puffing, would dash back and forth along his private track. It was also alleged that, when a high mood of adventure was upon

him, he would take his locomotive out on the main line of
the New York Central, when he knew no regular trains
would be coming through, and play at being the real thing.
These high jinks were great fun, and probably did no one
any particular harm, but it was nonetheless decided that,
somehow, it didn't look quite right. The trooper lost his
handsome toy.

As head of the state troopers, Governor Dewey appointed
Captain John A. Gaffney, a sturdy, intelligent, and good-
looking officer who had served in the Marine Corps in the
First World War. He had an excellent record with the State
Police. He was thoroughly familiar with the state, well
known among all local police officers, and recognized as a
good executive. The appointment of Gaffney as Superintendent was popular not only with the citizens who knew him
but among the members of the force as well.

The state troopers can proceed, unhampered by loafers
and chiselers, to add more fine pages to their already honorable history. Governor Dewey has every confidence in the
force as now constituted, and he uses troopers in a wide
variety of investigations and other duties. He gets along with
them as well as he got along with the New York police when
he was prosecutor.

XIX

THE O'CONNELL DYNASTY

THE name O'Connell in Albany means "boss." For six years Thomas E. Dewey has been training his guns on the Democratic machine built up in the capital by the O'Connell clan. In many quarters the fight has been anything but popular. The O'Connells, like comparable organizations in larger cities, have their devoted followers—and many of them are anything but disreputable. To Dewey the O'Connells are, in essence, little different from Hague in Jersey City, Pendergast in Kansas City, Kelly in Chicago, and so on.

In the state campaign in 1943, Governor Dewey, campaigning for the election of Joe R. Hanley to fill the vacancy in the Lieutenant Governor's office, again emphasized his determination to break the power of the O'Connell machine which has dominated Albany for a quarter century. The Governor listed this machine as among the "criminal political organizations" which he intended to root out. By the summer of 1944 he had gone a long way toward accomplishing his purpose.

Property assessments in Albany have been the main point of the Dewey attack, beginning as far back as 1938. The machine has many business ramifications, and it has a strong influence in state politics. A state election might easily hinge on the O'Connells.

The ostensible head of the organizations is John J. O'Connell, Jr., pleasant spoken and good looking. Old readers of crime news may recall that the kidnaping of John J. in 1933 created a national sensation.

John is chairman of the Albany County Democratic Committee. Behind him, as the real leader, is Daniel P. O'Connell, uncle of John—the "Uncle Dan" to whom Dewey has referred sarcastically in many speeches. Dan O'Connell is fifty-eight years old, broad-shouldered, heavy-set and bespectacled. He is the only survivor of the three brothers who brought the Democrats back into power in Albany following the decline of the celebrated Republican machine headed by the late William ("Boss") Barnes. In addition there is a fourth brother, Solly O'Connell.

"Uncle Dan" is no speechmaker and he talks but little for publication. Although an excellent mixer with a ready wit, he lives quietly. He has no children, and has long spent his affection upon his nephew and his nephew's children. He came from the south end of Albany and had only a high school education. He is, however—and this seems odd to many persons—a great reader. In particular, he is something of an authority on the Civil War, its development and the detailed history of its military strategy.

Dan O'Connell served in the First World War in the Navy. When he came home he ran for county tax assessor and was elected, the first Democrat to win a city-wide contest in twenty years. In 1920 he and his brothers, Edward J. and Patrick J., joined with the Corning brothers, Edwin and Parker, to lay the foundations of the present Democratic organization. The Cornings were members of an old and wealthy family in Albany, where old families are venerated. The alliance was shrewd politics.

The O'Connell-Corning combination elected the mayor of Albany in 1921 and won the county in 1922. In the mid-twenties the Republicans managed to elect a sheriff, but that is the only county office lost by Democrats since the O'Connells took over. In 1944 Democrats held all seats in the City Council and 32 of 39 seats in the County Board of Supervisors. In 1943, despite the Dewey charges and the election of Hanley as Lieutenant Governor, the O'Connells scored heavily. John T. Delaney, the Democratic District Attorney, was reelected by 23,160 votes; he carried the city of Albany by 25,942.

Backed by the O'Connell organization, Edwin Corning was elected in 1926 for a two-year term as Lieutenant Governor. In 1932 the Mayor of Albany, John Boyd Thacher, backed by the O'Connells, lost the nomination for Governor by a narrow margin to Herbert H. Lehman, who was supported by Franklin D. Roosevelt.

The Dewey administration first struck at the O'Connells in the late summer of 1943 with an investigation of assessment procedure, initiated by the State Tax Commission. Ernest B. Morris of Albany, son-in-law of the late William E. Woollard—a prominent Republican in the days of the old Barnes machine—was retained as special counsel for the inquiry. The inquiry went deeply into the system which, Dewey contended, made it profitable to vote Democratic in Albany.

A few weeks before the 1943 election, a second investigation, into the registration of voters, was started by Nathaniel L. Goldstein, the State Attorney General. He set up an Election Frauds Bureau, and appointed J. Edward Lumbard of New York City a special Assistant Attorney General. The bureau concentrated most of its work on Albany County; Dewey had charged that, in 1938, the registered Democratic voters outnumbered Albany's adult population. Lumbard's staff, aided by State Police, were able to report scores of election law violations—mostly in failure to provide the required safeguards, booths, curtains, etc., for privacy. Lumbard recommended that the Election Frauds Bureau be made permanent.

Frank C. Moore, the State Comptroller, in a surprise

move, sent a score of examiners into the City Hall at Albany to check city finances following a municipal request for Moore's approval of a refunding operation. The checkup uncovered what Moore called a "shortage" of $1,600,000 in the city's capital accounts fund, due to transfer of the money to a fund for payment of current expenses. Mayor Corning and other city officials disputed him, calling the transaction instead a "temporary diversion" of funds, and contended that it actually saved the city money by obviating necessity for short-term borrowing.

The Democrats began to fight back. District Attorney Delaney started a grand jury inquiry into spending by committees of the Republican-controlled Legislatures after 1935. He subpoenaed Comptroller Moore and Rollin Browne, President of the State Tax Commission, to obtain certain records; the validity of the subpoenas was questioned and the matter tied up in the courts. Republican legislative leaders asked Dewey to order an impartial investigation of legislative spending—let it hit whom it might. The Governor took the investigation out of Delaney's hands, superseding him with Hiram C. Todd as special prosecutor. Mr. Todd, a painstaking gentleman, has a long and notable record as an investigator.

Meanwhile the Governor ordered a broad inquiry into alleged crime in Albany County, and for this he named George P. Monaghan as prosecutor. Monaghan had worked with Dewey in New York. After the first few months of Monaghan's work, and after the first indictments came out, District Attorney Delaney resigned.

By the time Dewey was nominated for President, both of these grand juries had found indictments. One series of indictments was against an alleged ring of thieves who were charged with conniving in the theft of large amounts of property, mostly junk, from the New York Central Railroad. What will come of all these inquiries is anybody's guess. The Dewey record indicates that he would not have gone into the fight unless he felt that he was loaded for big game. On the other hand, the situation is highly complex, and breaking the power of the O'Connells may not be easy. The showdown may be at hand in time for the 1944 election.

The relations between the various Republican Legislatures and the O'Connell organization have been odd—a sort of gentlemanly game of blackmail. Time and again, when the Republicans in the Legislature would become indignant and threaten to look into the doings of the O'Connells, the Albany bosses would send word back, in effect: "All right. Go ahead. Then we will have a grand jury investigation of the Legislature. How would you like that?" Not until Dewey came along has there been a thoroughgoing inquiry. The old system of live-and-let-live is ended.

XX

LIFE AT PAWLING

DAPPLEMERE, the Dewey farm, lies among the rolling green and purple hills of Dutchess County, New York. It is within comfortably close striking distance of both Albany and New York City. Here the Deweys have had their summer home for the last seven years; they also have passed much time there in the winters. For two summers they rented the place, and then, in 1939, they decided to buy it with a cash payment and a mortgage.

Three hundred acres make up the Dewey place. In addition, the Governor leases 186 acres in order to take care of the herd of 100 Holsteins. Of the Governor's own acres, forty are in woodland and the rest either tillable land or pasture; of the 186-acre leased tract, about one-third is woodland, another third pasture, and the rest tilled land. The farm produces about one-third of the feed required for the cattle.

The Dewey farm makes money—not a great deal, but enough to make its owner feel that it is a going concern in addition to being a wonderfully attractive place to live. Many persons sold their dairy herds soon after the war started, when it became apparent that farming costs were going up. Dewey managed to hold on to the herd and even to improve it.

The Dewey farm is situated in a neighborhood known as Quaker Hill. It is two miles northeast of the village of Pawling, which has a winter population of about 1,200 and a summer population about double that figure. It is about 800 feet above sea level. The place was formerly owned by a Quaker family named Wanzer.

Besides the two large main cow barns, there are a hay barn, an implement shed, and sheds for the bulls and calves. A two-car garage, a pumphouse, and an old ice house go to make the ensemble complete. The Deweys raise 150 Leghorn chickens, as well as a few ducks and geese.

The house is a well-built structure of twelve rooms; most of it was built 150 years ago, and honest construction went into it. Its lines are charming. A white picket fence stands in front. The house is surrounded by fine old pines, cedars, maples, horse chestnuts, and tulip poplars.

The Deweys raise their own vegetables—potatoes, peas, tomatoes, beans, green stuff, etc. They have a food-freezing plant which assures them of a well-filled year-round larder.

Governor Dewey takes a close interest in the farming operations and knows exactly what is going on at all times. He makes no pretense, however, of being an authentic dirt farmer; he has never even had his picture taken running a tractor or pitching hay, although the temptation might have been strong.

The Dewey children, Tom and John, are the real dirt farmers in the family. They really work their gardens. They sell their produce to the Governor at fair but by no means fancy prices. Young Tom has a keen eye for pennies and has yet to be hornswoggled in any important deal around the place. He has put most of his profits into War Bonds.

The Dewey household at Pawling is cared for by Fred Stohl and his wife, Helen. They have charge of the gardens, and they run the house. Helen Stohl is an expert on cooking and canning. She bakes bread once a week. Her theory (and it is a workable theory) is that virtually everything needed can be raised right there on the farm. The actual farm work is done by Charles Frumerie, who, with his wife, Elsie, and two children, lives in a house near by, and by Kenneth Campbell, who lives with his wife and small son in another house on the farm.

When at Pawling, the Governor devotes part of his time to state business. He takes time out now and then for a horseback ride, goes swimming in a small body of water a mile away called Quaker Lake, plays with his sons, or indulges in a round of golf on a nine-hole course near by.

After leaving the office of District Attorney, Mr. Dewey had his way of life fairly well settled in theory: that is, he would keep a small apartment in New York, attend to his law office, and then two or three days a week he could relax, or work, as he choose, at Pawling. A neat enough arrangement, but the nomination for the Governorship in 1942 changed all that.

The Deweys first moved to Pawling at the suggestion of Lowell Thomas, the radio speaker, luncheon club orator, traveler and big-game hunter, who has a place not far away. Other neighbors include such persons, of widely different personalities and backgrounds, as Elliott V. Bell, now State Superintendent of Banks, who formerly served the *New York Times* and the *New York Herald Tribune* as a writer on financial topics; Dan Parker, the gifted sports editor of the *New York Daily Mirror;* K. C. Hogate, who went to New York from Indiana years ago and became publisher of the *Wall Street Journal,* which he revitalized; Charles E. Murphy, a lawyer, a Democrat, and former president of the New York Advertising Club; George Sibley, a drug firm executive and a leader in the New York Young Republican Club; and G. Lynn Sumner, a New York advertising man. Mr. and Mrs. Carl T. Hogan, who have known the Deweys for years, also have a summer place close by.

The Deweys prefer the farm at Pawling above any place they ever lived. Here, more than in any other spot, they have found the setting they wanted for the satisfactions of living.

XXI

THE GOVERNOR'S WIFE

THE Executive Mansion in Albany sprawls on a hill on Eagle Street, a ten-minute walk from the State Capitol. It is a vast and in some respects a terrifying edifice, built in 1877, when the governor was the great Samuel J. Tilden, the man who almost became President. Outside this house is a jigsaw of sharp angles, strange battlements, and inexplicable doodads; inside it has the charm of spaciousness, mingled with a touch of gloom. For all its shortcomings it is a comfortable place. It has seen its share of history.

The governors' wives who have presided as hostesses in this almost medieval monument to architectural whim and afterthought have been of many sorts—highly estimable ladies, but widely different in manner, looks, ambition and viewpoint. Some have been plain and motherly souls; others have been eager to make the most of the social position which automatically comes with being the wife of New York's governor; still others have used their position to promote worthy causes with great zeal, or, in their own peculiar ways, to improve the world. Some have been phenomenally thrifty, spending money only for what was absolutely necessary; others have expressed their individuality by spending thousands of dollars on new washrooms, startling wallpaper, and what not. Some have been recluses; others have had as many as 500 women in for tea—and, alas, missed a lot of fine silverware when it was all over.

The present incumbent, Mrs. Thomas E. Dewey, falls into

180

none of the usual patterns. Moreover, she is innocent of a deplorable practice, said to be common among women in high places, of turning up her nose at the personal oddities of her predecessors. If that strange Mrs. So-and-So, wife of the governor of the same name, wanted things a certain way and fancied a rather rococo combination of colors in the dining room, then that is all right with Mrs. Dewey. She may smile a bit wanly at some of the relics, but that is about all.

Mrs. Dewey, however, did not let the old place remain entirely as she found it. In some of the downstairs rooms she put in new draperies. She covered old chairs and couches with brighter material. She redecorated some of the walls. Without impairing any of the basic dignity of the house, she carried out a program—modest enough, in all conscience —which made the interior much more modern in tone, lighter, and more cheerful. Her task, as she saw it, was to try to make a home of this capacious old mansion, and to do it as economically as possible.

One of the first aims of Mrs. Dewey's regime in the Executive Mansion has been to make life uncomplicated. She dislikes hubbub, disorder, loose ends. The household runs smoothly. She has not interfered with what has for years been an orderly, going establishment. The staff of domestics, gardeners, engineers, and so forth carries on without interruption. The wonderful Whitehead, the talented major-domo who came from Australia long ago, is in charge of the household, a job he has held with only one brief interruption for some thirty years. The imperturbable Whitehead takes his governors and their families in his stride, likes them all so far as anybody knows, and does the best he can to make them feel at home.

The Deweys are not stand-offish; indeed, they like to have people around. And yet they have done very little entertaining on a large scale while at Albany. The first and most important reason, naturally enough, is that they have felt that anything suggesting ostentation—or even society as usual—would be improper in wartime. Albany has gradually come around to accepting this point of view. For another thing, the Deweys are simply not inclined to the giving of mammoth lawn parties, impressive state dinners, and receptions in observance of this or that occasion.

The truth about Mrs. Dewey is extraordinarily simple: Without being "plain," she shuns display. She has a mind of her own, but she ventures no political opinions except to her closest friends. She makes no speeches. She could make a speech but she sees no reason for making one. She joins none of those organizations, however worthy in purpose, which are dedicated either to the uplift or the annoyance of mankind. She has turned down all offers to write magazine articles, though she could doubtless have put the money to good use. She doesn't even have a secretary. She appears, in short, to have a great deal of common sense. She once remarked:

"I do not believe in piling unnecessary complications upon the ordinary business of living."

In 1938, when Mr. Dewey was running for Governor the first time, he asked Mrs. Dewey whether she wanted to accompany him on an upstate tour. She declined, saying:

"One young person in this campaign is enough. Two would be a little too much."

She has read many of her husband's speeches before they were delivered and at times has made sensible suggestions for revision of certain passages. These suggestions were usually heeded. She is a sound editor and can take the slips out of a manuscript with an almost professional touch. If she errs at all on this job, it is apt to be on the side of caution. As to judging persons who are under consideration for appointment to public office, she usually keeps her own counsel, though she is often helpful in giving her estimate of a man after having had a chance to size him up. So far, she has been right more often than she has been wrong.

An enthusiastic journalist offered the opinion early in 1944 to the effect that if the Deweys went to Washington, Mrs. Dewey would be the best looking mistress of the White House since Dolly Madison; here again the commentators roam in the field of futile and senseless comparison. The statement, even so, may be perfectly true. Not to beat about the bush, she is pretty. More, she has vivacity, graciousness, wit, and a quick intelligence.

Is beauty, in any sense, a regional matter? Impossible. Only a narrow sophist, and certainly no politician, would make such an argument. And yet the fact remains that Mrs. Dewey comes from the Southwest, the birthplace of many beautiful and talented women. More than a century ago Frederick Law Olmsted (he is the same genius who, with Calvert Vaux, laid out Central Park in New York City) rode through Texas on horseback, and even in that early day, he observes in his journals, he was struck by the beauty of many of the young women in the small settlements. A great department store in Dallas has become famous in catering to that same strain of beauty which the knowing Mr. Olmsted observed more than a century ago.

Such observers as Walter Winchell, such fussy entrepreneurs as Billy Rose, and such exacting critics as John Robert Powers have commented upon the uncommon beauty of so many Southwestern women—all of which, to be sure, is simply belaboring the obvious. The Southwesterner takes it all for granted and never speaks of it, which is precisely where he often makes the mistake of his life.

But, apart from mere good looks, the woman from the Southwest often seems to be endowed, to a very healthy degree, with the faculty of seeing things straight. She is not easily impressed by the artificial. She combines enthusiasm with skepticism.

Mrs. Dewey is on Mr. Dewey's side. She has been on his side for a long time. But to her he is simply Tom Dewey, much the same Tom Dewey she has always known. Sometimes the more effervescent members of the huge lodge of Original Dewey-for-President men use a language which is strange to her.

Late one afternoon Mrs. Dewey was sitting on the porch of the Executive Mansion talking to an acquaintance, a man who, after mumbling something about "man of destiny," had used the unfortunate word "superman" in referring to the Governor. Just then Canute, the enormous Great Dane which is the family pet, sniffed at a rag left by a painter earlier in the day, picked it up and ran out to the lawn with the apparent intention of hiding it in the shrubbery. The Governor, coming out of a side door, saw Canute and ran after him. The dog wheeled unexpectedly and tripped the Governor, who fell headlong on the grass.

"There," said Mrs. Dewey to her companion, "goes your superman."

•

Mrs. Dewey is five feet, four inches tall and weighs 120 pounds. Her brown hair, which is worn rather short, is beginning to turn gray. Her eyes are brown. She buys her clothes ready-made, mends them herself when they need it, and makes them last a long time. She still watches the family expenditures, but has abandoned her former custom of trying to keep an exact budget.

She is an excellent cook, although she doesn't cook much any more. Of the 250 or so ways to cook eggs, she has mastered most. She can do many Creole dishes to perfection—including, of course, shrimps. When she and Mr. Dewey were first married, she cooked their dinner most of the time. When they go out to dinner in New York City, they choose excellent restaurants, though they are never seen at the establishments made most famous by the writers about café (or saloon) society. Over the years they have favored, among several others, such eating places as the Plaza Hotel's Oak Room, Chambord, Christ Cella's, Charles à la Pomme Soufflé, and the Golden Horn, where shish kebab, the Armenian dish, is always on the menu. Before its lamentable closing, "Papa" Moneta's distinguished restaurant down in Mulberry Street, a short walk from the Criminal Courts Building, was another place where the Deweys were sometimes seen.

A large part of Mrs. Dewey's time is taken up with her sons, both of whom resemble the Governor. When they were smaller she managed them for various intervals without the help of a nurse and for five years has cared for them wholly without one. Before the family moved to Albany, she drove them every day to the public school at Pawling. Now the boys are in Albany Academy. Tom and John, now nearly twelve and nine, practice assiduously, one on the Dewey piano in the second-floor sitting room, the other on the Mansion piano in the ground-floor drawing room. Both have some musical talent and do not have to be driven to their lessons. They play most of the bloodthirsty games of their young contemporaries and follow the early evening radio programs. They say their prayers when they are ready for bed.

Sometimes Mrs. Dewey reads to the boys—more recently from Kipling's *Just So Stories* and *The Jungle Books*. They have also had a taste of James Fenimore Cooper, an author whom they tackled without much original enthusiasm.

As for her own reading tastes, Mrs. Dewey is first of all a reader of the newspapers. She reads all the Albany and New York papers every day, and occasionally sees newspapers from the West Coast and from Baltimore and Washington. She can recall with astonishing accuracy who said what and when. Being a diplomat, she has declined to name her favorite columnists. "Except," she says, "Ernie Pyle. I'll name him. But everybody likes him."

Mrs. Dewey is also a mystery story fan. She knows her Sherlock Holmes, but hardly well enough to qualify as a member of the Baker Street Irregulars. She is guilty of one heresy: she does not particularly care for *The Hound of the Baskervilles*. She has read much of Edgar Wallace, the Lockridges, Agatha Christie, and Helen Reilly. She agrees with connoisseurs on the excellence of E. C. Bentley's detective story, *Trent's Last Case*. She likes poetry and essays, and regrets the decline of modern essay writing. She is an admirer of the late Katherine Mansfield.

As for games, she sometimes plays hearts, double solitaire or backgammon with the Governor. The Governor has taught chess to both the boys, and they often steal an hour for chess or backgammon together.

Although she has lived through many a tense period with Mr. Dewey, so far as her closest friends were ever able to observe she never showed the slightest fear of what might happen—not even in the racket-busting days when many threats had been made.

Mrs. Dewey is the daughter of Orla Thomas Hutt, a retired railroad trainman, and the former Miss Audie Lee Davis, who live in Sapulpa, Oklahoma. They have made several trips to New York, Pawling and Albany to see the Deweys. On such occasions Mrs. Hutt seems to prefer the teas and the social life; Mr. Hutt, however, prefers to go off and talk to the men on a wide variety of erudite subjects, or to wander about New York looking at historical landmarks.

Mrs. Dewey (Frances Eileen Hutt) was born February 7, 1903, in Sherman, Texas, in the northeast part of the state, a spot with some reputation in the Southwest for its cultural development. When she was eleven she went with her parents to Sapulpa.

The first Hutt to settle in America was Daniel Hutt, who came from England in 1653 as master of a ship called the *Mayflower* (not the famous one) and settled in Westmoreland County, Virginia. He married Temperance Gerrard, daughter of Thomas Gerrard, a surgeon. Through the Hutt-Meredith-Gorsuch-Lovelace-Aucher line, the genealogists say, Mrs. Dewey's ancestry may be traced back to Charlemagne. One direct ancestor was a doughty pioneer bearing the stirring name of Nimrod Hutt and is said to have been a mighty slayer of panthers. He lived in Chillicothe, Ohio, as far back as 1812. Sir William Lovelace, father of Francis Lovelace, a Colonial Governor of New York, and of Richard Lovelace, the poet, was another ancestor. On her mother's side, Mrs. Dewey can claim a distant relationship to Jefferson Davis, President of the Confederate States of America. Coming closer to modern times, an uncle (her mother's brother) was W. D. Davis, a cattleman who was for several terms Mayor of Fort Worth, Texas.

Frances Eileen Hutt attended public school in Sherman and later in Sapulpa. She studied piano and singing and has always been distinguished by her musical ability. When she was seventeen she won a prize in the voice division of the State Fine Arts Contest at Norman, Oklahoma. In high school she was a member of the Tsianini Music Club. She helped her piano teacher and later had pupils of her own. On Sundays she played the pipe organ in church. Her singing lessons were under Miss Bess McLennan Hughes, who had been a pupil of Percy Rector Stephens in New York. Miss Hughes had so much faith in Miss Hutt that she arranged a concert, the proceeds of which were enough to send the young singer to New York for further study.

Mr. Stephens encouraged her. She was soloist in excellent church positions while she studied for a concert career. To obtain broader experience she took the leading singing role in a theatrical production for a brief time and later she was a soloist in a motion picture house production of a semi-classical nature. Thus, with the aid of church and other singing engagements, she was able to support herself during her first years in New York.

Mrs. Dewey retains her excellent mezzo-soprano voice, though she seldom sings. When she was married, although she kept her interest in musical affairs as well as in all other matters in her world, she devoted herself with a steady singleness of purpose to making a home and rearing a family. She has had a good time doing it. Still, very few days pass when she does not find a half hour at the piano for playing some Bach and Mozart. She finds this her one perfect re-laxation.

XXII

THE CASE AGAINST MR. DEWEY

ON serious levels, where sober, intelligent and fair-minded persons discuss such matters, the principal objections to Thomas E. Dewey's further political advancement at the moment are:

That he has not demonstrated that he possesses a firm grasp, a thorough knowledge, of national and international affairs;

That over the course of the last five or six years he has changed his mind somewhat on certain important issues—notably the wisdom of the Lend-Lease arrangements and the degree to which the United States should participate in world affairs;

That he has not had the benefit of personal contact and conference with the leaders of other nations, and therefore would come to the world scene more or less a stranger;

That, because of his background, he has the curious mental cast of the "prosecutor" as distinguished from the judicious and open-minded administrator;

That possibly he has come along too fast, and that he might be better with a few more years of what is known among the political pundits as "seasoning."

All the foregoing objections have been raised, and doubtless will be raised again, against Governor Dewey. To many reasonable persons they are considerations that deserve careful examination. Some of these points are sure to weigh against him; they are arguments which at least have the merit of a certain surface plausibility.

The supporters and well-wishers of Dewey—and these include many older men who have had the opportunity to watch the workings of his mind for a good many years— contend that none of these objections really contains much substance.

Their answer is that his perception of broad problems is unusually clear and that he can call upon the best brains of the country with the sure knowledge that they will respond; that he has for some years had an intimate acquaintance with the leaders of opinion in both national and foreign affairs; that when he has changed his mind, or shifted his position, he has done so because of new evidence and the logic of events—which is true of a large part of the American people; that personal meetings with Generalissimos, Prime Ministers and Premiers are not always necessary for an understanding of international issues and international agreements; that he, in fact, does have a long-standing friendship or acquaintance with many of the Ambassadors and Ministers of the leading nations of the world and has spent hours and long evenings with them in recent years; that he has already shown that he does possess administrative ability of a high order, and that many other men famous in American life first attracted attention as prosecutors; and that, far from requiring more "seasoning," he is now at the very peak of his physical and mental vigor.

Those two opposing points of view are already furnishing most of the talk about Dewey, and unless some wholly new and unexpected issue arises, they will constitute the main area of attack and defense.

But there is another vast and important field in which another type of argument will be used—indeed, where it has already been used: This is the field wherein operate the smear artists, the purveyors of snide wisecracks, the twisters of the record, the sly journalists of the left wing, the professional racketeers, the fearful bosses of the big cities, the dwellers in the foggy borderland of mystical idealism, the writers of chain letters and the disseminators of questionable documents—all that tatterdemalion crew whose members range from the merely foolish to·the downright malicious.

There remain, of course, a great many persons who, usually for vague reasons which they cannot precisely put into words, simply do not like Dewey. It may be some old epithet which sticks in their subconscious; it may be his mustache; it may be his snub nose; it may be something about his voice. Whatever the reason, they do not cotton to him, and the cut of his jib offends them. The Dewey supporters probably will be wasting their time if they attempt to argue with most of these people. Their minds are unyielding. At the same time, an analysis of some of the anti-Dewey talk may be instructive and even mildly amusing.

Anyone who gets around New York much will soon realize that Dewey is not popular among the more articulate leaders of that glittering class known as Café Society. He has often been damned at Jack Bleeck's Artists and Writers Restaurant in West Fortieth Street, where newspapermen, press agents, actors, old poets and horse-players often gather. The same is true at Frank Case's Hotel Algonquin, that wayward inn which may really be the intellectual center of America, though the point is debatable. It is true at Sherman Billingsley's Stork Club, where the leading customers often pause in their contemplation of the body beautiful and turn their minds to grave political prognostication. Likewise, Dewey-baiting goes on at the Twenty-One Restaurant, where the Messrs. Charles Berns and Jack Kriendler are hosts to some of the nation's best-dressed and most acute thinkers.

It may be asked, reasonably enough: Does anyone give a hoot what saloon society thinks about Dewey? Probably not, but still the matter has a certain importance because these people are not only very talkative but some of them, unless far gone in crapulence, can actually write—and write stuff that is widely read, at that.

Perhaps it would be going too far to say that the thinking of Americans is shaped by these rather delightful and giddy people, but that they do have considerable influence must be obvious. They fill the magazines and the syndicated newspaper columns to an extraordinary degree. And the truth is that a large part of them, perhaps the great majority, are not on Dewey's side. Worse, some of them exhibit clear signs of hysteria when his name is mentioned. In these circles being against Dewey is a fashionable pose.

Several theories have been advanced as to why this is true. One (a good one) is that these people as a rule do not like anybody, except possibly Franklin Delano Roosevelt. They do not like their drinking companions, for all their ecstatic greetings of "Darling!" On close examination, they do not appear even to like themselves—a prejudice which is often easy to understand.

For example, there is the case of one critic and feuilletonist, whose approval of anything is rare. He has had, in his voluminous writings, a good word for Richard Sylvester Maney, the Shakespeare-quoting theatrical press agent, but in giving the laurel wreath to Maney he just about reached his saturation point. He wrote a Profile of Dewey which was published in the *New Yorker* magazine in May, 1940, and which is still regarded in Café Society as the perfect example of how an accomplished artist can tear a man's hide off—and that without having actually met the man. How much, if any, this article hurt Dewey no one can say; in any event, to this late day the critics of Dewey still refer to it to bolster their opinions.

Another theory, held by many students of the question, is that a New York lawyer, Morris L. Ernst, has had a strong influence in turning saloon society against Dewey. Mr. Ernst is one of the most vociferous and well-heeled of all the prominent supporters of the underdog and also of such slightly tarnished "over-dogs" as the ex-convict Frank Costello, the slot-machine king. He is also the mouthpiece (and far from an incompetent one) for many of the writing luminaries of the New York drinking and thinking set.

Mr. Ernst is a dark, intense little man who darts in and out of the better eating and drinking establishments, and whose nervous movements once reminded Miss Ann Honeycutt, the retired wit, of the unpredictable gyrations of an enraged water bug. For some ten years Mr. Ernst has conducted a one-man jihad against Dewey, on the grounds that (1) he doesn't like Dewey, (2) he doesn't think Dewey is a good lawyer, and (3) he feels that Dewey is not a sincere friend of civil liberties. A great many of Mr. Ernst's listeners could not explain the difference between a subpoena *duces tecum* and a writ of certiorari, but they usually lend an ear to Mr. Ernst. With all his millions of words poured out on the subject of Dewey, Mr. Ernst could hardly have failed to impress a few persons—how many is anyone's guess.

An exceptionally smooth-reading sneer aimed at Dewey was published in the May, 1944, issue of *Harper's Magazine* under the title "The Man in the Blue Serge Suit." The author had never met Dewey, though he had been in the audience on at least one occasion when the Governor made a speech. The "blue serge suit" allusion must have been symbolical, for Dewey has not owned a blue serge suit in many years; the idea seems to be that a wearer of blue serge (spiritually speaking, in this instance) may be competent but that he lacks a certain dash and warmth which he might gain if otherwise garbed.

This writer conceded that Dewey had been an efficient prosecutor and that in many respects he had made an acceptable Governor—that is, acceptable in the sense that he could get things done. His chief complaint seemed to be that

Dewey was not a salty, hell-for-leather "character." He brought up the old story (very effective when coupled with the late Justice Oliver Wendell Holmes's dictum that wire-tapping is "dirty business") to the effect that as a prosecutor Dewey had allowed his investigators to tap telephone wires to obtain "leads" for evidence. He did not say, though it is true, that Dewey supported the bill, now a law in the State of New York, under which wires cannot legally be tapped except on court order. Reprints of the *Harper* article were circulated by the tens of thousands by the anti-Dewey forces just before the Republican Convention in June, 1944.

Another highly critical examination of Dewey appeared in *The Nation* shortly before the convention. The writer, after a visit to Albany, reported that he was bored—bored by the city, by the Capitol, by the way Dewey ran the state government, and by virtually everything he encountered. He reported that the Deweys, because they took no prominent part in the social life of Albany, were a disappointment. The upshot of the diagnosis was that Dewey and all his works were pretty much on the dull side.

However, for consistency over the long pull, the attitude of the newspaper (or What-Is-It?) *PM* has gone far beyond any of the other Dewey detractors. This paper is subsidized by Marshall Field, who lets the editors do just about as they please. As a result, the members of the staff have a great deal of fun, perhaps almost as much as if they were in newspaper work. The circulation of *PM*, though not large, is distributed in such a fashion that the paper's influence is by no means negligible. It is particularly well thought of by young radicals and by the editors of many college publications. The paper's first editor, now on leave from his editorial lucubrations and in the Army, was Ralph Ingersoll. Part of his platform stated that *PM* was to oppose people who "push other people around" and to favor "open-mindedness." The paper then proceeded to push a great many people around (some of them deserved it, God knows) and to forget all about any attempt at open-mindedness.

If Dewey has any virtues whatever, they are not discernible to a reader of the slanted articles in *PM*. There are people, many of them in the newspaper business, who feel that *PM* has done a great deal of good and that there is much to be said for its throwing over of the old-fashioned journalistic concepts of objectivity; others, naturally enough, have no confidence in its motives and no respect for its performance.

Among other things, *PM* has tried to show that the state Soldier Ballot Law (it is probably the simplest and most nearly foolproof law that could have been designed in conformity with the provisions of the state Constitution) means that relatively few of the New York men in the armed forces will be able to vote in 1944—and that Dewey, with consummate cunning, drew the bill with this end in mind. This charge became so widespread, and gained such currency even in some respectable circles, that Dewey issued a statement in July denouncing the whole scheme to smear him. The result was a concerted drive by both the Dewey and anti-Dewey forces to obtain as large a soldier vote as possible.

A curious criticism of Dewey's technique as prosecutor deals with his treatment of material witnesses when he was preparing a case against an important defendant. The fact is that he treated these witnesses well, gained their confidence, and kept his promises to them. The objection really boils down to the fact that he kept them where they could not be tampered with; here is the nub of the talk that Dewey is not really a friend of "civil liberties," which in this instance is like saying he is not the friend of shyster lawyers. Coupled with this is the objection to his method of trying several defendants at once on the same conspiracy charge—the joinder. The truth is that the joinder law which makes so many criminals and their mouthpieces unhappy, has been the practice in the Federal courts for 150 years. Mr. Dewey merely brought it into state law, and it has been upheld by the State Court of Appeals.

There has been talk that Dewey, at heart, is antilabor. This talk no doubt will continue, but it will be mostly confined to talk, as the facts would make it appear ridiculous in cold print. The Communist organs were the first to cry "labor baiter" at Dewey; even they have piped down somewhat. The trouble is that the more the charge is pursued the more embarrassing it becomes to the anti-Dewey forces. The list of crooked labor leaders he sent to prison is too long. He broke up many a scheme whereby racketeers were collecting from both sides. To condemn his actions would bring out all the old sordid story. The men Dewey sent to prison were guilty. Some of the unions which they dominated have been able to clean up their affairs and are in better condition than they ever were. A few of them have had the grace to acknowledge that Dewey had something to do with bringing on better days. It so happened, however, that Dewey did not function with an eye to obtaining the "thanks" or the "support" of anybody.

It is also said that he probably, as prosecutor, turned loose more criminals—prostitutes, pimps, sneaks, bums, tinhorns, hangers-on, fixers, musclemen, and so forth—than he ever put in jail. The fact is that his primary object was to convict the important and hitherto safely entrenched figures, to break up combinations, to stop organized crime. Some very wicked men and women turned state's evidence to save themselves. A current phrase among racketeers, of the smaller variety, who were in the mood to tell all they knew was, "Well, I think I'll go down to Dewey's office and cut myself a piece of cake." The charge that Dewey freed many sinful persons is a companion to the charge that he did not really abolish evil-doing in the County of New York. This also is true. Indeed, investigation probably would show that some of the madams who were once in the Dewey dragnet, far from reforming, are still doing business—if not in New York, then somewhere else. The total extirpation of sin was not on the Dewey agenda.

It is not enough for the critics that Dewey has been a consistent friend of the Negro. He appointed Francis E. Rivers, who was an Assistant District Attorney, to the post of City Court Justice at a salary of $17,500 a year—the largest salary paid to any Negro public official in the United States. Then he pitched in and helped elect Rivers to a full ten-year term. He appointed to the State Athletic Commission Dr. Clilan B. Powell, its first Negro member. This was a thoroughly logical appointment in view of the fact that so many outstanding boxers are Negroes. It was not easy to make even a sidelong attack on these appointments; about all the critics could do was to intimate that Dewey had made them for political purposes.

Talk has been widespread that Dewey is not popular with newspapermen, a defect which, if true, might be taken to indicate that he is not what is known as a "right guy." This charge is not made as often now as when Dewey was prosecutor. Certainly as Governor his relations with the press have been cordial enough. Many newspapermen are his friends. At the beginning of his career as prosecutor many veteran reporters were skeptical of him because of his youth and relative lack of experience. They had seen prosecutors—many of them false alarms—come and go, and were waiting to be shown. Some of them rode Dewey pretty hard. Some found fault with his occasionally abrupt manner and what they regarded as his jaunty self-assurance.

In particular, at the beginning, when he was laying the foundations for his far-reaching investigations, they were nonplussed by his insistence that at the moment he had "no news," or "no comment," and that he wanted no publicity. He was embarking upon an adventure which would have been ruined by premature publicity. News there would be—

but later. Old reporters found this attitude difficult to fathom. One day Arthur Brisbane, the high-domed editor, and his friend Bernard F. Gimbel, the department store owner, had lunch with Dewey at the Ritz Carlton. Dewey told them in confidence what he was trying to do, and then said he wanted "no publicity." Afterward Brisbane said to Gimbel, "I like that young man. He'll go far. But what was that he said about 'no publicity'? He must have meant just the opposite."

Brisbane had lived so long in a world of screaming head-lines and spectacular public officials that he could not believe it possible that here was a man who, for a time at least, wanted to do his job quietly.

The newspapermen (that is, the more ambitious among them) were displeased by Dewey's efforts to prevent "leaks" from his office. A few leaks he could not stop; some reporters had developed "pipe-lines" for information, and they resented any attempt to have these channels closed, even on the plea of public policy. In his most critical months, when the success of his whole program might have been endangered by one ill-considered story of news or rumor, Dewey lived in constant dread that something might happen to expose his hand before he was ready to show it. Much of his power lay in being able to keep quiet until ready to pounce. As the years passed, and the results of the Dewey methods became more apparent, the newspapermen for the most part forgave him. A few, however, still scowl at mention of the man who would not talk until he was ready.

In this reluctance to be stampeded, this refusal to make half-baked statements for the sake of headlines, the Dewey of today is essentially the same as the Dewey of yesterday. The trait, sometimes, can be exasperating; however, in the long view, there is much to be said for it. Like it or not, it is Dewey.

XXIII

MOSTLY PERSONAL

THOMAS E. DEWEY is religious, though devoid of any trace of what ordinarily is regarded as sanctimoniousness. He was a member of the Episcopal Church in Owosso, Michigan, as a youth. When he came to New York, studying both law and singing, his voice was heard in many choirs. After he became Governor and moved to Albany, he became a vestryman of old St. Peter's Episcopal Church there. He gives to parish matters the same careful consideration that he gives to the government of the State of New York. One of his friends, and a frequent guest at the Executive Mansion, is the rector, the Rev. Dr. Erville Maynard. When at their farm at Quaker Hill, the Governor and Mrs. Dewey attend the local church, where the Rev. Ralph Lankler conducts services. Occasionally, in the summers, Mrs. Dewey has played the organ in this little church. Once a year it has been the custom for the Deweys to give a Sunday School picnic at the farm, where Mr. Dewey lends a hand with the frankfurters and hamburgers. Governor Dewey invariably says grace before dinner.

Mr. Dewey, having made the money he has (which is not a great deal) the hard way, is conscious of the value of a dollar. He remembers what Earl Putnam paid him on the farm —$30 a month. He understands that his $25,000 a year as Governor is not to be squandered. Out of his own financial experiences, which included making ends meet while living in a two-room walk-up apartment as a young married man, he likes to figure out the cost of things—any costs, whether private or governmental. He is quick to spot a man who is living beyond his means and to draw reasonable deductions. He is also quick to sense the distress of a friend.

Governor Dewey has consciously and carefully tried for the greatest possible effectiveness on the platform and over the air. He believes it would be something of an affront to his listeners to go before them with a slipshod performance when he is capable of a finished performance. As a result, his voice is something new in American political life. Never a banger of tables, he still carries unusual force in his voice; he can get the effect he wants from a seemingly casual statement of the facts. He also knows how to take care of his voice, which is something that many public speakers have never taken the trouble to learn. On only a few occasions has he had the slightest trouble with his throat. His voice comes over the air with no trace of affectation or condescension. Although he came from Michigan and Mrs. Dewey from the Southwest, the origins of neither could be determined readily by hearing them speak. They are "American" voices, right enough, but not bearing the mark of any section.

The Governor is a trifle more than five feet, eight inches tall, almost precisely the same as the average of the men in the armed forces of the United States. He is about three inches taller than Joseph Stalin, and almost two inches taller than Winston Churchill. His shoulders, which he carries well up and back, are unusually broad for his build. Sometimes he has a cold in winter, but otherwise his health is perfect. He weighs 160 pounds, only slightly more than he weighed back in the racket-busting days. He keeps himself in excellent condition, though he could hardly be called a

THOMAS E. DEWEY

THE GOVERNOR AND HIS MOTHER, AT HOME IN OWOSSO

TOM DEWEY AT THREE

THE BOY AT TWELVE

FARMHAND AT SEVENTEEN

EARL PUTNAM, MICHIGAN FARMER, CHATS WITH
HIS EX-FARMHAND

THE DISTRICT ATTORNEY AFTER A NOTABLE TRIUMPH

THE DISTRICT ATTORNEY SCORES AGAIN
At the signing of the Cafeteria Employees Union contract; with
William B. Herlands (l.) and Father John P. Boland (r.)

NOMINATION AT SARATOGA

OPENING SESSION OF THE STATE LEGISLATURE

GOVERNOR AND STAFF
Seated, l. to r., Miss Lilian G. Rosse, Governor Dewey, Paul Lockwood, Charles D. Breitel. Standing, l. to r., James C. Hagerty, Lawrence E. Walsh, Hamilton Gaddi

Press Association

Elliott Bell

Aimé DuPont

Rollin Browne

Press Association

John E. Burton

Acme

Edward F. Corsi

Press Association

John Foster Dulles

GOVERNOR'S AIDES

Press Association

Harold Keller

Press Association

Paul Lockwood

Press Association

John F. O'Connell

Press Association

Charles H. Sells

GOVERNOR'S AIDES

Acme

With Warren of California

Acme

With Vivian of Colorado

Acme

With Baldwin of Connecticut

Press Association

With Bacon of Delaware

Acme

With Bottolfsen of Idaho

Acme

With Green of Illinois

REPUBLICAN GOVERNORS ALL
Candidates Bricker and Dewey meet their fellow governors at St. Louis.

Acme

With Hickenlooper of Iowa

Acme

With Schoeppel of Kansas

Acme

With Willis of Kentucky

Acme

With Sewall of Maine

Acme

With Saltonstall of Massachusetts

Press Association

With Thye of Minnesota

REPUBLICAN GOVERNORS ALL

With Kelly of Michigan

With Donnell of Missouri

With Ford of Montana

With Griswold of Nebraska

With Blood of New Hampshire

With Edge of New Jersey

REPUBLICAN GOVERNORS ALL

With Snell of Oregon

With Martin of Pennsylvania

With Sharpe of South Dakota

With Wills of Vermont

With Langlie of Washington

With Goodland of Wisconsin

REPUBLICAN GOVERNORS ALL

OFF FOR A ROUND OF GOLF AT PAWLING

Acme

DAPPLEMERE AND THE FAMILY
The Governor with his wife and sons at their Pawling farmhouse.

GARDENERS AT PAWLING
John (1.) and Thomas Jr. with their father in Dapplemere's garden.

AN AMERICAN FAMILY OF THIS CENTURY

fanatic about exercise. He keeps a close watch on his waistline. To the observer he seems to have little reason to worry. As to diet, he eats virtually anything he likes—and that includes almost everything. He likes an occasional taste of Italian or Armenian cooking. Sometimes he works late into the night, though not so late as many of his assistants. He usually gets a full night's sleep. He has never tried to astound his associates by getting to his office at some fantastically early hour. He smokes, on the average, a little less than one package of cigarettes a day.

Governor Dewey likes to play golf, and takes a turn almost every week end when he is at the farm; sometimes even when the weather is bad. He is only a fair golfer, shooting usually in the middle nineties. Usually his golfing companions are Charles E. Murphy, G. Lynn Sumner, and Carl T. Hogan. Mr. Dewey has been known to burst into short—very short—snatches of song on the golf course. He has also been known to swear. As a cusser, however, he is adjudged by experts to be less than adept. He doesn't seem to put quite enough zest into it, for one thing, and his imagery is not picturesque or startling enough. At the game of softball, which is the most strenuous sport he has allowed himself in recent years, he is anything but a champion. He has a peculiar and ineffective stance when batting; Ty Cobb could show him many things about sliding into second base. He seldom plays poker, and then only for small stakes; he is never spectacularly successful. He will take a drink or two, preferably Scotch and water, but he has always gone easy on the alcohol. He has some friends who drink to a point that is known as "heavy," and others who do not drink at all. He rarely tells jokes. He is excellent, however, at remembering effective phrases or striking aphorisms. What is known on Broadway as the "gag" or flip wisecrack has little appeal to him.

Occasionally in the course of the investigations into New York's rackets, Mr. Dewey and many of his aids received threats of bodily harm. Many of these threats were from the never-dying army of crackpots; some of them, however, were undoubtedly on the level. If at any time Mr. Dewey was perturbed by any of these threats he showed no sign. He was usually accompanied to and from his office by one or more detectives. When he and Mrs. Dewey took a stroll, a detective followed twenty feet behind. For a time Mr. Dewey had a habit of slipping off by himself and taking walks about New York without notifying his guard. He stopped this practice when Paul Lockwood reminded him:

"You may not care about yourself. But think of the detective. He's supposed to watch you. If anything happened to you he'd lose his job."

The contemporaries of Mr. Dewey's singing days are agreed that he not only showed promise but that he actually was a good singer. Indeed, there are ladies who were students at the University of Michigan when he was there who still remember that a song by Tom Dewey was about the best thing in those parts.

The occasions when Mr. Dewey has sung since he became a public figure have been exceedingly rare. He once sang for a small group of political workers who were eating with him late one night in an East Side restaurant. He and Mrs. Dewey sometimes run through a few songs. When her parents, Mr. and Mrs. Orla Hutt of Sapulpa, visit the Deweys, a quartet may be organized. Mr. Dewey was greatly taken by the songs in the show "Oklahoma"—"Oh, What a Beautiful Morning," "The Surrey with the Fringe on Top," "People Will Say We're in Love," and so forth. He learned them all. He sings them in the bathroom.

There was once a Governor of New York—and not a bad one, either—who said that so far as he could recall he had only read one book, and that was the life of John L. Sullivan. Mr. Dewey will take a turn at a novel, a mystery story, or a book of essays, but most of his reading is on the slightly heavy side. When he becomes interested in a certain subject, such as the farming problem, world-nutrition schemes, or international trade agreements, he will read all he can find on the subject. He will also call on experts to give him their opinions, which sometimes are served to him in the form of detailed memoranda or abridgments of important but lengthy reports.

He has an excellent library in the Executive Mansion which includes most of the current books. Unless he has guests he usually cleans up some work in the evenings, but he is often able to spend an hour or two catching up on his reading. About the Mansion, he is polite and easygoing, and thoroughly relaxed. He likes best of all the company of such old friends as Mr. and Mrs. Carl T. Hogan and Mr. and Mrs. Roger W. Straus, who are frequently at the Mansion for dinner.

Governor Dewey knows a great deal about the lives of his friends and associates. He will perform such simple acts of thoughtfulness as getting up early Sunday and driving the young daughter of a Quaker Hill neighbor to Mass when he knows her parents are away and cannot take her. Again, he will go out of the way to encourage a friend. Once he heard that a friend of his (a prominent Democrat) was deep in the doldrums, about ready to give up. Dewey drove over to see him, bawled him out, and then gave him a pep talk to end all pep talks. Whatever he actually said, it was enough to bring the gentleman out of his despair.

The Governor's regard for the straight, simple, and un-adorned truth is sometimes cited by his friends as an excellent trait politically, but trying socially. If a man, or a woman, has told Dewey that a certain thing is true, and then, sometime later, changes the story, the Dewey memory will go into action and he will call them for it—sometimes sharply. Maybe the change is of no great importance; nevertheless, when the stories do not jibe the Governor wants to know why.

"He could save himself a lot of trouble," says one of his friends, "if he would learn the art of telling a few harmless lies. Most people are liars in one way or another. Why can't he learn the art?"

Maybe so, in ordinary social gatherings. And yet this uncompromising regard for truth is beyond doubt one of the fresh virtues which Dewey has brought to American political life. Not himself geared to the habit of prevarication, in big things or little, he has a profound scorn for the prevaricators and breakers of promises who sit in the seats of the mighty.

ENEMIES OF LABOR

At American Labor Party Notification Rally in Carnegie Hall, New York City, September 30, 1937

TONIGHT we launch the first organized campaign by workers of New York to insure to our people four years of clean, liberal and honest municipal government. You have nominated me for District Attorney of New York County. With a deep sense of personal satisfaction I am proud to accept that nomination.

I want you to know how that nomination came about. For more than two years now, ever since I undertook the task to which the Governor of this State appointed me, I have sat regularly for days and for nights in conferences with leaders of organized labor, many of whom sit upon this platform tonight. These two years of conferences have been devoted to the purpose of making sure that the frontal attack on organized crime should never be of injury to the labor movement. And so it was that some two months ago, when I was being urged to become a candidate for District Attorney, I sat again with these same leaders, who told me that I owed a duty to the people of New York to become a candidate.

I shall never forget the statement of the president of a great international union when he said to me, "Labor has committed itself to the cause of good government in New York. In doing that we have incurred the wrath of the corrupt political machine which has controlled the district attorney's office for twenty years. If we do not also break their control on that office, labor will suffer a four year war of retribution. Labor will again have to submit to the invasions of gangsters. For the safety of our workers, the office

205

of district attorney must be saved and you have got to do it."

And so it is that I have become your candidate for district attorney to deliver that office back to the control of the people.

To anyone who knows and understands the aspirations of the labor movement, it is clear why labor is and must be united behind this fight for decent municipal government. The day has come when the workers need no longer accept the crumbs which drop from the table of vote-seeking politicians. The day has come when labor can and will assert as a matter of right that the government of this city be permanently freed from the control of any special group or class and most of all from the control of that small group of selfish politicians who brought it to the brink of ruin four years ago.

In the long struggle out of which have arisen the great collective agreements of today, the great fight of the labor movement has been against prejudice. We all remember the employer who used to say that unionization would close up his shop. He did not realize that sound industrial relations were sound business policy. Today we see those very same employers, freed of their suspicions, working happily and in mutual confidence, under successful collective bargaining.

It is becoming understood that there can be no advance in our industrial society without collective bargaining. But there still remain two major obstacles to sound collective bargaining. There are still business men who regard a picket line as a signal for a criminal investigation. For two years people have come to my office who still believed that the exercise of the right to picket was a criminal conspiracy. In these two years we have made real progress in public education. The incidents of the struggle for honest collective bargaining are at last coming to be sharply distinguished from the invasion of the industrial field by gangsters.

ENEMIES OF LABOR

Less than a year ago the officers of a great shipping company publicly demanded the intervention of my office in a strike, and at that time—long before I yielded to any suggestion to become a candidate—I announced publicly, as we have on so many other occasions, "Bona fide disputes arising from an effort to improve the conditions of men working in any industry are under no circumstances any part of the purpose of this investigation." And I repeat, they are not a part of any criminal investigation.

The gangster has been the second obstacle to industrial progress, of which I speak. The racketeer is in no sense part of the labor movement. He is no more a labor racketeer than a business racketeer. Years ago, when some short-sighted employers first used professional criminals in the industrial struggle, the gangster gained his foothold. Under the supine indifference of a machine-controlled district attorney, the gangster rapidly became an institution. A hundred dollars paid to the underworld this year means five hundred dollars next year. Employment of a gangster one year becomes domination by him another year and so under the paternally closed eye of the public prosecutor, both capital and labor came to find the gangster in the field, sitting in at conferences between employers and workers, as the uninvited guest.

Let us take from the record a specific case. It is now a matter of sworn testimony in the criminal courts that five years ago the "Dutch" Schultz mob invaded the restaurant field. Electing their own men as officers of two great unions in that field, they used those unions for the exploitation of the workers and extortion from the employers. The stench bomb became familiar to the restaurants of the City and the good name of legal picketing was sullied by demands of gangsters as the price of peace. Picket line after picket line was placed for the sole purpose of enforcing demands for money, in case after case every offer of settlement was re-

207

jected until the demands of extortion were met. Then the picket lines were withdrawn and the workers betrayed.

Employers were forced into a trade association owned and operated by the gangsters for the purpose of additional extortions. A whole industry was brought to its knees by the mob.

These conditions were no secret. Articles exposing them were published by liberal leaders and friends of labor. Protests were made at the international conventions of the unions involved. Yet such had become the power of the mob, that every effort, even to raise the question, was defeated.

Where was the District Attorney during this hijacking of an industry? The record shows that in October 1933, after the restaurant racket had been going for a year, a group of heroic workers in one of these unions dared to rebel against the mob and they caused the arrest of the gangsters who operated the racket.

Without a vestige of investigation the case was brought to trial resting only on the testimony of those poor workers who had taken their lives in their hands to complain and during three days the case was so badly presented that every defendant was freed. The tragic results of that failure are now written as a matter of record.

The mob was there in court. The whole case was there available to the district attorney if he chose to go out and get the evidence. Instead, the wrecking of that case was taken as a license to the gangsters to rule and ruin.

The complaining workers were driven from the unions and deprived of their right to work. The other workers gave up in hopeless despair. Protected shops became a matter of city-wide scandal.

From the dues of the workers of those two unions, thousands of dollars were taken out by the mob for their private profit. From the restaurant industry more than a million dollars was extorted while the workers were betrayed.

This is the price our people paid in one industry alone for the kind of public prosecution they have had for twenty years. When I undertook the investigation of that industry these conditions were public property throughout the city, but so deeply entrenched had the racket then become that it took eighteen months of most intensive and gruelling investigation to get the proof. A fear stricken industry had learned its lesson once when the district attorney allowed the mob to walk free.

Every kind of false propaganda was spread as to the purpose of that investigation. But last January the case was brought to trial and after ten weeks, every defendant was convicted and every witness was protected.

Six months have passed since those convictions in March of this year. Let us look at the results of that prosecution. In each of those unions the workers have adopted and re-established new and model constitutions of labor democracy. They have elected their own officials, in many cases the men who led the long and hopeless fight. The disrepute which once attached to their picket lines has vanished; the workers have become real trade unionists and not mere paper members without rights. Contracts have become a living reality and decent working conditions have been actually procured. But more, the day that criminal trial started the paper membership of those two unions totalled 6,900 members. Today, in six short months the actual paid-up membership for those unions stands at 15,100—more than doubled. And in those same six months wage increases have been procured totalling over a million dollars.

These are the facts on the record. These are some of the achievements on the record of less than two years, and these are only samples of the list I could give you if time permitted.

These, my friends, are the proof of what happens to the progress of industrial peace and collective bargaining when the gangster is driven from the conference table. For twenty years the accumulated obstacles to industrial peace have been permitted and indeed fostered by a succession of machine controlled district attorneys who neither knew nor wished to understand the problem of industrial progress.

With your help we shall go forward to industrial and economic peace under a city administration which represents all the people to a new day of progressive municipal government under the continued leadership of Fiorello La Guardia.

Never again must the criminal underworld be permitted to sit between the employer and worker, extorting from the one and beating down the wages of the other. Never again must the process of the law in this County be so abandoned as to permit organized crime to victimize organized labor. With your help these conditions will never again exist.

CRIME AND POLITICS

*Fourth in a Series of Five Broadcasts on "The Inside Story
of a Racket" by Mr. Dewey, October 24, 1937*

TONIGHT I am going to talk about the alliance between
Crime and Politics in the County of New York.

I am going to tell you about a politician, a political ally
of thieves, pickpockets, thugs, dope peddlers and big-shot
racketeers. Albert Marinelli, County Clerk of New York,
powerful leader of half the Second Assembly District, dominates the whole. He attained power by staying in the dark
and keeping his mouth shut. Tonight we turn on the spotlight.

The people in the Second Assembly District in downtown
New York know what gorillas they have met at the polls,
how they have been threatened, how their votes have been
stolen; and I am going to tell them how it came about that
gangsters roamed their neighborhood immune from prosecution.

For years racketeers used the name of Marinelli to
frighten victims—and not in vain. Back in 1932 there was
a pair of rising gangsters known as James Plumeri alias
Jimmy Doyle and Dominick Didato alias Dick Terry. They
had never driven a truck but they were handy with a knife
or a gun. They decided to take over the downtown trucking
industry. They started by forming a so-called truckmen's
association at 225 Lafayette Street, which just happened to
be the building where Marinelli has his office and his Albert Marinelli Association. They elected themselves President and Treasurer of this Five Borough Truckmen's Association, and were ready for the business of intimidating
truckmen. For front men and to help with the rough work

211

they took on Natale Evola and John Dio. They went to work on the truckmen. They set themselves up as dictators. They told decent truckmen whom they could truck for and whom they could not. They enforced their rules by beatings, stench-bombs, and the destruction of trucks. They boasted of their political connections.

William Brown was a typical victim. Together with his wife he ran a small trucking business on West Twenty-first Street. The Browns had three trucks. They were struggling along in 1933, making a fair go of it, until the racket got after them. As a result of their troubles, his wife had a nervous breakdown, Brown's brother was beaten black and blue, and their best truck was wrecked.

Brown and his wife were sitting in their trucking office one night working on the books. Terry and Doyle walked in. Brown had just got a new customer.

"What's the idea of your taking this account?" Doyle demanded. "We are from the Five Borough Truckmen's Association. You can't get away with taking any of these accounts around here."

Now, Brown had courage. He told them where to get off. Doyle threatened, "You know what happens to guys that don't play ball with us. They are pretty soon out of business."

Then they shoved Brown up against the wall and told him that unless he gave up that account they would put emery in his truck motors and beat up his drivers. Then Doyle said, "We've had a lot of complaints against us in the last year and we've beat every rap. All we got to do is call up Al Marinelli and the rap is killed. He's the man we got higher up that's protecting us."

Brown defied the gangsters, and within three weeks there was emery powder in the crankcase of his best truck. It wrecked the motor. Seven gorillas entered the office one night, threw monkey wrenches at Brown's brother and beat him with an ax handle. He was in bed for two weeks. A fellow worker was slugged at the same time.

Mr. and Mrs. Brown were terrified. They remembered what Doyle had said about protection from Marinelli. They were afraid to go to the District Attorney's office and so they kept quiet. Then one night in May, 1933, Brown was listening to the radio and he heard a speech by the man who was then the Police Commissioner who said racket victims should come in and he would see they were protected. The very next morning Brown was at the Police Commissioner's office, and he was sent at once to tell his story to the grand jury. Indictments for coercion and conspiracy were voted against Dick Terry, Jimmy Doyle, and Johnny Dio. Brown and his wife went home believing they had found justice.

But the case dragged on for a year with no trial. Finally, Brown got a subpoena calling him to the Court of General Sessions for the trial. He handed his subpoena to the clerk and the clerk said, "Why, that's a wrong date on that subpoena; your case was dismissed yesterday." And the record shows the dismissal on recommendation of the District Attorney.

All of the charges, fumbled by the District Attorney, together with others, were brought to trial in the spring of this year by my office. After a year of investigation we procured an indictment exposing the entire brazen history of the trucking racket. Finally Jimmy Doyle and Johnny Dio pleaded guilty on every count, after my assistants, Murray I. Gurfein and Jacob Grumet, had presented the people's evidence. The men the District Attorney turned loose are now in State's prison.

Who is this Albert Marinelli? Officially he is your County Clerk. You elected him four years ago. He survived the La Guardia landslide because the people did not take the trouble to know who was running for County Clerk, just as the

213

machine controlled District Attorney survived, with the help of Marinelli and his boys.

It was Marinelli's office which affixed his signature to the extradition papers for his friend, Lucky Luciano, which my office used to bring that worthy back from Hot Springs, Ark.

Al Marinelli today is one of the most powerful politicians in New York. This shadowy figure gives no interviews to the press. His history is shrouded in mystery. No one even knows just how he rose to power. In 1931 he took over the leadership of the Second Assembly District of Manhattan. Rapidly his power spread to other districts. In 1935 he put up a handpicked candidate named Joseph Greenfield and unseated David Mahoney as leader of half of the First Assembly District. Mahoney charged that two notorious racketeers, Socks Lanza and John Torrio, were active in that election which led to Marinelli's triumph. Lanza was the gorilla who dominated the Fulton Fish Market for years. Complaints were made to the District Attorney of New York County against Lanza but they were ignored. Lanza was the cause of one of those frequent scandals in the machine dominated District Attorney's office which resulted in an investigation ordered by Governor Roosevelt. It took the Federal Government to catch up with Lanza and save the fish industry from his terrorism. Torrio, once the boss of Al Capone in Chicago, is now under indictment in Federal Court. When he was brought to Court, he put up $100,000 in cash for bail. Somehow or other, Torrio was also indicted on a forgery charge last year by the District Attorney of New York County, but the indictment was quietly dismissed last December and Torrio walked out a free man.

Mysterious as he may be in New York, Marinelli's supporters may be interested to know that he has a luxurious estate surrounded by an iron fence, on Lake Ronkonkoma, way out on Long Island. From his several motor cars, he chooses to drive back and forth in a Lincoln limousine; and his Japanese butler, Togo, serves him well.

Regularly, you will find Al standing in the basement of the Criminal Courts Building in Manhattan, quietly chatting with bondsmen, lawyers, and hangers-on. Your County Clerk has many, diversified interests.

In 1932, when Marinelli set out to attend a function in Chicago, there was with him a well-dressed, pasty-faced, sinister man with a drooping right eye. He had an air of quiet authority. Together, they turned up in Chicago, playing host in a suite at the Drake Hotel, and were constant companions at the race track in the afternoons. Marinelli's companion was Charlie Lucky Luciano, then almost as unknown as Marinelli, later revealed as the Number One man of New York's underworld, master of many rackets. Luciano is now in Dannemora Prison, serving a sentence of thirty to fifty years.

Some of the facts about Al Marinelli and his organization are matters of record and you are entitled to know the kind of man who helps to pick your public officials—who helps select those who are in charge of criminal justice.

Back in 1933, while I was a Chief Assistant United States Attorney, the United States Government conducted an investigation of election frauds under the Federal Law. Election inspectors in various districts of the city were indicted and convicted but nowhere were conditions worse than in Al Marinelli's Second Assembly District. In that district alone, the records indicate, they had added 4,534 votes to their own set of candidates and stolen 3,535 from the others. You know, in some districts the dominant party will bribe or intimidate the officials appointed by the other party. And both become parties to the corruption of the ballot. Democrats and Republicans alike were indicted.

Let us take just two election districts in Marinelli's District. We'll see who was running the election for Al. In the 28th Election District, the chairman of the Election Board was George Cingola. He was the man directly charged with preserving the peace at the polls and seeing that there was an honest count. He was imported into the district for the election and registered from the home of his sister. Back in 1927 he had once before been arrested for an election offense and beat the rap. But less than a year before he was appointed to his 1932 election day job, he was arrested no less than three times—twice for assault and once for bootlegging and he served a term for one of the assault raps in the county jail in Mineola. And just a few months before that, three detectives of the Police Department Narcotic Squad, upon arresting him in his home found him sleeping with two loaded revolvers under his pillow. He was convicted in the Court of Special Sessions for his double violation of the Sullivan Law. He was let off with a $25 fine. And so he became qualified to serve as an election inspector. Marinelli made him the public official in charge of the polling place and graced him with the title of chairman of the local board of elections.

He was indicted by the Federal Attorney's office, but he has not been heard from since, and the indictment has now been dismissed.

The members of Al Marinelli's county committee faithfully elect him year after year and faithfully work for his candidates. They ratify the party choices and work desperately for them, this year most of all. You are entitled to know what kind of people some of them have been.

I have the official criminal records in front of me. Here's the first one. He has eight arrests to his credit but the only charge which stuck was one in the Federal Court for selling dope. They sent him to prison for that one but on the other seven arrests, going way back to 1918 when he was locked up for robbery, he has "beaten the rap." These include two charges of robbery and one each of felonious assault, disorderly conduct, malicious mischief and grand larceny.

Here is another who has a great personal interest in law enforcement and municipal government in New York. He began in 1924 with a sentence to Atlanta for counterfeiting. Some years later, he was picked up for extortion and carrying a gun, but it took him only two weeks to get out. Only a month later, he was again in the hands of the police, charged with homicide with a gun. But he beat that rap too. Last month he was named as a member of Al Marinelli's County Committee.

Here's some more. But these men are probably not particularly important in the councils of the Second Assembly District. They've never been convicted of crime. But perhaps I'm wrong—it may be that their achievement in avoiding conviction entitles them to special honor in the Marinelli councils.

One of these was just selected County Committeeman last month. He has to his credit discharges on complaints of stealing an automobile, robbery with a gun, and vagrancy. Another of his fellows who was just chosen has a vagrancy discharge. A colleague of his, likewise selected last month, beat an attempted robbery charge. Another of his fellows was turned out on a grand larceny charge. Here is a precious pair who each beat two raps. The first one on a felony assault charge and for stealing an automobile; another for toting a gun and for coercion. Here's another charged with being a fence for receiving stolen goods. Then we have one who ran up against the liquor law a couple of times and another who was in conflict with a policy charge.

All of these, as members of the official county committee of the Second Assembly District! Aside from those who always beat the rap, the ex-convicts alone include a counterfeiter, a stickup man, and others convicted of assault, injuring property, gun toting, impersonation of a public officer and larceny, both grand and petty. Worst of all are the six convicted of dope charges. What an intense interest these men must have in electing the public officials who administer criminal justice! What an interest these men must have in decent municipal government! But that is not all. These criminal records on more than a score of Al Marinelli's county committeemen tell only part of the story. There are also the election inspectors.

Inspectors of election are public officials, certified to by the county chairman from a list provided by the Leader. Let's look at Al Marinelli's election officials. Perhaps we will find out the reason for some of the things that have been going on in New York. Here are some of the men officially designated to keep the peace, certify to the honesty of the election and count the votes in the Second Assembly District. This faithful worker who counts your votes started as a pickpocket in 1908. He wasn't out long before he was convicted of grand larceny, and later of assault. But he won't serve as an election inspector this year. On June 1st he ran up against the Federal Government and a United States Judge sent him to Lewisburg Penitentiary for a year and a half.

Here are three more vote counters. The first has three arrests to his credit but went to jail only once. That was for petty larceny. Three years ago he was arrested for felonious assault but it took him only a day to get out.

Another was convicted of attempted grand larceny in New Jersey and still another, whose pedigree I have here, was convicted on a policy charge. But he acted as an election inspector last year, and you will probably see him at it this year too.

Of course some of the election inspectors in the Second always manage to beat the rap. Here is one who wiggled out of two burglary charges. Another was acquitted of burglary and a third was discharged on a grand larceny count.

Well, these are some of the County Committeemen and Inspectors of Election in the 2nd Assembly District. I have police records for thirty-two of them. Twenty of this fine assortment, who have been selected to serve on the County Committee or to count votes, have been convicted at least once. The other dozen have thus far succeeded in beating the rap. Their attainments include seventy-six arrests on a varied assortment of charges ranging from robbery to sex crimes, with dope peddlers heading the list. No wonder they are desperately fighting to keep the office of the District Attorney in the same hands it has been for twenty years. No wonder Marinelli is joining with his pals, running the fight of his life.

The people of the second Assembly District are entitled to know the facts about those who have been misrepresenting them in the political councils of New York. For years they have been terrorized at the polls and forced to submit throughout the year to the domination of the gunmen who paraded their streets. And don't for one moment believe these are the only cases.

These are the sinister forces who are fighting to keep the right to select assistants for the office of District Attorney of New York County. These are the living obstacles to everything that's decent and clean in the conduct of our city.

This is not a political issue. There can be no difference of opinion on the questions involved. Gorillas, thieves, pickpockets, and dope peddlers in the political structure are not the subject of argument. There is nothing political about human decency.

The issue is defined. The decision is in your hands on Election Day.

LOOKING FORWARD

Delivered at the Closing Rally of His Campaign for Governor at the Academy of Music, Brooklyn, N. Y., November 6, 1938

TONIGHT we are here to complete the victory for clean, progressive government. This great demonstration proves that the people of Brooklyn are determined this year to be free.

For eight years now I have been at work across the river from you, fighting against the criminal and political monopolies which once oppressed the people of New York County. This year at the polls we shall crush the power of those forces which have so long betrayed you in Brooklyn.

In this campaign we have dedicated ourselves to the principle that the freedom of the people can only be preserved by free leaders; that corrupt political machines shall no longer be allowed to dictate the choice of candidates or of elected officials; that the influence of those machines shall be removed.

I have carefully read all of the speeches made by our opponents in this campaign—all of our opponents. Tonight not one of the major issues before the people has been met by them. Instead they bring a single indictment against me.

I stand before you accused of one crime: I was born in the 20th Century. To that charge I plead guilty.

I am of the 20th Century. We look forward, not backward.

When I accepted the nomination of my party for Governor, there was a unanimous call for new leadership. The heavy hand of the past was cast off. In this election I look for support only to the people of the State of New York.

In this campaign we look forward to a better and a hap-

pier day for the people of our State. We look backward
only to learn by the mistakes of yesterday. We look forward
in the hope of curing those errors.

Another generation has passed on to us a sick world. It
is sick economically with 11,000,000 of our people still unemployed. It is sick spiritually, poisoned by hatreds. It is
sick politically when a candidate for Governor of the great
State of New York does not dare repudiate corrupt elements
of the party which support him. Right here in Brooklyn last
night he had an opportunity. He ignored it. He didn't even
mention them.

Only with courage can we meet the problems of tomorrow. In this campaign I have met every issue squarely and
promptly. My economic and social philosophy and that of
my associates on this ticket have been placed squarely before the people.

We are pledged to restore individual dignity and human
freedom. First comes economic security. To this end relief
for the needy must and will be maintained.

The right to a job at fair wages and the support of government to that end is another major objective. To that we
are pledged.

The right of the small business man to protection against
unfair competition shall be preserved.

We shall carry forward the fight to protect the very young
and the old, the sick and the infirm, from economic and social injustice.

We shall advance the cause of the workers of our State
and their right to bargain collectively through representatives of their own choosing. For all of labor's hard-won gains,
we shall fight.

These beliefs are not new. They are part and parcel of
our generation. We of the twentieth century move forward
with clear eyes toward our goal of economic and social justice. During eight long years of struggle in one county, I

have fought for these beliefs. I've been down in the trenches, fighting as a common soldier for the lives, the liberties and the freedom of our people; fighting for the freedom of labor; fighting for the freedom of a community from the throttling forces into whose hands corrupt local machines of the Democratic Party betrayed it; fighting for the business men oppressed by criminal monopolies; fighting to protect the home; fighting for the right of every man and woman in our community to live and to work as free men and free women. After January 1, I will carry on that fight with the same vigor and willingness in a larger field.

It was well said last night by the President, and I quote:

"New ideas cannot be administered successfully by men with old ideas, for the first essential of doing the job well is the wish to see the job done at all."

That is what the President said. I agree.

This year we offer the people of New York not only the wish to see these things done, but the will to see them done well. There are many tasks before us.

We shall strengthen the unemployment insurance law of our State. We shall cure that breakdown which has prevented our people from receiving their just due. Weeks ago in this campaign I pointed out a major reason for that failure. I showed that more than half of the 5,000 employees of the unemployment insurance division of this State are temporary employees not protected by the civil service. Good laws break down under bad administration. No wonder my opponent has not lifted his voice in answer or even in apology. After January 1 there will be an effective and progressive civil service system in this state.

I have pointed out that in the State of New York, after six years of political argument about the electric companies, a broken down and ineffective administration leaves us among the nine most backward states in the nation. And to this there has been no answer, because there is no answer.

I have pointed out that in six years not a single low-cost housing project has gone forward with the aid of the State of New York. Two million people in New York City and hundreds of thousands in other communities in the state are still living in ancient fire traps which were unsanitary the day they were built. And to that there has been no answer from my opponent. Not even an apology.

How true it is that new ideas cannot be administered without the youth and the vigor to carry them into effect!

Again, it was well said by the President last night, and I quote his words:

"By their promoters ye shall know them."

In this campaign I am promoted by no man. No man or group of men told me what office I could not run for. No man or group of men on an easy chair, on a bed, or otherwise, told me what office I could run for.

"By their promoters ye shall know them."

We are all agreed that the rights of the people can be preserved and extended only by vigorous and aggressive leadership. We must be agreed that the ability of a public officer to serve the people is dependent upon the freedom with which he obtains that office.

To you people of Brooklyn these things are more than theories. You have lived them. You have suffered under them.

The political machine which dominates your county has day after day, year after year, betrayed you. Three times in five years has the protection of your homes and your lives so broken down that outside help was needed. And still, my opponent dares not repudiate that machine. After six years in power my opponent has not yet raised his voice to demand its overthrow. Instead, he relies upon it for support.

The Albany machine, which registers more votes than there are adults in the city, is now well known to the people of the state. Two weeks ago I laid bare the facts and in those two weeks no mention of the City of Albany, of the oppression of its people, or of the sponsors of that oppression has passed the lips of my opponent.

Our opponents still rely upon the discredited and repudiated forces of old and reactionary political power in Albany, Buffalo, and here in the City of New York.

As I have pointed out on other occasions in this campaign, this is a fight between two political philosophies. On our side we maintain that humane, progressive and clean government can be procured without the help of those forces which my opponent dares not repudiate. I have pointed out name after name of men convicted, either in the courts or before the people, as betrayers of the public trust. These men remain high in the councils of the Democratic machine in this State, choosing its candidates and dominating its affairs.

After exposure they have maintained their political power. Some of them have actually been promoted.

To this there has been no answer—no word of explanation—no word of apology. Night before last, speaking in the Bronx, my opponent, instead of answering the major issues, pointed to five Republican office holders who had been guilty of wrongdoing. Five out of the thousands of Republican office holders in the State.

Last night I pointed out the difference between two political philosophies. Were those five promoted? The answer is on the record. Each of the five office holders who stole public funds was prosecuted and convicted by a Republican District Attorney and sent to prison. Each of those men betrayed their trust. He was never again allowed to hold public office. He was and is today no longer in the party councils.

One other was mentioned by my opponent. He told a story about a former Republican sheriff in Cayuga County. I quote him:

"Believe it or not, Dutch Schultz was appointed a deputy sheriff in Cayuga County. This Sheriff was a leading figure in the Republican organization of that county."

Last night I added another chapter to that story about the Republican Sheriff in Cayuga County. I pointed out that this appointment of Dutch Schultz was discovered after the Cayuga Sheriff was out of office and that the Sheriff was then read out of the Republican Party. That Sheriff will never again be in the Republican Party councils.

My opponent suggests that I should have known that Dutch Schultz had once been a Deputy Sheriff of Cayuga County. Since his address in the Bronx last Thursday night, I have investigated the activities of Dutch Schultz as a law enforcement agent.

Now when my opponent gave his speech in the Bronx last Thursday, he didn't have to go as far away as Cayuga County. He could have talked about Bronx County. On July 31, 1925, Arthur Flegenheimer, alias Dutch Schultz, was appointed a Deputy Sheriff of Bronx County. At that time he was in the rogues' gallery of the Police Department and was already an ex-convict.

Let's look at his oath of office, now reposing in the records of the County Clerk of Bronx County:

"I, the undersigned, Arthur Flegenheimer, do solemnly swear that I reside at 875 Brook Avenue, in the County of Bronx, and am a citizen of the United States; that I will support the Constitution of the United States and the Constitution of the State of New York and faithfully discharge the duties of a Deputy Sheriff to Preserve the Peace in the service of the Sheriff of the County of Bronx, under and pursuant to my commission to the best of my ability.

(Signed) "ARTHUR FLEGENHEIMER"

Now let's look at the copy of his warrant of appointment. I have it here. Let's see who was Sheriff of the Bronx in 1925? Who appointed the man who at that time was a trigger man for Legs Diamond and Owney Madden, and was preparing to build up his own vast racket empire. Let's see the name at the bottom of this certificate—the name of the Sheriff who made the appointment, administered the oath, and gave the badge of a law enforcement officer to this notorious Dutch Schultz. Let's see the name. Here it is. Edward J. Flynn!

Boss of the Bronx—then and now Democratic Chairman of the County Committee, Chairman of the Executive Committee of the Democratic Party in the Bronx.

Let me read you the warrant of appointment.

It reads as follows:

"To all to whom these presents shall come or may concern:

"In compliance with the provisions of Chapter 523 of the laws of 1890, and the acts amendatory thereof, and of the provisions of Chapter 548 of the laws of 1912, and the acts amendatory thereof of the State of New York authorizing the Sheriff of the County of Bronx to make certain appointments,

"I EDWARD J. FLYNN, Sheriff of the County of Bronx, having appointed, designated and approved and by these presents do appoint, designate and approve

ARTHUR FLEGENHEIMER

to be a Deputy Sheriff during my will and pleasure without compensation.

"Given under my hand and seal this 31st day of July, 1925.

(Signed) "EDWARD J. FLYNN,
Sheriff of the County of Bronx
State of New York"

Now was this Ed Flynn thrown out of the councils of his party? No. He was promoted. Six months later he was appointed Chamberlain of the City of New York under the old regime. And in that office he had the custody of trust funds belonging to widows and orphans.

You all know the record of the City Chamberlain's office under Boss Flynn s administration. You all know about the notorious State Title and Mortgage Company, many of whose officers have since been convicted of crimes. You all remember how $6,500,000 of these trust funds were invested in so-called guaranteed mortgages and certificates; how more than one-third of that amount, over $2,000,000, was invested in the certificates of the State Title and Mortgage Company. It is this man to whom the widows and orphans whose funds he had held in trust look in vain for payment on the investment of their funds.

Now the damage caused by Flynn's reckless investment of other people's money wasn't really known until the crash came some time later. And when the crash came, where was Ed Flynn? Again he had been promoted. He had arrived at the exalted office he now holds—Secretary of State of the State of New York, at $12,000 a year, by appointment of the Governor of the State of New York! As Secretary of State, he has custody of the Great Seal of the State. He has official custody of the laws of the State. He administers the oath of office to the Governors of the state, to other state officers, and to members of the legislature.

He is still Democratic boss of the Bronx. He is still one of the most important leaders in the councils of his party.

And only recently he was again promoted. Today he is the Democratic National Committeeman from the State of New York.

My opponent raised this subject. Investigation brings out the devastating facts on the record.

Again they illustrate the difference between two political philosophies. They illustrate the issues in this campaign.

During the past few weeks it has been my obligation to leave no doubt in the minds of every citizen of New York State: first, as to where I stand on every issue in this campaign affecting you and the public welfare; and second, as to exactly the kind of government you may expect under my administration. I believe I have fulfilled that obligation.

Because I am devoted to our form of representative government, I have stressed the necessity of ridding it in New York State of those who betray it. This must be done to make sure that our form of government will not go the way of those ancient, as well as modern, democracies which have decayed and rotted away under the domination of politician overlords. This must not happen here.

My opponent, with all of his honorable intentions, is helpless after six years. I believe I will accomplish what he has failed to do.

The answer must come from every voter who wants efficient, humane administration of government, in which the rights of none are neglected and none are favored to the exclusion of others, regardless of religion, race, or color.

I pledge you that I will not fail you. After January 1 we go forward together.

AMERICA IS NOT FINISHED

Excerpt from an Address at Minneapolis, Minn., December 6, 1939

TONIGHT I am going to talk about the state of mind of our national government and the resulting state of mind of the nation. We have grave problems in agriculture, in labor, in business, in unemployment, in finance. Tonight I am not going to attempt to state solutions of those specific problems. Our difficulties must be dealt with as a whole. I wish to discuss the thing we must first get clear in our minds if we are to be successful in dealing with any of those problems.

First of all, we must make up our minds whether we believe in the continued growth of this country or whether we believe we have reached our economic limit.

Our greatest national enemy is defeatism. We have Republicans who do not think that our party can win through. We have Republicans and Democrats who do not think that our country can win through. We have Europeans and Americans who do not think that civilization can win through. I am not ashamed to confess the abiding faith that our party, our country and the world will win through.

It is true that we have a crisis here in America. But ours is a crisis of faith—faith in ourselves, in our system, and in our own traditions. On the solution of that crisis everything depends. If here we can rout defeatism, if here we can regain courage and unbounded activity, if here we can unite industry and agriculture and labor for an invincible America, then, and then only, can we contribute to the peace of all the world's people.

.   .   .   .

When President Roosevelt was inaugurated, he said: "Our greatest primary task is to put people to work." He defined

229

the issue but has failed to find the solution. After seven years, putting people to work is still our greatest primary task.

One person out of every five employable persons in this country is today unemployed. The great unanswered question is: What keeps him out of work?

Some people say he does not want to work. That is a vicious slander on the American people.

The other day, in New York, the city authorities announced that they needed fifty-eight automobile mechanics. Hundreds of men stood in line all night to try to get one of those jobs. Six thousand five hundred men applied for those fifty-eight jobs. Those men could have been on relief. But they didn't want relief. Nor will the ten million others prefer relief, the day they are offered work with any reasonable belief that it is a steady job.

Now, some people say that unemployed capital does not want to work. Let me tell you a little story about that.

Last September 1st, the Booneville Savings Bank, of Booneville, Iowa, closed its doors after having been in business for thirty-three years. There was nothing the matter with the bank. It was entirely solvent and it paid out in full the $267,000 of its deposits. In a letter to the depositors, the president of the bank explained the reason for closing. Here it is, and I quote his words:

"The principal reason for quitting is that we do not know what to do with our money."

Now, why didn't that bank know what to do with its money? Obviously, because the customers of that bank were not seeking loans. They were not branching out into new and increased ventures.

Unemployed capital today is about the same as it has always been. It will go to work if it can find a place to work with a reasonable chance of not losing both its job and itself.

I say to you that both capital and labor want work, that both detest idleness. We are going to get exactly nowhere telling lies and libels about one another. We have been getting nowhere for seven years, telling lies and libels about each other.

So I ask you once more: What keeps the unemployed man out of a job? This time I ask it in broader terms.

The New Deal has a committee called the Temporary National Economic Committee. The New Deal has been in power nearly seven years—in case you forget. Its Temporary National Economic Committee this year reports as follows. I quote:

"The American economic machine is stalled on dead center."

After seven years of lending and spending, seven years of priming the pump, seven years of pushing the accelerator down to the floor on more and more and more public spending, seven years of warming up the cylinders of the machine with more than twenty-one billion dollars of new national public debt—after seven years what does the New Deal repair crew tell us? It admits defeat. It says: "The American economic machine is stalled on dead center."

I have been asking: "What keeps the unemployed man out of a job?" Here is one of the answers. This New Deal repair crew does not believe in this machine.

It believes in public spending. But does it believe in what has always hitherto made the machine pick itself up and bound forward again after every temporary slowdown? Does it believe in those absolutely necessary new, great, adventurous private enterprises that create jobs?

Just so there shall be no doubt about it, let me quote the President himself. The whole of the basic economic theory and of the basic economic practice in the New Deal is in the speech the President made in San Francisco in 1932.

In that speech he said some fine things. For example:

"America is new. It is in the process of change and development. It has the great potentialities of youth. We can still believe in change and in progress."

Splendid! And true! But listen now to the part of the San Francisco speech which discloses his real philosophy. I quote excerpts: but I quote them in harmony with his full actual meaning. Here are his words:

"Our industrial plant is built. The problem just now is whether under existing conditions it is not overbuilt.

"A mere builder of more industrial plants . . . is as likely to be a danger as a help.

"Our task is not . . . necessarily producing more goods. It is the soberer less dramatic business of administering resources and plants already in hand. . . ."

Here is the whole outlook of the New Deal: The established plants are all right. But the new plants, the new adventures, the new industries, are unnecessary and even possibly undesirable. There is nothing left to do. All that remains is to divide up what we got from the Indians.

Such is the theory of the New Deal administration. Such is its practice.

With this philosophy I totally and absolutely disagree.

Our country has lived through this sort of theory several times before. One time was in the eighties of the last century. I want to read to you from the annual report of the United States Commissioner of Labor for the year 1886. Note these words carefully. They are so full of pessimism they will encourage you. In 1886 it was there solemnly reported:

"It is true that the discovery of new processes of manufacture will undoubtedly continue . . . but it will not leave room for a marked extension such as has been witnessed during the last fifty years."

Note that! The time of extension of expansion is over. In 1886!

And finally, it said:

"And it will not afford remunerative employment for the vast amount of capital that has been created."

Note that! No more use for idle money. No more chance for profitable, new investments. No chance for the future of our growing population. All this in 1886.

Aren't we lucky that the men who put their money into the early hazard of the automobile industry didn't read this report? Aren't we lucky that our radio pioneers, and our motion picture pioneers and our aviation pioneers, in their ignorance, never heard of it? Aren't we lucky that a host of other pioneers, since 1886, have given us new commodities and new services with no recollection of the economic defeatism of 1886?

The fifty years which followed 1886 make the defeatists of that day seem ridiculous to all of us and yet today the apostles of despair are with us again. They have learned nothing from history. Again they occupy high places in the national government; again they tell us the same old story. I venture to say it will sound as silly fifty years hence as do the statements by the Commissioner of Labor of fifty years ago.

But today we have that same economic defeatism all over again. It seems to come back upon us every so often, and not only here but in all the rest of the world.

In the year 1880 the British statesman, William Pitt, said:

"There is scarcely anything around us but ruin and despair."

In 1849, another British statesman, Benjamin Disraeli, said:

"In industry, commerce, and agriculture, there is no hope."

Here we are, at it again. Here we are, at a time when the American Federation of Labor reports that there are 53,000,-000 employable workers in the United States compared with

48,000,000 just ten years ago. A net increase of half a million new workers per year! And, yet, the President says:
"Our industrial plant is built."

In effect, he says there is no place in this country for the people who are growing up in it. And the tragedy is they are beginning to believe him. Only last week the Young Men's Christian Association reported on a wide-spread survey among our youth. They told us that 80 per cent of the young men and women believe that ability no longer offers assurance of success in America. The philosophy of despair is indeed taking root. What the New Deal means to them is that it would have been better had they never been born.

Its theories have infected the thinking of many of the rest of us. Industrialists, labor leaders, social workers talk about "vast permanent unemployment." In the 1920's we had no unemployment that was "vast." But now they say we must face an unemployment that will be "vast" and that will be "permanent."

The President has said we have a rendezvous with destiny. We seem to be on our way to a rendezvous with despair.

Fellow-Republicans: As a party, let us turn away from that rendezvous and let us start going in the other direction and start now.

The one ultimate unforgivable crime is to despair of the Republic. The one essential to the survival of the Republic is to know it will survive and will survive into a future that is always larger, always better. In every era for a century and a half it has been doomed to death by gloomy young theorists and by tired and hopeless elders. And history laughs at them as each time the dynamic forces of a free Republic led by free men have given the lie to the defeatists while the system of free economic enterprise has marched onward, sweeping the nation's increased population to full employment and even higher living standards.

Nor is history the only answer to these gloomy predictions.

For we have about us in every state, in every city, on every farm, the answer. Here in our own America we have the man-power, the wealth, the natural resources, the genius to invent and create. We have the industrial skill to release the ever-flowing stream of new inventions and greater productivity wherein lies the future of our own America. I don't say to you, close your eyes and have faith—I say to you, open your eyes, look around you and be convinced.

Here is the final answer to the defeatism of the New Deal.

All history proves it is wrong. Our own eyes and our own brains tell us it is wrong. And because its basic theory is wrong, it has done only half its job. It is a duty of national government to perform its social obligations. I believe this administration has sincerely attempted to fulfill those obligations. But that is only half the job. The other half is to maintain, to encourage the economic system which supports the government and makes performance of social obligations possible.

Society has a permanent-deep-rooted obligation to its aged, its blind, its sick, its unemployed. But it is not enough to say no one shall starve. It is a cruel illusion to pass laws which are a mere promise without also taking measures necessary to fulfillment of that promise. The present administration has thought it well enough to make the promise, leaving the performance to come from the savings of the last generation, achieved under Republican administrations, and mortgaging the earnings of the next generation, which will also be under Republican administrations. Our obligation—and I say ours because the Democratic administration has failed—is to start producing the goods and earning the money so that those promises can be fulfilled.

Our first task is to sweep away the obstacles to that fulfillment. There is only one source of real money in any free country and that is private enterprise, the enterprise of the farmer, the worker, and the business man. It is our first, our

primary task, to create the conditions under which this enterprise can go to work.

Until we first make up our minds that this is our purpose,
there is no use discussing particular problems.

Do we believe in the continued growth of this country or
do we believe we have reached our economic limit? All history and every observation of your own eyes prove that
America is not finished. It need never be finished. There is
no limit to America.

There is a force in America that has been held in check
which once released can give us the employment that we
need. It has nothing to do with slick monetary schemes. It
has nothing to do with slick economic panaceas. This force
is the energy of American enterprise, great and small. Given
a chance, it can produce employment, can generate new pur-
chasing power and set in motion once more the surging flow
of commercial venture.

Government hostility, repressive taxation and economic
quackery have kept this force from going to work. Our firm
resolve must be to give it a chance and to encourage enterprise.

Nor does this involve tolerance of abuses in business or
in any other element of society, civil or criminal. Where
there are abuses in business, it is the function of government to correct them as they arise. But we can cure abuses
in business without creating abuses by government.

Tonight I propose that we Americans, of whatever party,
make up our minds that we do believe in the continued
growth of this country.

Let us know the truth that the frontiers of social and economic expansion of America have not yet been discovered;
that there is room and plenty in all this land for all the
young men and women who are growing up in it; that there
is work to do for them and all that follow.

Is it true that America is matured and completed and

overbuilt and incapable of further expansion and new achievements? Is it true that all we can do from now on is to administer the achievements we already have? I do not say no temperately. I say no with resentment and anger.

Let us again learn to believe in the ability of a free people to solve its problems if given a chance. We can and we will again go forward. The one thing I want to do in whatever way I can is to help make the courage of eternal youth run once more in the veins of my party and of my country.

A CALENDAR OF UNPUNISHED CRIMES

Excerpt from an Address in Chicago, Ill., March 28, 1940

LAST evening I spoke of the erosion of character in the administration of our national government. I pointed out that a basic cause of the failure of the New Deal was its lack of integrity and its cynical disregard of the principles of common honesty.

Let us look tonight at the abuses of power of the last seven years which were committed for the simple and ugly purpose of corrupting the electorate of the United States.

This Administration professes great concern for the underprivileged. It parades its generosity toward the unfortunate victims of its own economic failure. To hear them tell it one would almost think the New Dealers invented kindness and human decency. The fact is that every responsible person believes in the obligation of Government to provide relief for the needy. Every decent citizen goes one step further than the New Deal. Every decent citizen insists that relief must be free of politics.

So let us look at the record of the New Deal.

We have the official report of a Committee of the United States Senate. Four of the five members of that Committee, including the Chairman, Senator Sheppard, were Democrats.

Take the evidence state by state.

During the 1938 Democratic primary election in the State of Kentucky the New Deal wanted its Senator Alben Barkley to win. That decision was not to be left to the Democrats of Kentucky. It was decreed by the high command of the New Deal. So the WPA was called into action. The official record shows that in 32 counties of Kentucky government employees on government time prepared lists of WPA workers for the Barkley primary campaign. These were mimeographed on official WPA stationery. In county after county the workers were asked to sign pledges to vote for Barkley. Men who refused to sign this political pledge were discharged.

That's only part of the record. WPA workers in Kentucky were receiving as little as $32 a month. But they were not permitted to keep all of that. They were openly solicited for campaign contributions in county after county. They were told to kick back for the benefit of the New Deal. Relief for the needy was put on the auction block of partisan politics. And all this was done for the New Deal leader of the Democratic majority in the United States Senate.

The records show that in Tennessee foremen and other petty officers of the WPA used "intimidation and coercion" in soliciting campaign funds from relief persons and those employed on WPA.

Ordinarily men go to jail for the crimes of intimidation and coercion. But not the officers of the WPA. Under the New Deal this is high statesmanship. For New Dealers this is the way to the more abundant life.

The primary election in Tennessee was important. So they went still further. WPA workers and materials, paid for with funds appropriated for emergency relief, were actually used to improve private drives and roadways where it was thought the owners would help win the election. Campaign contributions were ruthlessly levied on those least able to pay. Employees of the postal service, of the Bureau of Internal Revenue, and workers on the public roads were notified to pay up—or else. Yes, even the employees of the Soldiers Home at Mountain City were shaken down with the rest.

What kind of people are these who will pick the pockets of road workers, mail carriers, and servants in a Soldiers Home? What kind of people are these who hide behind the smiling mask of the New Deal? The time has come to tear away that mask. The time has come to look at the ugly facts. There stands revealed the lowest form of political life.

In Arkansas $500 was collected from twelve WPA workers for the 1938 Senatorial campaign. That was $42 from each worker. Forty-two dollars out of the meagre earnings of a man on WPA! And by a crowning touch these contributions were described as "voluntary" by the men who collected them.

In Pennsylvania there was another primary election. There they went even further. WPA workers were summoned to Democratic Headquarters, where they were solicited for campaign contributions. Owners of trucks used by WPA were shaken down for $100 each. Republican workers were shifted from jobs near their homes to jobs 40 miles away from their homes. In Northampton County, supervisory officials on a sewing project took $1.50 apiece from the women workers for tickets to a Democratic meeting. In Luzerne County numerous WPA workers, including women, were threatened with loss of their relief employment if they refused to change their registration from Republican to Democratic. This threat was actually carried out.

For ordinary people extortion is a felony. But in the New Deal it is known as remembering the forgotten man. These are things the American people can never forget and will never forgive. These are things no decent Administration would tolerate. . . .

These are not isolated cases. The Chairman of a County Democratic Committee in Pennsylvania addressed the following letter to a woman employed on a local sewing project. Listen to the suave extortion:

"DEAR MADAM:

"I am very much surprised that you have not responded to our previous letter requesting your contribution in the amount of $28.08 to Indiana County Democratic Campaign Committee, as I was sure that you appreciated your position to such an extent that you would make this contribution willingly and promptly. I must, however, now advise you that unless your contribution in the above amount is received promptly it will be necessary to place your name on the list of those who will not be given consideration for any other appointment after the termination of the emergency relief work, which as you know will terminate in the near future."

Precisely $28.08—exacted to the last penny. The women on relief could go hungry. But the New Deal must have its tribute.

Never before has an American political party descended to such brazen abuse of the needy. Never again must such an administration be entrusted with power.

Here in Illinois the record of abuse is the same. . . . Look with me at what the official record says about your 1938 primaries.

Those elections meant a lot to the New Deal. So here too the relief organization was pressed into political action. Three weeks before Primary Day, 450 men were especially hired. It was called road construction work. Yet every one of them was under political orders and actually working in a primary campaign. Every one of them was used by the New Deal machine until Primary Day—and practically every one was dismissed the day after. Every one of those 450 men had his card signed by the New Deal campaign manager in the primary contest! A total of $23,268 taken from the relief of the needy and put to what the Committee itself branded as "a mis-use of Federal aid road funds."

The law calls that grand larceny. But of course nobody went to jail. That's not even petit larceny under the New Deal. Because petit larceny from the needy is no crime at all in the code of the New Deal.

.   .   .   .

241

The trail of abuse leads through state after state. There was a special set-up in South Dakota, all arranged for election day. Let me read the buying order for nine votes. Listen to these instructions from the Democratic County Chairman to the Director of WPA:

"Please place this man on WPA on the special set-up you have that takes care of rush men as Welfare will not certify. Have looked into affair—has nine votes in family."

Here's a letter from a United States Senator to a humble applicant for a WPA job in his own State of North Carolina. The Senator advises the applicant—and I quote the letter:

"If you will furnish this office with a letter of recommendation from the Democratic chairman of your county, I will be more than glad to take up your case with the WPA. . . . This procedure is followed in all instances."

There it is over the signature of a member of the United States Senate. To get on WPA a man has to get a letter from a New Deal politician. And this procedure, he says, is followed in all instances.

This Administration has boasted of its abuse of powerful men. By its own words it shows that it has no scruples about even greater abuse of friendless and unfortunate men. The shame of the New Deal is spread from coast to coast. The record of WPA shows that we are dealing not merely with the vicious practices of subordinates. We are dealing with official policy of this Administration.

This policy of corruption of the ballot is practically the only policy which the Administration has consistently followed. And it is that policy which an incorruptible American people will this year bring to an end.

Look at the great election of 1936.

During the four months preceding that election, private employment increased by more than a million men. Yet during these same four months of increasing business activity and employment, 300,000 men were added to the WPA payrolls—and the WPA payroll itself increased from 122 million to 137½ million dollars a month. The month after election 300,000 men were dropped from the WPA. Three hundred thousand men and their families moved on and off relief as pawns of New Deal politics.

Let us see what happened in the next year when there was no election. Look at 1937. In the four months preceding November in that year, business was rapidly declining. Nine hundred thousand men lost their jobs. Were they assisted by WPA? There was no election that year. No less than 127,000 men were thrown off the WPA payrolls during those same four months of decreasing employment. Was the New Deal saving money for the next election?

Let's see. In 1938, in the four months preceding the election in November, the number of employees in private industry increased by over a million. Was WPA reduced accordingly? Not during an election year. In the same four months before election 327,000 men were added to WPA payrolls, and the payroll itself was increased from 151 to 172 million dollars a month.

I have been citing facts and figures but they tell a human story. It is a story of men struggling to support themselves and their families on the slender pittance of relief money. It is a story of men and women held up for contributions for political campaigns, thrown on relief and off relief to meet the election needs of a power-hungry administration. Under the threat of loss of desperately needed aid, tribute was exacted. That tribute was paid in food out of the mouths of hungry men, women and children.

What kind of people can these be who do these things for political profit? What do they think of themselves? Listen to a member of the inner circle of the New Deal. He gaily writes in his syndicated column:

"Indeed, much of the political success of the New Deal

is due . . . to a shrewd use of relief funds and Federal projects to keep the faithful in line."

I particularly resent this kind of thing. I know something of the WPA people. For the past five years I have had twenty-five WPA employees doing special accounting investigation in my office. They are earnest and competent men who, through no fault of their own, have been kept out of jobs by the economic failure of this Administration. These and the thousands like them are not statistics to be added and subtracted from the rolls for election purposes.

I have said these abuses are an Administration policy. The final test is what happened when the whole shocking story was laid bare by the Senate Committee. At the conclusion of the investigation what happened to the responsible head of the WPA?

What happened to Harry Hopkins? Did the President dismiss him from office? Did the President so much as rebuke him? The President promoted him. As a reward for the things I have discussed tonight the President elevated Harry Hopkins to the Cabinet of the United States where he sits today.

Is it any wonder that many a political veteran has been heard to say, "You can't beat five billion dollars."

But you can beat five billion dollars. The American electorate is not for sale. Once they know the shameless corruption that is going on behind the smiling visage of the New Deal they can beat fifty billion dollars.

Need we go over any more of the nauseating evidence? It is all on the record. It is a calendar of unpunished crime—broken covenants, disloyalty to the Constitution, abuse of power, intimidation, coercion, extortion and larceny—all committed against the underprivileged and the helpless unemployed.

THE DEFENSE OF AMERICA

An Address at Dallas, Texas, May 27, 1940

In the past fourteen months, nine nations of the world have been subjected to ruthless military conquest. For this there was no provocation—save that they were peace-loving and weak. We have seen brutally trampled under foot everything we in this country hold dear—individual liberty, the right to peace and security, the right of the people to govern themselves. We are sick at heart at the tragedy of millions who are homeless refugees tonight.

We need not deny where our sympathies are, nor need we be ashamed of our emotions. Great Britain, France and their Allies are fighting against a system of despotic government, religious persecution and military aggression which we hate and abhor. Our convictions and our sympathies are wholly and unhesitatingly with the Allied nations.

As news comes to us of reverses to the Allied arms and success to the aggressors, there is an ever-increasing tendency to yield to the feeling that this country should go into the war. There is no fever so contagious as war fever. It might even sweep this country off its feet. As a people, we are already deeply stirred and it is imperative that we should not allow our emotions to overcome our reason.

In the twenty years that followed the last World War, the people of this country reached a solemn determination that they would not become entangled in any future European conflict. We resolved that we would not again send our young men to fight on foreign battle-fields. That decision was made in the calm thoughtfulness of a period of peace and not under the stress of emotion. I, for one, stand by that decision.

This does not mean that we should be or can be indifferent to the frightful tragedy in which the world finds itself. Brute force has been unleashed upon the world. That force respects nothing but force. We must not be blind to the possibility that we might be called upon to defend ourselves. Our first and imperative task is to create a strength of our own which must be respected.

The ugly facts are that the United States is not even prepared to defend itself against attack in its own territory, let alone to wage a war abroad.

Let us consider some of these facts.

We have a good fleet—in the Pacific Ocean. Our Atlantic seaboard is protected by a "shadow" fleet headed by three old battle-ships in need of modernization. The whole Navy is handicapped by aged and slow auxiliary ships.

Our Army has only 75,000 fully equipped troops ready to take the field. We have not a single complete mobile division of infantry and artillery which could be rushed to a point of attack.

The Army has on hand only 38,000 modern infantry rifles. It needs more than 240,000 for its present plans alone. It has only 14 per cent of its anti-tank gun requirements. It has less than 2 per cent of the light tanks and less than 10 per cent of the medium tanks that it needs.

We have only one 37-millimeter anti-aircraft gun for every one hundred that our Army needs under its present plans. We have less than 2 per cent of what the Army requires in anti-aircraft ammunition.

Our whole Army air force includes only 863 combat planes—a week's toll in the battles of Europe. Major General H. H. Arnold, Chief of the Army Air Corps, testified before a Senate Committee this month that the Army has only 52 first-class heavy bombers. He further testified that if our twin-motor bombers were sent against modern equipment, "it would be suicide." And when he was asked how many of the Army's 2,700 planes could be modernized, he said: "Off-hand, I should say half a dozen." None of the Army planes has armor, self-sealing fuel tanks or sufficiently heavy firing equipment.

In the Army we need over three times as many gas masks as we have. In the National Guard there is only one gas mask to every eight men.

We are dependent upon foreign countries for twenty-three materials essential to our national defense.

In citing these facts, I am giving no aid and comfort to potential enemies. All this and much more has been disclosed in official testimony before the Congress. It is all well-known in the War Offices of foreign powers. They know the condition of America. It is high time the American people themselves knew it.

But even our lack of military preparation does not tell the whole story. Behind the military front there is an economic front where decisive battles are won or lost. On that economic front also, this national emergency finds us desperately unprepared.

There has been a seven-year war here in our own country. It has been a war by the Administration against business and against every vital and productive force of the nation. It has been a selfish war for power, waged against the men and the brains and the industrial plants we now need so urgently.

Under the harrying and abuse of recent years our productive industrial plant has slowed down, deteriorated. The national debt has been staggeringly increased. And all of this in a time of world crisis.

In the last seven years the Administration has spent six and one-quarter billion dollars in the name of national defense. This is the largest peace-time expenditure for defense in any seven years of our history. In spite of these unprecedented expenditures our national defenses are wholly inadequate.

Such, in brief, is the solemn situation in which we find ourselves. Hysteria will not help. We have facts to face. We have a duty to act effectively. The paramount question before us is, how can this nation best protect itself?

When the people became aroused to the urgency of this question, the President called for another billion dollars for defense. He called for an air force of 50,000 planes and an annual productive capacity of 50,000 planes.

Now, what about those 50,000 planes?

Last Monday, 100 representatives of airplane manufacturers were called to Washington. For the benefit of newsreels and press, Secretary Morgenthau made a welcoming speech. News pictures all over the country were to show that the Administration was on the job.

But was it? The assembled manufacturers were also addressed by the Secretary and Assistant Secretary of War, the acting Secretary of the Navy and others. These high officials had little more to say than that the airplane makers were welcome to Washington. When the plane-makers asked what they could do to help, they got no information.

Those hundred manufacturers from all over the United States went back to their plants in complete bewilderment.

It was a good publicity stunt. But publicity will not produce planes.

We cannot produce airplanes the way the New Deal produces a billion dollars—by printing government bonds. You can't print airplanes. A blue-print is no protection against a bomb.

This country wants planes—plenty of planes—and it wants them as fast as it can get them without interfering with the delivery of planes to the Allies. In fact, our effort should be to help speed those planes to the Allies.

But what is the good of talking about 50,000 planes unless we know what we are talking about and are prepared to do something about it? What are the facts about airplane production in this country? What does such a program mean?

Our actual production of military planes, without their engines, is now at the rate of 6,000 a year. By the end of this year with present floor space and floor space actually under construction, plane capacity will be at the rate of 10,200 planes a year. This is the estimate of the men responsible for building the planes.

To produce 50,000 planes a year, it will take a plant about four and a half times as large as our present plant, including all plant capacity now under construction. Experts estimate that it would take at least four years to accomplish this. It means recruiting and training a whole army of skilled airplane workers. It means more than 500,000 men to build those planes.

And this does not include guns, ammunition, or bombs.

To use airplanes you have to have an air force. To maintain and fly 50,000 planes, an air force of about 750,000 men is necessary. That is more than three times the size of the Regular Army of the United States. At least 75,000 of these men would have to be pilots, and it takes the most skilled instructors a year and a half to train a military pilot.

The average cost of a military plane is $84,000, including necessary spare parts. Allowing for increased efficiency in mass production, experts estimate the cost of 50,000 planes at 3½ billion dollars. And that is without factories, without guns, without flyers. The cost of training and equipping ground crews runs to another 3½ billion dollars. That means 7 billion dollars as a starter.

These are sobering facts. But they are only a fraction of this enormous and complex problem. It is important that we realize what we are facing. We should move along the road to preparedness in the way of a free people—with our eyes open.

Airplanes are only one part of any plan of national defense. We need tanks, artillery, rifles, ammunition, bombs; we need battle-ships. The national defense must be balanced and complete. France found that a Maginot Line which protected only half of its frontier was no protection at all.

There must be no half-way measures in safeguarding the future of this nation. The revival and mobilization of depressed and disorganized industry is a staggering job. The technical problem requires coordination, construction and planning of a great national effort.

And what is being done?

Every man in America who understands these great industrial problems has been driven out of the councils of our government. So the President takes personal charge of this job in addition to his manifold other duties. He permits the Secretary of the Treasury, who knows nothing whatsoever about the subjects, in addition to his own large duties, to take personal charge of all defense outlays and, incidentally, to coordinate the vital machine-tool industry.

This job cannot be done in this way. This national emergency cries aloud for experts to take complete charge of this program. America has the greatest engineering and mass production administrators in the world. In Heaven's name let us put this program in their hands. Let us do it before it is too late.

The needs of a nation are far greater than the desires of any man or men for political power. This job must be taken out of political control now and it is the patriotic duty of the President to do it at once.

. . . This country is under the leadership of Mr. Roosevelt. He is the President and on him rests the responsibility of obtaining prompt measures of rearmament.

But this does not mean that the country should relax its

efforts to free itself from the destructive policies of the New Deal.

It is very disturbing to find the President so blandly confident in our hopelessly inadequate defenses. It is even more serious to find that he fails to recognize that the job of national defense is one for expert industrial leadership and must be taken out of the hands of his appointed incompetents who have made a mess of national defense. The President has shown no comprehension of the necessity for hard work and sacrifices to meet our urgent needs for preparedness.

France today is paying a frightful penalty for the bungling experimentation of a socialist Popular Front modeled on this New Deal. England is reaping a whirlwind from the failure of government to provide adequate defense. Both countries are now in agony because of the failure of their opposition parties to expose the truth and offer the people constructive leadership. I say to you with all the earnestness and vigor at my command: the Republican Party will not let that happen here.

Soberly and with a full sense of the responsibilities involved, let us consider our problem and agree as a nation upon the essentials of a program for American defense.

1. We must first decide what we are going to defend.

It is imperative that the Army and the Navy know what areas they must protect.

The two basic principles of American foreign policy have been, first, to avoid foreign entanglements, and second, to uphold the Monroe Doctrine. Let us redeclare these policies in ringing words and then prepare our defense program accordingly. Then, in cooperation with the other countries of the Americas we shall secure the peace of this hemisphere.

2. A non-partisan National Defense Board to plan and direct our program of rearmament should be immediately established.

This board should not be mere window-dressing. It should have real power and full authority.

It is not enough to appropriate more billions of dollars. Our problem now, more than ever before, is not to be solved by the mere spending of money. It must be solved by the skilled production of the things we need.

The President should move forthwith to see that the work of the Board is not sabotaged from within the New Deal. I say this, because we had a War Resources Board within the past year. The President himself appointed the Board last August. And what happened? The business-baiters who surrounded the President did not like that idea. It looked too much like a truce in their war on industry. So after three months the War Resources Board faded out. Its members were quietly told to go home—they weren't needed any longer. That was last November, after the war in Europe had been raging for three months.

3. The national Administration must remove from office its Socialists, Communists and fellow-travelers.

It has been shown repeatedly that the government departments are plentifully sprinkled with subversive activities. We can preserve our civil liberties without placing the conduct of our government in the hands of men whose first aim is the overthrow of that government. Whether Nazis or Communists, we want no Fifth Column in our government.

4. The Administration must abandon its war on business.

We need the full cooperation and the full resources of a revitalized and energetic industry. For seven years the New Deal has pursued policies which have restricted production and prevented industrial expansion.

We cannot wait until next January. Enterprise must get going now. The unemployed must be given a chance to go to work. National defense will not support the nation. A working and producing nation must support the national defense.

5. Our national morale must be revitalized.

It is a delusion to believe that effective defense can be secured by arms alone. The effective use of arms requires a people who as individuals are determined and energetic, who are physically and spiritually strong—individuals who are ready to accept hardship and sacrifice to preserve liberty and freedom. We cannot rely alone upon our love of peace to keep America secure. The time has come for every American to realize that the safety of this nation and of its institutions may depend upon him. We must recapture the self-reliance which made our country great.

Let us not minimize the gravity of the situation that confronts us. But let us not exaggerate our difficulties. Let us understand them and proceed with intelligence, vigor and unity. To take any other course is to trifle with the whole future of human freedom. And there is a future for human freedom. There is a place for decent and honorable human beings to live in peace with each other. There is a place for the worship of God on this earth. And there is a future for your children and mine.

Despite the ravages of the last seven years, the Republic still stands. Despite the attacks on it, our Constitution remains unimpaired. We have freedom of the press, freedom of speech and freedom of worship. These things we can preserve for ourselves and for the world. Let us pledge ourselves, our every waking hour and our sacred honor to that end. United and at work we are a powerful nation and can face the world with fearless confidence.

A STATEMENT OF PRINCIPLES

Excerpt from a Radio Address, June 21, 1940

UNDER our republican form of government, the responsibility of the party in opposition is hardly less than that of the party in power. In a time of national stress, the responsibilities of the opposition party are multiplied. The nation's very life may be at stake. Then is no time for unsound policies and slipshod administration. The need for honest and effective government is paramount. At such a time the relentless vigilance and unhesitating frankness of the opposition party are the chief safeguards of the national welfare.

In this hour of danger, the Republican Party has a solemn duty. It must make clear to the people the things for which it stands and the things to which it is opposed.

For my part, I believe that the national welfare demands the reaffirmation of certain basic principles. I have discussed them in various parts of the country during the past seven months. These principles are:

1. The United States must be strong enough to control its own destiny. We must have

A navy capable of repelling simultaneous attack in both oceans.

An army and air force able to crush every attempt at invasion of this hemisphere.

An industrial system capable of producing all modern military equipment in any needed volume.

2. The United States must pursue a strong and consistent foreign policy designed to protect our national interests. To this end, we must

Continue to work for peace.

Avoid foreign entanglements.

254

A STATEMENT OF PRINCIPLES

Defend the Monroe Doctrine.

Work for closer relations between the nations of the Americas.

Resist every effort at military, economic or ideological penetration of this hemisphere.

Extend to the victims of aggression all proper aid.

But steadfastly refuse to send American forces to Europe.

3. Society has a permanent, deep-rooted obligation to its aged, its blind, its sick, its unemployed. This obligation must be met for the benefit of the people and not for the profit of a political party.

4. As the first requisite of a strong nation, we must provide for everyone an opportunity to work. Meanwhile we must

Continue government aid for the unemployed.

Eliminate corruption from the administration of relief.

5. Agriculture must be restored to a position of parity with the rest of the national economy. Essential parts of this program are

Cash payments for soil conservation.

Conversion of sub-marginal land to more economic uses.

Crop loans to provide for orderly marketing, and

Effective action to increase the use of farm products in industry.

6. Labor must be assured of its fundamental right to the protection of constructive labor legislation.

Such legislation defeats its own purposes unless it is provided with fair and competent administration.

The American worker is also entitled to protection against racketeer and Communist control.

7. We must encourage the expansion of private enterprise.

The restoration of freedom of enterprise is essential to national recovery.

A STATEMENT OF PRINCIPLES

We must reverse the seven-year trend toward government competition with business.

Regulations affecting the conduct of business must be made and administered in the public interest and not for punitive purposes.

Violations of the laws against trusts and monopoly should be energetically prosecuted, but these laws should not be misused for the purpose of harassing business generally.

8. The seven-year trend toward national insolvency must be reversed.

We must eliminate waste and extravagance.

Taxes should be levied to bring in a maximum of revenue without needlessly hampering business enterprise.

The power to tax should not be used for punishment or vengeance.

9. A stable currency and a strong, independent banking system constitute the safeguards of the people's savings.

The Federal Deposit Insurance System should be maintained and strengthened.

The laws giving the President discretionary power to change the gold content of the dollar and issue paper money should be repealed.

10. American agriculture, American labor, and American industry must be protected against foreign economic aggression.

We should cooperate with friendly nations to restore world trade to a prosperous level.

Finally, we must reaffirm our unshakeable belief in the integrity of the individual and in the American tradition of liberty and justice for all.

An administration guided by such principles would restore health and strength to the nation and its economy. But we cannot have that kind of an administration unless we recognize and remove the barriers in the way. To remove those barriers, therefore, becomes the great task of the Republican Party. Every ounce of its energy must be devoted to telling the people of this country the truth, the whole truth, and nothing but the truth.

The task will not be an easy one. For seven years the country has been drenched with misleading propaganda, charming super-salesmanship and political hypnotism. Many are still under the spell. But every man and woman in this country must have an opportunity to see the truth. For when the truth is made available to the American people, their judgment will not fail. And the truth shall keep us free.

THE WORLD WE WANT TO LIVE IN *

WE are passing through a crisis, the outcome of which will determine whether this is to be a free world or a slave world. It is the largest issue our nation has ever faced. In our will to victòry we are united to the greatest degree in our history. And this time we are united to a larger purpose. We shall not only win the war but we shall also win the peace.

America is young and does not know defeat. Somehow, with the tragedy of war, there are many compensations to sustain us. The most important of these is this greater unity among us all—a unity fused by the white heat of patriotism. Only a complete singleness of purpose will sustain us. Past differences must be forgotten. Political passions must be rationed. Personal interest must be subordinated to the common welfare. The American people will not stand for the feuds and bickering that attended the downfall of France.

The President of the United States is our elected leader in this fateful war. We shall all support his every effort to win the war. We shall even support him in spite of mistakes provided they are solely the result of zeal to win the war.

Many of us have criticized the administration severely. We shall continue to criticize the acts of the administration when we believe that criticism is helpful to our common effort. That is one of the very sources of the strength of a free republic. We should betray our country if we failed to make useful criticism. We shall do our duty in support and in criticism. The one acid test in each instance shall be: Will it help win the war?

All of us had hoped against hope that we could be spared participation in another great war. Even after the first year

* A résumé of three speeches made in May, 1942, by Thomas E. Dewey.

of the war our leaders, from the President down, had voiced that hope and expectation. In the election of 1940 the platforms of both parties and both Presidential candidates gave repeated and firm pledges to avoid direct involvement in the war. We were all eager to lend full aid to all who resisted aggression. But it seemed incredible that American lives would again have to be sacrificed to stop a few madmen who had temporarily acquired superiority in modern instruments of destruction.

Our hopes were not to be fulfilled. The waves of war broke over our own shores. Now we are in this war until we win total and crushing victory. To the service of our nation we have dedicated ourselves and every resource at our command.

To this end we are united. There are, of course, those who would divide us here at home. There are the apostles of appeasement—those sympathizers with alien ideologies who seek to impede American action. And there are those who can see only defeat in war and who despair of our future afterward. We shall give no heed to those apostles of despair whether alien or home-grown.

We shall win the war and then we must win the peace. For as the most powerful of nations, we have learned that power begets responsibility. Never again shall we forswear hard-won victory.

We have the will and the tools to win. I believe it is time we began to acquire the intellectual capacity to win. We no longer have to deal with generalities or emotionalism. Our people are educated and intelligent. They deserve to be treated as adults by their leaders.

MISTAKES BEHIND US

The attempt is sometimes made to lay the blame for the whole disastrous course of world events since the last war to America's refusal to join the League of Nations. That is an absurd over-simplification. The whole truth lies in many factors.

In retrospect we can see now that the period between the two wars was an unreal truce. The world tried to live on borrowed time and borrowed money without facing its problems. The United States played a decisive role in the war, then withdrew from an equally decisive role in the peace. We were half in and half out of the affairs of the rest of the world.

Our failure to take a realistic attitude toward the war debts made difficult the solution of reparations. Our generous lending to Central Europe and subsequent sudden withdrawal of short-term credits put an intolerable strain upon the finances of that area. This ultimately spread to Britain and precipitated the universal breakdown of currencies. Our stock market speculation of the twenties put London under constant pressure and contributed to the world-wide scramble for gold. We were much concerned about the post-war stabilization of currencies, yet we did not recognize that central bank credits alone would not do the job. More complex matters of price levels, trade balances, interest rates and debts were involved.

There was the refusal by our government, even after Hitler came to power, to cooperate in joint plans for economic stabilization at the London Economic Conference with the nations of Europe—Britain, the Netherlands, Belgium, France and the Scandinavian nations. There was our total failure in the 1930's to recover from the most profound of all depressions and the resulting distress throughout the world. Those are some of the many mistakes which contributed to the breakdown of world security. For those failures neither party is without blame.

It will not do now merely to voice again the aspirations that were shattered twenty years ago. The world has greatly changed since then. Even after the total victory upon which we shall insist, it will be impossible to put back into their bottles the genii which have been released. National and racial aspirations, long subdued, have been awakened. The hopes of hundreds of millions of people all over the world are on the march. The victory at arms will not be the end but only the beginning.

WORKERS AT WAR

It is essential that we remember always that our power in this war and our influence in the peace must rest upon our own integrity and strength as a nation. Out of the war we are going to learn something about the real nature of the American productive plant. We will learn, I hope, more of the relationship between our economic system and our free way of life.

The people of this country are achieving an industrial miracle. The real story has not come through the veil of censorship. But it is coming. The evidence is so all-prevasive that it cannot escape us. It is important to have a censorship which withholds confidential information from the enemy. Fifth columnists and saboteurs must not be aided by details about the places and size of our productive plants. But there are facts not known to the public that should be known—facts that would put courage and buoyant faith into the American people—facts which would strike fear and defeatism in the hearts of our enemies.

The truth is that miracles of energy and ingenuity are being performed by our productive forces. I wish it were possible for all to see the great aircraft plants scattered over the country. They are turning out planes of a variety, a quality and a quantity that exceeds the wildest dreams of two short years ago. As the fragmentary news of the achievements of our planes drifts back, and we turn from it to the actual production in our factories, our wonder grows. For many of the very planes that are scoring triumphs abroad are considered already obsolete in our American factories. New models, enormously improved, are rolling off our production lines. There are fighters with speed and fire-power that will write the name of America in every sky over Germany and Italy and Japan. There are bombers to avenge London and Crete, Rotterdam and Dunkirk, Pearl Harbor and Corregidor. There are transport planes that will revolutionize all methods of hurling force where force is needed. The genius of America is at last released.

I cannot be discouraged when I see the great army of men and women in these plants inspired by the same indomitable will and patriotism that carry our men-in-arms to the far corners of the world. I cannot be discouraged when I see the leaders there—the managers of American industry—men of brains and integrity. Speed of production has been not only increased. It has been multiplied. Managerial skill has, in one type of tank alone, reduced the man hours by 50 per cent. There are MacArthurs in American industry. There are fighting men in overalls.

Take another example—shipbuilding. For ten years our national policy has starved the American merchant marine. It has been reduced to a pitiful shadow of our once-proud preeminence on the seas. But there, too, miracles are under way.

The same drive and ingenuity have made our automobile and other industries a veritable Vulcan's forge. Everywhere the men who made American industry the envy of the world are now making it the greatest power in the world. They are turning out planes and motors, ships, guns and tanks at a speed which makes new records of production every day. Wherever you go, this fact is coming home: American business enterprise is showing in this war the same daring, the same skill and ingenuity, the same incredible ability to get things done that built this country. The brains, the muscle and the spirit that gave our country the highest standard of living in the world are in this war to win.

What did this madman Hitler think America was made of? What could have been his thought when he drove us to rise, an avenging nation in arms? Did he think we would do less than this? Hitler has been building for nine years. We have been building for less than two years. Hitler hasn't seen anything yet.

The result is clear. This man Hitler will not have to live much longer to say what Hindenburg said about the United States in 1918: "Her brilliant, if pitiless, war industry had entered the service of patriotism and had not failed it."

Hitler will then have learned the lesson—but he will have learned it—too little and too late.

A FUTURE FOR AMERICA

Our experiences today will stand us in good stead when the time comes to meet the problems of post-war reconstruction. In that period, I see an America, with proved capacity to produce the greatest quantity of implements of war, just as capable of producing the greatest quantity of peace-time goods for human consumption. I see an America whose frontiers have not only not been reached, but whose frontiers have not even been discovered. I see an America with an absolutely limitless future.

During the depression years before this war began our industries had found 10,000 new metal alloys alone. There were discovered 250,000 chemical compounds. It is impossible to imagine how greatly the list is being expanded by our war production drive. Most of these discoveries await new peace-time uses. The pent-up demands for durable and consumer goods which we cannot now meet will open a new era in production. That will only be a starting point for a new high standard of living.

Let us review a few of the possibilities that a free system

can realize. In 1937, two of our leading housing experts estimated that 16,300,000 homes had to be built by 1950 simply to maintain the standard of 1930. Nearly 1,200,000 homes should be built each year to keep pace with that standard. In 1937, 1938 and 1939 combined, we built less than enough to meet one year's schedule. Again in 1940 and 1941 together, we built less than enough to meet one year's schedule. As of this year we still have 14,000,000 homes to be built by 1950. That would mean over one and one half million homes a year. After the war we must build as we have never built before. We must overcome the building deficit of the 1930's and the current war.

Economic wants are insatiable. New ideas crying for practical expression are being turned out year after year by the thousands.

The future of air transportation is limitless. There will be stream-lined diesel-engined passenger trains made of new metal alloys. They will transform the railroads of tomorrow. We have new textile fibres, in many ways better than the fibres of nature itself. There is the whole field of plastics, which in its infancy before the war created a $200,000,000 industry. The field of chemistry is just on the threshold of its industrial future. From the laboratory comes synthetic rubber. It is better than natural rubber for many uses and it will have to take the place of natural rubber for some time to come. When the war is over it will be there for new and ever-expanding peace-time uses.

Refrigerators have been designed that are better than any we have seen. New materials and new methods of production will make them available to every American home. Air-conditioning, technicolor movies and television are today where the automobile was in 1920.

Does all this sound as if we have to plan for a post-war collapse? The answer is clear. This nation's future is a growing thing. We face the opportunity in these United States to write for posterity a record that will outshine the best that has been written in the past. Today we are the most productive, the most potentially powerful of the world's peoples. With this heritage, we must go forward. If we do not, we will have broken faith with those who are fighting now.

There are more than 100 government and private agencies of one sort or another engaged in post-war planning studies. Some of these are staffed by men who see in the post-war era an opportunity to fasten upon America their revolutionary schemes. They are the men who have the know-it-all, but do not have the know-how. For the time being they have taken a back seat. For they cannot help win the war. But when the time comes, they will be ready with their plans. Their propaganda already crowds the air waves. If the business community has nothing constructive to offer, these busy schemers may win out by default. Even in the midst of their extraordinary war effort, the business men of America should be planning for the future. With its record of achievement in this war, American enterprise can be sure of public support if it is ready with sound, workable proposals for meeting the post-war problems.

THE DANGER OF INFLATION

Adequate safeguards can tide us over the transition from war production to peace production and from military life to civilian life. Our great danger may very well be that, having succeeded in suppressing, in part at least, a price inflation during the war, we may give way to a post-war inflation. If the history of the last war is any guide, we may have strong popular insistence for throwing off all such controls and for getting "back to normalcy." That, rather than any business collapse, may be our test. For at that point we shall have to make decisions which will be vital to our future.

If we suddenly discard all controls and give way to a post-war inflation, we will have still another reaction. That revulsion may carry us, by another swing of the pendulum, far into a peace-time system of regulated economy. Our people will not want that, but there will be those who will point to the episode as conclusive proof that private, unplanned enterprise is incapable of giving us sustained employment except under the stimulus of war and the restraints of full government control.

I do not believe either extreme swing is necessary. Neither is necessary if the genius of American business which is producing to win the war starts now—today—to win the peace. Some work is being done. But it is not enough.

It will not be sufficient for private companies, working individually, to devise schemes for making work and for pioneering with new inventions. One or two enterprising companies cannot sustain even their own businesses if other enterprises are not advancing with theirs. Rather, all industry should be seeking ways and means to keep production rolling. We ought to have learned by now that in the post-war world we shall need to have firmly established as our national policy the goal of full employment and full production.

If anyone asks: "Can we afford it?" the answer is: "How can we afford anything else?" We shall have a national debt of possibly $150,000,000,000 to $200,000,000,000 with minimum annual interest costs of $3,000,000,000 to $4,000,000,-000. We shall have, even after the war, a very large military budget and a normal budget which, judged by pre-1933 standards, will be fabulous. To sustain such a budget we shall clearly have to be a nation fully producing and fully employed.

It is my firm conviction that we can meet these burdens and fulfill our future responsibilities as a free people and only under a system of free enterprise. But if we do not meet them well and fully under free enterprise, the school of collectivist planners will surely be here to take over the job. And that will be the last chance of free men to solve their own problems.

AMERICA NEVER GOES BACKWARD

I feel confident that America can achieve stability and lasting prosperity without the loss of any essential part of its political or economic freedom. To do this it is not necessary to talk about going back to any specific type of economic theory. That would be reaction. The American people never go backward. I do not believe in reverting to the theory of laissez faire, nor am I willing to go back to the nearer past and accept the creeping collectivism of the past few years.

Facing the world ahead and recognizing the necessity of a government active in promoting the best interests of individuals and of individual enterprise, we should establish two principles at the base of such regulation.

The first is that government intervention must be of a character consistent with the American free enterprise system. Its objective must be to widen—not restrict—individual economic opportunity. It must do this without any reservations as to its faith in private enterprise. In short, it must promote fair trade and not treat trade as a thing to be tolerated.

Second, in the administration of government intervention in private business, the personnel must be composed of people who believe in and understand both American workers and business men. This is impossible where a supreme qualification for holding public office seems to be complete innocence of any experience in the matter which is to be the subject of regulation.

But in meeting the problems ahead, do not think that all the faults which must be cured are on the side of the government. Business men must learn to work with government. They must learn to think in terms of national well-being as well as in terms of their duty to their stockholders and their partners.

We must greet the future, soberly aware of its dangers but clear in our appraisal of our capacity to meet them. We cannot fail. Defeat is not in our tradition. Poverty is not our birthright. Scarcity is not our watchword.

When this war passes we shall never again tolerate a pinched standard of living or a lowered horizon of production. We shall never again tolerate scarcity or the politics and economics of scarcity. Our burdens of debt and taxation must be lightened by pushing ever upward the levels of national production. The national income must be more equitably divided. Business will have no monopoly of power, but it will have the assurance of stable policies in law and government. Agriculture, vitally necessary to an impoverished world and new industrial outlets, must not subsist upon reduced production, but thrive upon increased consumption. The hard-won rights of labor will be taken for granted and fortified in a growing, free economy.

The America of the future will have within it not merely material success—but a stability and sanity and devotion to principle that will serve as an instrument by which all men can remain free. It will serve as a symbol of the dignity of the individual and his rightful place as master of his free system of government as against the regimented totalitarian system.

A FUTURE FOR THE WORLD

We cannot think about the future of America without considering the future of the world. On this subject there is need for hard-headed thinking. Every time we get into a war we tend to think only in terms of idealism. After the war we tend to think only in terms of domestic materialism. In each phase the thinking of the other phase is denounced by extravagant orators.

We cannot build the next peace on sentimentalism alone. We of America are tough-minded realists. We strive for a world where peace will endure not only for the welfare of the world, but for the elementary self-interest of every American. Unless our thinking includes that premise, the American people will reject it. And that must not again occur. We must use our industrial might with a full sense of responsibility. The young and vigorous America that will be reborn out of victory must play its part in building a peaceful world to come.

No man can chart a blueprint of the future of the world. But any man who thinks of the suffering and horror of war must think with a clear mind and a resolute spirit about the future. Twice now the people of the United States have entered a major world war which they hoped to avoid. But it was not to be. As a result our people should be determined that we must not continue this process of periodic sacrifice of the flower of youth. We must know while we are fighting the war that it is for great purpose and great achievement. We must have in our hearts serene confidence that our sacrifices will be made worthwhile by a lasting peace after the war.

Clearly the well-being of every American will be affected by the future of all men and women. This is now a world that is spanned in the space of hours by bombing planes. The economic mechanism is so balanced that events in one part of the world necessarily have their repercussions in other parts. In such a world we cannot hide behind the boundaries of geography.

I do not for one moment subscribe to the notion that the United States was wholly or even primarily to blame for the economic dislocations of the period between the wars. But I do think that it is well for us now to recognize that, in our own interest, we must assume greater responsibilities in the future for political and economic security among nations.

PLANNING FOR INTERNATIONAL TRADE

In our own economy we will have to deal with a brand new set of obstacles to the exchange of goods between nations. We must learn what they are so we will be prepared to meet them. One outstanding aftermath of the last war was the rise of economic nationalism. This was particularly true of the Central Powers which had felt the pinch of blockade and which strove for self-sufficiency through the development of synthetics. Now in this war we ourselves are blockaded. We are completely shut off from rubber and partly shut off from sugar, to name only two important commodities. This condition will have important repercussions.

To some thinkers, beet sugar has for years been as a red flag to a bull. It has been argued that it was unsound and uneconomic to encourage our Western farmers to grow sugar beets at the expense of cutting down sugar imports from foreign countries. But what is the situation going to be after this war? Are the sugar beet growers who are now helping to meet our sugar shortage going to be content to plough under their acreage and give up their increased share of the domestic market for the purpose of furthering foreign trade? Or can they develop substitute crops and the sugar factories be converted for other uses?

Take another significant case—that of synthetic rubber. It has been said that before Pearl Harbor our government was reluctant to push ahead with plans for the development of synthetic rubber because we should continue to provide a market for the natural rubber produced by friendly nations. It is difficult to appraise our rubber situation accurately because of the conflicting reports from government sources. But we can be sure of one thing: the natural rubber is in enemy hands and we are struggling to create a synthetic rubber industry. Once that industry attains size and experience, it may be able to produce rubber as good and as cheap

270

as natural rubber. Moreover, under the stimulus of war we have undertaken to experiment with the production of synthetic rubber from corn, wheat and other crops. The possibilities of such a development are enormous.

Consider the situation we may have if, instead of being burdened with surplus crops which we have paid the farmers not to grow, the farmers are told: "Produce all you can— industry will make it into rubber for your automobiles, tractors and trucks." That is a revolution in the way the American people have been expected to think these last ten years. The limitless productivity of the soil has been regarded as a curse rather than a blessing in recent years. Now we would be urged to use it as the source of vital industrial raw materials.

Here again there are involved great complications for international trade in the post-war world. If we emerge from the war with a great synthetic rubber industry, especially an industry which helps us to solve our farm problems, will we turn all that back into the ground in order to be able to trade with our Netherlands and British allies?

I raise these questions only to illustrate the point that those who are today talking of post-war conditions in terms of the lost opportunities of twenty years ago are greatly oversimplifying the problem. We shall have to contend in the post-war world with new problems fully as difficult as those which we failed to solve between the wars and we shall have to find new solutions. The answers to these questions are not to be found in slogans, epithets and catchwords. They will only be found in thoughtful study of the facts. The answers will in part be flatly controlled by economics. We should, at least, know the facts. Let us not be defeatist about finding the answers, but likewise we must not be dreamers, blind to realities.

Assuming that the lease-lend debts will be cancelled and that there is to be no repetition of the futile attempt to collect reparations in the form of money, there will still be difficult transfer problems. After the war we shall have to lease, lend and give both to our allies and to our defeated enemies, food, medical aid, machinery and equipment to rehabilitate their destitute peoples and rebuild their bomb-torn lands. We must build the peace so a free world can be reborn. But we cannot establish a sound post-war economy, beyond the first period of emergency reconstruction, on a basis of international charity. We must find means of exchanging with other nations the things they can use and the things we can use.

In this aspect, it is clear we will need planning. In the field of foreign economic relations we must expect a large and continuing measure of government guidance.

INTERNATIONAL JUSTICE

As the shape of the world to come emerges we must and shall meet it with understanding. We must be prepared to formulate and participate in sound solutions for the future. There are some things about our place that we can already foresee.

That place must be neither narrow nor imperialistic. Dollar-diplomacy must never again be written on the pages of history. It is the well-being of 130,000,000 Americans that must be our primary concern in assuming our position as a great nation. That means the well-being of every farmer, every man who works with his hands, every housewife, every section of our business life. With this objective before us, our foreign policy will never become the tail to any other nation or aggregation of world powers.

We are carrying our arms to the continents of the world not only to resist aggression—not only to destroy the threat to our free way of life. We have sprung to arms to make certain that, in the end, we shall attain a completely victorious peace. That peace through victory will enable us to do our full share in the plans for a freer and better world. It will be a world in which sacrifices will be well worth the cost if we can by a long view of the future prevent the rise of new Hitlers and assure the essentials of justice.

In the interest of our own sons it must be our purpose to participate in making effective a new and permanent justice among nations. There is no reason to be defeatist about the possibilities of an orderly future under law—no more than there is to be defeatist about the future of America itself.

Among other things, we have learned that a peaceful world requires a more even distribution of the world's goods. The privilege of acquiring raw materials should, in the peace, be denied to no nation which accepts its responsibility for peace. Equal opportunity for self-development is a fundamental American doctrine. It can and should be a part of our foreign as well as our domestic policy. In assuming such a role, we shall play neither the knave nor the fool. The hard-headed common sense of the American people will not be sold down the river. But we must be prepared to give and take. In so doing, we must also recognize the place of small nations in the problems of the future. We will learn to think of them not so much as states as of groups of people with the same aspirations as our own for a better life. It will be necessary to get them back on their feet by joint and comprehensive programs of stabilization. Such action will prevent the existence of economic vacuums in the world where other systems can move in to destroy the freedom so hard won.

There will be other and more immediate questions that will arise soon after victory. We should be prepared to meet them. They will involve geographical problems. They will involve the possible voluntary movements of certain populations. They will involve the needs of minorities. We must meet from a humane and understanding point of view the

273

problem of the homeless Jews and other dispossessed peoples. We must meet constructively the legitimate desires of a free Polish people, a free Czechoslovakian people, a free Dutch and a free Belgian people, among others. We will deal, when the time comes, with a free France and we will recognize the aspirations of those great peoples of the human family—China and India.

To chart the solution of these problems in detail at this time is, of course, impossible for any human mind. But we can dedicate ourselves to the proposition that the United Nations, having come into being for the prosecution of the war, shall become a symbol of justice to legitimate aspirations of all peoples in which men of good will everywhere will join.

It is too early now to speak of the German people, the Italian people and the Japanese people. Anything that might be said as to their political and economic future trenches upon the conduct of the war and, as to these matters, our government must determine its policy as events shape their destiny. One thing we do know. We shall never deal with Nazis, Fascists, or the Japanese military dictatorship.

In looking at the future, let us refuse to be taken in by slogans of the past. Let us not repeat the mistakes of the past generation. Let us not approach the problem with the belief that any of us knows all. We can not correct the mistakes of history by a stroke of the pen. The words that will be written in documents will survive the ravages of time only if our conduct after they are written allows them to survive.

There is no going backward. We refuse to believe, despite the scourge of Hitler, that civilization is dying. We refuse to believe that the economic possibilities of this land and of other lands are exhausted. We refuse to believe that the future is inevitably laden with the burden of past error. It is my hope that after complete victory, none of us will ap-

274

proach these problems with partisanship based on a desire for party or sectional advantage.

If we are firm in our purpose, we shall yet emerge to a new freedom and a new and expanding future. We will discover even greater economic frontiers. We will harness machinery and invention for the social betterment of a happier and a peaceful mankind.

Providence has decreed that in a great moment in the world's troubled life America should hold the sword of destiny over many seas and continents. She also holds the scales of justice. Her duty in war will become a duty in peace. Her great influence must be justly used to the proper ends of world stability and order. At home she can, if she will, ward off the dangers of the aftermath. We must not fail to meet that challenge. Our record now will lie open before the high court of the future. Let us build that record well.

THE FAITH OF MILLIONS

A Radio Address, November 2, 1942

TONIGHT we have come to the end of a political campaign, conducted in a period of grave national anxiety. Tomorrow the people will go to the polls as free men and women and render their decision. The next day, all rivalry forgotten and bitterness forgiven, we shall press forward with increased faith, a united nation with but one objective—total victory. That is the miracle of democracy. That is what Hitler can never understand.

We are fighting this war for the right of men and women everywhere to lead free lives. We are fighting to defend the principles by which men and women remain free—freedom of speech, freedom of religion, freedom of opportunity, freedom of election. In time of war these ideals take on deeper significance.

The eyes of all the world have been upon us here and will be upon us tomorrow. We have been engaged not merely in a political campaign. We have been vindicating the faith of millions. We have been proving that with us democracy is alive and vigorous. We have dared to keep it vital even in the midst of total war. We have shown that even in the midst of such a struggle we still cherish and can make stronger our heritage of freedom.

Tonight, on the eve of election, I want to summarize briefly the principles which have governed the members of my party in this campaign and to look ahead to the principles which will guide us in the future.

First. It was clear at the outset that the war itself was not and could not be a political issue. An issue is something upon which people disagree. But we are all united in this war, Republicans, Democrats, Independents—men and women of all parties, all opinions—we are as one in our devotion to the war effort. We are as one in supporting our Commander-in-Chief in every measure necessary to the winning of the war. Let Hitler, Goebbels and their creatures choke on that.

Second. Because the war was first in all our thoughts, it was imperative to make our campaign brief and to the point. To that end we of the Republican Party were determined from the outset to confine the period of the active debate to the minimum necessary for a simple, straightforward statement of the real issues. From that resolve we have refused to be diverted.

Third. Because the war was first in all our thoughts, the single, fundamental issue that had to be discussed was this: How could we in New York best organize our energies and our resources to play a strong and vital part in the winning of the war. For my own part, I have tried to be direct and specific. I have given a program to meet the problems of our threatened food shortage, the problems of our wartime tax-payers, the problem of maintaining the security of labor, of strengthening our social advances, and of improving the relations between labor and industry; the problem of giving New York's unemployed and New York's small business enterprises an opportunity to do what they most desire—to get into the war effort. My associates and I have pledged our whole energies to specific plans for throwing the full force of this great State—one tenth of the nation—into the all-important task of winning the war. We stand pledged to fight with every force at our command the corrosion of our democracy by corrupt political machines.

Today's problems cannot be met by minds long trained to comfortable routine. They cannot be overcome by men who defend their lack of enterprise by claiming to have inherited other men's experience. The great problems of today cannot even be honestly faced by men who court the support of corrupt enemies of the people.

I wonder if we all realize how great a privilege it is to be able to vote as we will do tomorrow in a free election. I wonder if any of us in this country can wholly understand the full significance of the right to enter into that little booth, to draw the curtain, and to vote, alone, in secret. It is said that only those who have been utterly alone can understand the deep meaning of friendship. Only those who have been very sick can know the real exhilaration of health. The men and women who have seen all their freedoms lost when they lost the freedom of election could best tell us what it means to be able to vote as free men and women in a free election in a free country. From behind the barbed wire of Nazi oppression they look with hope and longing to America. If they could vote, what a mighty plebiscite for freedom they would cast!

Let every man and woman remember tomorrow that freedom can never be kept by default. Some one always exercises the power to govern. Never forget that when you fail to vote, others who do vote are exercising your right for you. Many an election has been lost by over-confidence, just as many an election has been won by the unrelaxing vigilance of a corrupt political machine.

It is my earnest hope and firm conviction that tomorrow every man and woman eligible to vote will do so. By a mighty concourse of our citizens to the polling place we can strike terror to the hearts of our enemies.

In this great affirmation of our faith women will play a more vital part than ever before. When they go to the polls tomorrow thousands of them will be voting not merely for themselves. They will be voting to keep alive the system of free government for men who will one day return to ask how well we have kept the faith.

In this election we seek to strengthen government so that

our State can make its rightful contribution to the war. This State must and shall throw every ounce of all the energy of its people into the winning of complete and crushing victory.

These are dark and troubled days but America never has retreated in the face of adversity. America will drive on without compromise to a victorious peace.

When peace is won we shall face massive problems. That is clear. But we must not face them in any spirit of dejection or discouragement. If the problems are great the opportunities are even greater.

We have among us prophets of despair who tell us we can look forward only to a new depression and new agonies of unemployment. That point of view I totally reject. Our men are not fighting for that kind of future. When they come home we must be prepared to welcome them not merely with guarantees of security from economic want. There can be no question of that. We must see to it that the country they have fought to defend is a land of broad economic opportunity—a land where every man and woman has the right to work and get ahead.

We are conquering the problems of production for war. Certainly we can conquer the problems of full production and full employment for peace. We shall not forget the lessons we have learned. America never goes backward. America goes forward. I have been saying for years, and I will say it with my dying breath, there is no limit to our country. There is no limit to America.

We need not fear to face our destiny. We can go forward boldly and in confidence to meet it.

I see emerging from our victory a new America. And yet, not altogether new, it is the America for which our fathers, from whatever lands they came, fought, worked and prayed. It is the land in which our people never lost their faith, even in the dark days of our generation.

It will be an America that has put behind it the selfish

struggle of the twenties, the dismal bickering of the thirties and the desperate struggle of these war years.

Look what it holds. The richest, fairest land in all the earth—a people strong, courageous, enterprising.

We have the men, the tools, and the resources—the skill and the will—to lift our people to new heights.

Today we are the most productive, most potentially powerful of the world's peoples. When this war passes we shall not be content to fold our hands.

If there is one clear thing that has emerged from all the troubled thinking and confusion of the past decade it is this: The American people believe in full production and full employment. These we can have in time of peace as well as in time of war. These we must have if America is to take its proper place and carry its responsibilities in the community of nations.

This nation's future is a growing thing. This State's future is a growing thing. New York has always been a leader in the nation. It must always be the Empire State. It is to that purpose that we dedicate ourselves.

INAUGURAL ADDRESS OF
GOVERNOR THOMAS E. DEWEY

The Capitol, Albany, N. Y., January 1, 1943

THE new Administration of your State is committed to the proposition that our society must provide full employment through full production. We know that these objectives are attainable at a price, for twice within our generation they have been attained at the price of war. They must also be achieved in peace. We must achieve them by methods which do not destroy but rather strengthen the ideals of political, religious, civil and economic freedom. For material things are not in themselves the all-sufficient end. They are rather the means which assure men the opportunity to possess spiritual and intellectual values which are essential to a rich and happy life.

These are not partisan objectives. Nor will they be achieved by partisan action. It is a part of the genius of the American people that they can contest political elections with vigor and intensity. But once the decision has been fairly made, they can unite wisely and generously behind the parties and individuals who have been given the responsibility of government.

Your State Administration which takes office today will be, God willing, not only a wartime but also a peacetime administration. Its responsibilities in the period of readjustment after the war will be no less than its responsibilities in war.

To meet these obligations our State Government must emerge from the war with unimpaired strength. But it can do this only as the strength of its citizens and its institutions is maintained against the ravages of war. We shall find a

State geared to great war production; and much of industry, commerce and small business will face grave problems of conversion to peace. At the same time the members of the armed forces will be triumphantly returning home expecting to enjoy the benefits of the free system they have successfully defended.

I state it as a cardinal objective of your new State Administration that these young men and women are entitled to expect something better than the hopeless period of government-made work and relief, of which they have seen so much in the past decade. They are entitled to a fruitful, productive place in a free economic society, dependent on the favor of no man or political party for their livelihood or for their security. They are entitled to come home to a State in which employment can freely be found and in which a man can work and look forward to a future limited only by his own skill and ability.

To achieve these ends there must be a sound economic structure in this State. We must prepare for the prompt and full utilization of technological advances in commerce, agriculture and industry so as to carry the staggering peacetime burdens we will be assuming.

Beyond this, the State will have a duty constantly to adjust its social welfare agencies and educational facilities to meet the special needs of a post-war community.

The readjustment of family and social relationships torn apart by war is a problem that will call for wise and sympathetic handling.

Just as we achieve unity in war, we must sustain unity in peace. In that unity there shall and must be no place for distinctions among us by reason of race, creed or color.

STOP HITLER NOW

For the "Stop Hitler Now Demonstration" Held at Madison Square Garden, New York City, March 1, 1943

THE purpose of this meeting goes to the hearts of everyone in the United States, in the United Nations. The problem at issue is without precedent, without even a parallel since time began. Not in the Dark Ages, not even in the history of barbaric peoples was there such selective savagery as the Nazis are even now perpetrating in Eastern Europe. Neither Huns nor Tartars nor Mongols of old were as methodically unspeakable as the minions of Adolf Hitler.

Never before has the complete extermination of an entire people been compassed deliberately, officially, systematically, wantonly. The Nazi Fuehrer not only admits what he is doing but now he boasts of it. His leaders have put it on paper in pseudo-scientific jargon as an explicit policy of State.

One such is Werner Best, a mouthpiece for the Nazis. Speaking officially for Heinrich Himmler's Gestapo he wrote a recent article in which he used these words: "Historical experience has shown that the destruction and elimination of a foreign nationality are not in the least contrary to the laws of life, provided that such destruction and elimination are complete."

This is not the sadism of an isolated individual. There is no such thing as isolated opinion in Germany today.

It is the official dogma of the Nazi that murder of a people is the law of life provided the whole of such a people be murdered. Such a blasphemous concept can only serve to speed the day when the wrath of the Lord God of Hosts will destroy its exponents. But during the process of their

283

destruction it is our high duty to frustrate to the limit of our capacity the savage purpose of the murderers.

It is our duty and our will to do everything we can to protect American prisoners—any prisoners of the United Nations—in enemy camps. To this end we are committed not only by human feeling but by military practice. By the same token we are justified in doing all we can to save those internal prisoners of slave nations—those whom the Nazis are wiping out. The Nazis exterminate them because they look upon them as enemies of the Nazi State. That makes them our allies. Every victim of Nazi hate is an American ally. Every life we save will speed the victory—will aid in the task of creating a free world after the war.

Therefore, we have a right to call upon the United Nations for action—action now. We ask for the immediate pursuing of every negotiation possible by the Foreign Offices of the United Nations to prevent the continuance of the monstrous process of extermination of minorities. In our growing might, we too can carry out reprisals—but ours should be for acts in the violation of the laws of humanity. As we speed ultimate victory, we too can bomb and punish. We can also bargain for freedom for many of the victims and provide places of refuge for them. And so, too, can we serve notice through the governments of the United Nations, that the peoples of the Axis powers will pay now and later by every means at hand, for every act of savagery, for every failure to permit the passage of their victims to a place of refuge.

The one purpose of all of us in the United Nations today is victory. Without victory the ultimate objective toward which we dedicate ourselves tonight cannot be attained. We must, we shall devote ourselves with ever greater vigor to the prosecution of the war, to the end that we shall win that victory speedily. Each of us has his part to do in the forefront of battle, either in combat or in production in the battle of supplies and food. And for those in combat we shall preserve here at home the sacred freedoms for which we fight, as we seek to procure freedom for all, now and in the future. Nothing less would prove us worthy of the pledge we make tonight to our fellow men overseas.

GOVERNMENT CLOSE TO THE PEOPLE

At a Regional Meeting of the Council of State Governments, New York City, on April 9, 1943

In approaching the problems of the post-war period, it is well for all of us, and particularly this Council, to re-examine the relationships between the people, their states and the federal government.

In the last ten years it has been the trend of the federal government to by-pass the states and attempt to deal directly with the local communities. This trend has extended prodigiously the scope and power of the federal government, somewhat at the expense of the local communities, greatly at the expense of the states.

Now, with the intensity of total war naturally accelerating that concentration of power, we are getting a clearer picture of what it does and how it works.

There have been a number of results. One such result has been the siphoning of the funds of the people direct to the national government. Thence, after paying large administrative expenses, the balance, other than war expenditures, is distributed according to the varying social and economic philosophies prevailing among the groups which dominate from time to time in the shifting Washington scene. This growing trend is based on the theory that the people in their states are incapable of deciding how best to use their own resources.

Ultimate power remains always with control of the purse. That is one measure of the extent to which the people have been losing power to the federal government—power, influence and the opportunity to share in working for the common good.

286

Of course, with power goes leadership. The inevitable result has been the tendency for the promising younger men as well as those of mature experience and ability to be drained off from their cities and their states. Big men become small cogs in a vast federal machine. The majority find themselves wasted, when they could be doing creative work in the war effort as leaders in their home states.

This is the second result of the present trend. The federal government now has a civilian staff of more than two and a half million people—two and a half times the number needed in the last war. To put it another way, this is a staff of adults almost as large as the whole population of the Kingdom of Norway.

Aside from the countless numbers in routine work, this great number includes many of the ablest scientists, scholars, business and professional leaders of the nation. At home they were great producers, great leaders. Lost in the catacombs of Washington, their capacity seems to be so sterilized and counterbalanced that their usefulness is lost to their state and also to their country.

This poses not merely a question of the most efficient way to win the war. For the whole future, is it the best way to solve our problems after the war?

The basic question to be decided in the next decade is whether the present trend is sound. Is it wise to divert our resources, our leadership and our technical skills into the bottomless pit of a government far removed from the people themselves? Can a free Republic the size of ours operate that way? More important, can it remain free under such a system?

It raises the fundamental question: Do our people want to make their own pattern of life? Or do they want it made for them?

Our recent experience here in New York with the farm problem has afforded us one of our most important lessons and at the same time one of the most costly. Not only here in New York but in all the adjoining states which you represent, we had for many months foreseen the catastrophe that was facing the country in the production of food. The catastrophe arose simply because the national government never saw the problem—never acted on it until a few weeks ago—never even reversed its crop restriction program in time. The misfortune obviously arose as a direct consequence of the siphoning of all responsibility and power into the hands of the national government.

There have been many similar lessons which lead to a major conclusion. It is clear that when mistakes are made by a county government, they affect only that county and can quickly be remedied. When mistakes are made by a state government, only the people of one state suffer. But when mistakes are made on a national scale, they become disastrous for the whole people.

The farm catastrophe which is already upon us is one that we cannot erase—we can only attempt to repair it by local effort and by the resumption of local responsibility, as we are now trying to do. It demonstrates the dangers and the difficulties attendant upon the direction of local problems from the seat of national government.

Under the stress of war, we have relearned the obvious truth, that no central government can solve at one time the problems of the Indiana corn grower and the New York potato grower or fruit grower. No power in Washington can fit into the same pattern the needs of the Colorado rancher and the Virginia tobacco grower. No set of national controls, however much they be multiplied, can do anything but hinder total agricultural production.

I take it as an axiom that in the years immediately following the war our difficulties will be more complex than in the war years. After all, our present task has one simple underlying motive. We subdue all our personal interests, we stop at no sacrifices to win the war. After the war will come the tremendous job of winning and keeping the peace. To that end it is of paramount importance that we keep ourselves not only free, but strong. How best shall we be strong enough to win a new lease on freedom?

It seems to me imperative that we must bear in the forefront of our minds at all times that this war is a struggle to uphold the dignity of the individual. Certainly it would not be worth the candle if it were for a lesser purpose. After total war, with its concomitant total powers, we shall find ourselves faced clearly with the problem of translating victory into reality for the individual.

One of the grave mistakes we can commit in fighting total war is to forget our objectives. Our war objective is to abolish totalitarianism and restore the dignity of the individual. The very thing which brought this war about was the possession of total crushing power in the national governments of our enemies.

The totalitarian trend spread all over the world in the 1930's. One of the questions we must determine for ourselves is: Shall we permit the continuance of the totalitarian trend in our own country or shall we recover the rights of the individual for which we are sacrificing today?

The true relationship of a national government in a free republic of states is too often lost and confused in arguments over symbols. It is not merely a matter of states' rights or of community rights or of national rights. It is a question of the human rights which keep a people free to live the kind of lives they choose in the varied types of communities which exist across the breadth of a continent.

It is basic that the national government must have the power to deal with national problems. In many fields there exist problems which overflow the borders of states. Combinations of financial, industrial or political power become national and cannot be met by any state or even by a group of states. There must always be in the Federal government power and authority to deal adequately and decisively with any amalgamation of financial, industrial or political power which exists on an interstate basis.

Such broad national powers are essential to freedom of the individual.

By the same token, these powers which are essential to the freedom of the people can be endangered when polluted by the exercise of control over essentially local matters.

The exercise of powers which infringe upon liberty can cause revulsions against all delegated power. We must clear our thinking for the days ahead so that there shall be no revulsion against the proper exercise of full power by the national government in national problems. We can preserve such necessary national power by recovering for the states and for the localities the authority to deal with the vast majority of problems which are essentially local.

After the long years of war, therefore, our first problem will be to reverse the reactionary trend as exemplified by the growing exercise of total power over local problems by the national government. We must revive the rights of the individual—the strength, the character that is the essence of America. That strength and that character lie in the independence, the intelligence and the initiative of the individual.

We have learned that lesson all over again in the war. For example, we have learned from our armed forces that however great the mass of troops, however powerful the mechanization, in a crucial moment we depend on the individual strength, the hardihood and the initiative of every single soldier. Granted equal ammunition and firepower, the final protector of our destinies is the individual soldier, his discipline, his courage, his intelligence. We have seen it in Tunisia; we have seen it on Guadalcanal; we have seen it in the battle of the Bismarck Sea, we have seen it in every theatre of the war.

The same is true of the difficult process of keeping alive freedom. Its vigor depends on the devotion of each individual who shares it. Only by continuous vigilance and positive exercise of our rights as free men in state and local government can we continue to practice and keep fresh the rights we have taken for granted.

As we shape our thinking for the peace to come, let us determine whether we shall again bring government close to the people. Shall they make their own decisions as robust, clear-thinking free men or shall they abandon their rights to an aggressive oligarchy at the seat of national government? There is only one course by which we can retain and bring to its full flower the freedom which shall again be so hard-won at such great cost.

The natural evolution of a free society is a constant process of trial and error—a constant competition between men of ability, a constant contest between ideas welling up from within our communities.

There is nothing fixed about a free society. If it is healthy, it is always fluid. That is fundamentally the secret weapon of freedom.

One of the great advantages of the freedom for which we are fighting is that it makes it possible for all of the people to receive the benefit of the thought and the productive genius which society produces. Neither power nor opportunity is confined to the selected few. Where opportunity and freedom of expression are available to all the people, there is the structure of a free society. But it is not truly a free society until opportunity and freedom of expression become not only available to all the people but become natural to them. Then they are not only free to try out the products of their minds but they actually do so. The sound contributions are successful. The mistakes, having been tried out, fall into the discard. Then and only then does the mass of the people receive the benefits of a liberal society. Only then do such benefits spread throughout the nation.

That must be the ultimate purpose of any good government, of a government that wishes to remain strong, the free government of a free people.

THE BATTLE OF FOOD

Speech at the Governors' Conference, Columbus, Ohio, June 21, 1943

I AM happy to find myself asked to talk here about the farm problems of the State of New York. Everyone has thought of New York as a great industrial state. It is doubly gratifying that it should finally be recognized as also one of the great agricultural states. But I must recognize that, as a New Yorker coming to Ohio to talk about farm problems, I am carrying a good many coals to Newcastle.

One of the most urgent problems facing us at the first of this year was the shortage of farm manpower. A group of farm leaders in the State had long been organized and were thinking earnestly about the problem. Collaborating with them was a technical committee of young, relatively unknown men from the State College of Agriculture, the farm organizations, the Department of Education and the United States Employment Service. They had a complete program worked out.

All we needed was to translate their program into action. So one of the first things we did was to set up a Farm Manpower Service with one of these young men in charge of it as Director with every facility of the State of New York behind him. We did not retire to an ivory tower to invent something new and different. We did not reject the program already worked out by people who knew the problem just because they knew it. We simply gave funds and legal authority to translate into action the program which rose from among the farmers themselves.

The result has been that short training courses for new farm workers have been given in State agricultural schools from Long Island to the Canadian border. Thousands of boys were let out of school early for the planting season and will be excused again next Fall for the harvest. Thousands more will be available during the harvest season in camps under good supervision. Business men in many cities have organized to give additional help with the crops. In cooperation with the Farm Security Administration, we have brought additional permanent workers into the State, and have trained them in our schools for work on New York farms.

All this was done by the process of collaboration between all farm groups and Federal, State and local agencies. During this process the Congress had a flash of true wisdom. It transferred the federal funds for farm manpower away from Washington to the land grant colleges of the country, to be administered by their Extension Services. Our people had worked closely with the Employment Service, which had only two years ago been taken over from the State. So we were happy to have the farm placement work continued under contract made directly with Cornell University. There was no interruption in the work and even better local integration resulted.

I do not pretend the farm labor program has been solved in the State of New York. But it is greatly improved and I am now satisfied that we will be able both to plant and harvest our crops.

One of our happy discoveries in this process has been that the most effective way to avoid surrender to the failures of the National Government is to step out and do the job ourselves as a State. And in so doing, we have found that there are enough men in Washington whose primary concern is to get the job done, so that we have had many examples of fine cooperation. This has also been the experience of our Emergency Food Commission, established three months ago.

The creation of the Emergency Food Commission was the second step we took to meet the food situation in our own State. In this Commission we revived the forgotten principle that if you want a good job done you call on a busy man who knows how. You do not call on a cattle grower to solve an industrial problem and you do not call on a professor of astrology to help out a dairy farmer. The Commission brought our eleven best experts in their fields to the service of the State. They were not just a collection of heavy thinkers. Each of them was a man of action. Each carries a specific responsibility for a specific group of agricultural necessities and keeps in touch with it daily. They have met regularly for all-day sessions.

The information services of our Department of Agriculture and Markets have been speeded so that in every critical situation we have daily and sometimes hourly reports from every section of the State.

The Commission has foreseen and solved in advance many of our problems. Confronted with a shortage of apple crates, they have been lining up sawmills to make them, long before the harvest. Similar procedures have been followed with everything from wire for hay balers and twine for tying up asparagus to substitutes for crushed oyster shells for laying hens.

During the early spring, the Commission foresaw a complete lack of fertilizer in the State. The difficulty centered in Maryland. It was never quite clear whether the trouble lay in wage ceilings which kept the fertilizer people from getting labor, or price ceilings which made it more profitable to serve only local trade. But the Commission went to work with both the fertilizer trade and the national farm organizations. They turned on all the heat they could muster, and we got the fertilizer in time.

There have recently been times when critical shortages of gasoline have existed in as many as twenty farm counties. As many as 400 farm tractors in a single county have been without gasoline. But plowing cannot wait for red tape. The Food Commission took vigorous action to get and distribute gasoline. Finally an official of the Petroleum Administration for War took desk room right in our State Office Building, to work with the transportation member of the Food Commission. Only by day to day action and cooperation are we keeping the farm tractors running.

Today the cooperatives and the independent feed dealers have been brought together by the Commission to find the answer to our most urgent long range problem—how to find feed for our dairy cows and our laying hens. As many of you know, the State of New York is the best customer of the Midwestern grain fields. We buy from the Middle West more than 60% of the feed necessary for our great dairy and poultry production. We need at least 2,000,000 tons of concentrate feed from outside the State this year and we are not getting it.

No purpose would be served in analyzing the incredible deficiencies of the National Government in its 10-year campaign to restrict food production in the United States. We are just now reaping some of the harvest of these policies. But as a sardonic final touch, we now find that out of the genius of the OPA there was developed a theory that it would be a good idea to repeal the natural law of economics that corn and hog prices are tied together. The result is a ceiling price on corn of $1.05 at Chicago. Meanwhile, the farmer can get $1.45 for the same corn right on the farm, just by throwing it over the fence to his pigs.

In short, the Iowa hog can pay 50 per cent more at the farm for a bushel of corn than a New York cow is allowed to pay. The result is we have no corn.

I hope you of the Midwest will forgive us, then, if we cannot wait forever for Washington to discover the laws of economics. We have to get feed wherever we can find it.

Accordingly, our Emergency Food Commission is now in the process of arranging, not with State funds, but by the joint cooperation of the cooperatives and the feed dealers, to buy millions of bushels of grain from Canada. That grain has to come down the Great Lakes to Buffalo and for that we must have shipping space. The Emergency Food Commission has been negotiating in Washington for the necessary bottoms. They are receiving the most sympathetic cooperation from Mr. Chester Davis and we hope and expect somehow to get the bottoms. Unfortunately, Mr. Davis, who understands the problem, has been left, like too many others, with a title but inadequate authority. There is still no spokesman in the new super-Cabinet for the food for 130,000,000 Americans, to say nothing of the starving peoples of the world whom we all hope to feed when they have been liberated.

We have had too much in this country of waiting for crises to reach the breaking point and then using emergency measures to pick up the pieces. Our Emergency Food Commission, under the Chairmanship of Mr. H. E. Babcock, has conceived it to be its duty to approach the food problem with foresight rather than with panicky afterthoughts. With that purpose it has prepared an analysis of what we have to look forward to in the way of food—not what is going to be on the butcher's counter next week but what will confront us two, three, five years from now.

They started from the fact that for many years this country has not had a real surplus of food. Despite the past six years of bumper crops, we have eaten virtually all we have produced, except wheat. Thus under the vastly increased demands of war and victory we are certain to have an increasing scarcity of food.

Inevitably under such conditions one result occurs. The livestock population is cut down and human beings stretch the food supply by eating grain themselves instead of feeding it to pigs. This happens, not because anyone is less fond of beefsteak and pork chops, but because it takes seven pounds of corn to make one pound of pig. A shift to a cereal diet is the only way to make our food go around.

Right now the meat situation is a jumble of paradoxes. In New York this week our cupboard is bare, not because of any present shortage in meat animals, but because of price manipulations which have cut off trade. Actually in this country we have a livestock population so vast that we never can support it and at the same time fulfill an obligation to help feed the starving survivors of a wrecked world. Right now in this country our meat animals are eating into the precious food reserves which must be increased if we are even to begin saving the undernourished people of a rescued Europe.

There can be only one result of this. Human beings will inevitably push the pig away from the trough, to eat his corn themselves. Livestock will be reduced, and its slaughter will for a time give us the illusion of a continuing meat supply. I think the illusion may last until election day next year. But then will come the time when we will really know what a meat shortage means.

Already our people, like yours, are discovering that the war and the food scarcity programs of the past are taking out of their diet the things on which they are accustomed to live. We have the greatest concentration of people in the world in New York City, with the widest variety of eating habits. Our other cities are faced with the same problems, to a lesser degree. They are finding the staple items of their diet ranging from eels to kosher meats disappearing from the market. So the Emergency Food Commission is tackling this job too.

Once again we had, right at home, the people who were leaders in the rapidly developing science of nutrition. Again we did not need to go out and create something new. We just had to use the brains and the facilities at home. And we put in charge the people who knew the problem best.

The Commission's scientists have been seeking new foods to cushion the shock of that time when we get less and less of the foods to which we have been accustomed. They have already made one tremendous contribution. Adopting a principle which for centuries has maintained China's strength on a cereal diet, they have brought forward the sprouted soybean as a food new for this country.

In the last twenty years we have become familiar with the great value of the soybean as an animal feed, rich in protein and fat. Now it is discovered that when the bean is sprouted a miracle occurs. It becomes easily cooked and palatable for humans. Moreover, while it sprouts it not only retains a high value in the nutrients we find in meat but it also creates within itself a new and precious supply of Vitamins B, C and G. Our Food Commission now is acting to make these sprouted beans available to our people. They are not a substitute for meat. No one wants or will find any substitute for good red steak or lamb chops. But for the days when there is little or no meat they make a splendid supplement with all the nutritive value of meat and more too.

The strength of our country is in its roots. The battle of the home front is not going to be won by any master-mind anywhere. I have spoken with unabashed enthusiasm about our Emergency Food Commission, not only because I was invited to speak on this subject, but because it is the kind of job being done everywhere, once our citizens are given the chance. I do not pretend that we in New York have any disproportionate share of brains or experience. On the contrary, I know that at every crossroads, in every county, in every state of America, there are men who, because of their knowledge and ability in their own familiar surroundings, have an infinite amount to give to our war effort. It is our job as Governors to give them the green light so they may go ahead under their own power.

Our conclusions in New York have been fairly simple and direct. Because the national government would not or could not see or understand as a whole the problem of feeding our people, we moved in to meet it ourselves.

Because the national government still cannot or will not understand the food problem of America, the war Governors of the United States, who are close to their people, can and will do the job.

In so doing, I am sure that none of us will suffer from the misconception that either the national government or we as Governors can ourselves meet the need. What we can do is to use the great reservoir of ability, character and courage among our people. We can release that ability to serve the needs of the nation.

Winston Churchill once said, at a time of crisis for Great Britain: "Give us the tools and we will do the job." Our people are in that situation today. As war Governors we can, because we must, understand the ultimate truth,—that no government either state or national produces money, goods or food. We can revive the long forgotten truth that it is the people of the Nation whose funds support government. Their sweat produces the goods and food. They are both the rulers and the makers of their country's destiny.

We can remove all obstacles. We can insist on giving our people the tools. As always, the people of America will, themselves, do the job.

TEAMWORK

At the New York State Federation of Labor Convention in Buffalo, N. Y., August 23, 1943

IT seems long ago, but, in truth, it was only last year that the gallant men under MacArthur and Wainwright were fighting the Battle of Bataan inch by inch. Those who escaped have told us that they were driven back by overwhelming enemy superiority in planes, guns and all armament. As they fell back they cried out: "If we only had the weapons we would not be the ones who are retreating."

The truth of their cry has been amply proved throughout this year. Today it is our men who have the weapons; it is the enemy who is retreating.

Great, stirring victories have come to the armed forces of America. All of us have been deeply proud of the achievements of our fighting men. After long months in which our Army and Navy were handicapped by lack of material, we have seen the tide turn. We have seen American airplanes sweep the skies in overwhelming numbers above enemy territory. We have seen the courage and ability of our troops at length backed up by the weight of weapons needed to roll back the aggressors upon their own soil. These victories on the fighting front abroad were made possible by victories previously won on the production front at home.

Too often, understanding is one thing and action on that understanding is another thing. We know it will take great sacrifices to win the war. But it is easy to let the other fellow make the sacrifices. We know that winning the war is greater than the issue involved in any strike. Yet it is too easy to let little issues become big issues which roll up into strikes.

301

TEAMWORK

With such fateful events hanging upon the continued outpouring of arms from our factories here at home, we have a single task ahead of us. We must redouble our every effort. We must be vigilant against the relaxation which is so apt to follow initial success. We must be vigilant against the human impulse to slacken effort in the face of a hard task long continued. We must be vigilant against those who would impede our production by dividing us against each other. The stream of supplies must flow to the fighting fronts not only in equal but in ever-increasing volume and without cease. Of these things, organized labor in the State of New York has shown its deep understanding.

Accordingly, we can all take particularly great pride in the fact that there have been no industrial strikes of any moment in the State of New York. There have not even been any industrial controversies here which are worthy of the name. The New York State Federation of Labor can point with similar pride to its record of having authorized no strikes in the industrial shops where it represents the worker. Labor in this State has kept its no-strike pledge.

In other parts of the country the production of coal, the production of steel and the production of other essentials to the machines of war has been critically hampered by industrial disputes. That has not happened in this State. In New York there has been no interruption in production.

At the height of the war effort, the people of the State changed Administrations. They brought a different party into power and a complete new set of State officers. And with that change there was not one second's interruption of the public service or the production of goods, services and food for war. On the contrary, I can confidently say that this State is more vigorously in the war effort in every department, than ever before.

In the entire session of the Legislature which ended last March, there was not one provocative incident which might impair the war effort. Not a single law was recommended by the Executive or passed by the Legislature affecting either industry or labor which would cause dissension affecting the war effort.

In this critical year we have had no contest between the executive and the legislative branches of the State government. We have had no squabbling between department heads in the public prints, or, to let you in on a secret, in private. In order that the Nation might fight better abroad, we made certain that in this State there should be no fighting at home.

Yet, not for one moment has there been an impairment of the two party system of free discussion or of differences of opinion. There have been plenty of differences. But we have settled them after full debate in the American way and then got along with our job.

In the same way, and perhaps for somewhat the same reasons, labor has kept to the job. Of course, there have been differences between workmen and employers. Of course, there have been hotheads among both. But among men of good will there have been earnest discussions and peaceful settlements. And the men of evil will have not lasted long in important positions.

There has been little or no disposition among our leaders of labor, to use the war to advance their personal power or their private ideologies at the expense of the people as a whole. Aside from limitations imposed by the war, through the National government, the rights of working men of this State have been scrupulously preserved—even advanced—and the welfare of the Nation as a whole steadily served.

This free society of ours can wage total war and remain free. This we are proving in the State of New York. I am sure that you will wish to share some of the credit for this with the several State agencies that mediate between industry and labor. They have lived up to their responsibilities as you have, disinterestedly and intelligently.

The prime reason for the lack of major internal friction in our State can be put in one word, teamwork. We have had in New York a reasonable and cooperative attitude by enlightened employers devoted to free enterprise. We have also had a reasonable and cooperative approach by enlightened leaders of labor who also see in the enterprise system the only economic society we know under which labor can advance and remain free.

There was nothing magical about the teamwork which averted interruptions in production within our State. It has been achieved by hard work and the employment of common sense and good will. It is founded upon the basic principles of this free Republic—a decent respect for the welfare, the opinions and the rights of every citizen whether he be in the majority or the minority, whether he be rich or poor, white or colored, employer or employee.

Democracy in a republic is not merely a word or a formula. It is not something for which we cheer on public occasions and which we then go home and forget. We cannot achieve it just by voting occasionally and considering that to be the end of our duties. Good, free government must be a habit of our lives from day to day.

It is good democracy in industry for free men to get together and solve their problems as free men. That means to solve them man to man, without force, without violence, without coercion. It is good democracy in government for free men to get together and solve the problems by which they govern themselves as free men, without force, without violence, without coercion.

In other words, democracy is a faith and a political philosophy, which we practice in a constitutional republic. Its principles rest upon the ideas that should guide us in all our human relations, the relations between neighbor and

304

neighbor, the relations between electors and the people they elect, the relations between employer and employee.

We are sometimes told that the growth of America, the great development of its industries, has made impossible the human understanding that used to prevail when the boss knew every soul that worked for him and called him by his first name, and was called, in turn, by his first name. It is true that the early, friendly period was followed by unhappy days when labor relations were decided at meetings of a board of directors far distant from the plant. This is not true today and what has been happening in New York State is proof of it.

Both labor and management are increasingly learning to have competent, trained men on the job where the work is done. Each learns the problems of the other. Differences are adjusted by people on the spot, by those closest to the problem. That is a condition we need to encourage and expand not only in industry but in government. Good government in a free republic depends inevitably upon good local government. By the same token good relations between industry and labor are being steadily built by good human relations between those on the job, united in the will to do a good job for their country.

The war has inexorably brought us closer together in the solution of our common problems. We are learning that free men living in mutual respect can solve any problem. We are also learning to lift our eyes above immediate irritations of the day and look to larger objectives. Today, those larger objectives are all submerged in the winning of the war. Tomorrow, let us make sure we keep our eyes lifted up to the objectives of a happy and productive peace. It is not too early to discuss the direction in which we want to go when that time comes.

Under the pressure of war we have all willingly submitted to restraints by the National government which are foreign to our most vital principles. In fighting total war, we have learned we must mobilize our every resource and our every moment. A multiplicity of Federal regulations have been promulgated, governing hours, wages and conditions of employment. In large measure these regulations supersede the functions of collective bargaining. They have superseded private management, and, in some cases, have even taken plants away from their owners when the owners were without fault.

In time of total war such an abridgement of our rights is probably inescapable. But it is a condition which can only be justified by the sacrifices of war. We are fighting to make sure that such totalitarian conditions cannot exist in time of peace.

For, whether we recognize it or not, the peacetime effect of government control over the terms and conditions of labor would inevitably be to regulate out of existence the whole purpose of labor unions.

It is a fundamental truth that there is no place for genuine collective bargaining in a regimented economy. We have seen that strikingly demonstrated in the Fascist economies against which our whole Nation is today fighting. Collective bargaining is a right of free labor which can only be exercised by free labor. And there can be no free labor except in an enterprise economy conducted by free men.

It will take vigilance and understanding to make certain that the wartime change in the relations of government to organized labor is not carried over into peace.

The hard-won rights of labor which have been abridged by wartime controls are as fundamental as freedom of speech and freedom of the press. Like these other rights, they must be restored intact to a people who have temporarily yielded them in the cause of freedom.

We can be sure of this only if we make certain that the regimented economy of war is succeeded by a peacetime economy of freedom under law. We can preserve it only in an economy of full production and full employment. For we can never, as a nation, consume more than we produce.

So that we shall truly regain and keep the vital freedoms for which we fight today, I invite you to join with all your vigor in the struggle to restore them at the end of the war. We can be neither free nor strong in a peacetime regimented economy. We can be both free and strong if we recover for labor and enterprise the dignity and unfettered strength which only free men can enjoy.

We are all fighting for the same thing, total victory. Workers and employers are equally interested in that goal. They are all gladly making every possible sacrifice to win the war and to win the peace after the war. An indispensable part of that peace will be continued progress in all our relations—the relations between labor and management, between both and government. The teamwork that we have set up in New York State must not be a temporary arrangement. It must be something that will last—that will enable us to live together and to work together, more keenly alive than ever, to the ultimate truth that what benefits one group will benefit all.

America never turns back. Whatever our calling, we Americans look forward to the sharing of an ever greater future.

THE WIDENING SOCIAL HORIZON

At Carnegie Hall, New York City, October 3, 1943, before the Combined New York and Brooklyn Jewish Federations

THERE is no part of our way of life that is so appealing and heartwarming as that part of it in which you are engaged tonight. Of what can be accomplished by the spirit of voluntary helpfulness in the field of social welfare, this Federation of Jewish Charities is one of our country's finest examples.

One of the oldest expressions of the primary obligations of citizenship in a free republic is the friendly concern of one man for the welfare of his neighbor. This tradition is rooted in our human sense of pity, in that quick, instinctive reaching out of the hand to those who suffer. More importantly, however, it is rooted in our basic American political faith. For we hold that every human being has a right to the decencies and the opportunities of life. And this is all an inseparable part of that deep religious faith in which we see our fellowmen in terms of brotherhood under the fatherhood of God.

A world which has suffered as much as our world has will never be the same again. It does not follow, however, that it will necessarily be a better world than the one we have known. With its exhaustion, brutality, poverty and starved peoples, it will for some time be a worse world. But, if we will it enough to labor for it, we can make it a better one.

But this can only be with our earnest effort and cooperation. The desire for whole-souled cooperation is and must be a fundamental feature of our relations with other nations and other peoples.

Exactly the same is true of our own State and Nation.

We, too, will bear heavy scars, both spiritually and physically. Only by a determined continuance of our unity and high purpose can we build a better world at home. In this work, our social agencies and the voluntary enterprise which has built them, will find new and larger fields of usefulness than ever before.

Your Federation President tells me that never before has there been such a warm interest in Federation, or greater eagerness to work for its good cause. I believe this is true of most other volunteer campaigns throughout the country. And when you add up the people serving as volunteers in the traditional social agencies and in the war-time protective services, and the people serving as volunteers in raising the money, you have a huge civilian army.

I believe all of this has the deepest significance for all who are concerned with the future of American life. How heartening it is to know that this part of our American life —the spirit of voluntary helpfulness—is sound at the very core!

At the very time when government takes on larger and larger authority, when we accept all kinds of rules, regulations and limitations to win the war—it is at this very time that the citizen's sense of what he is willing to do, not by Government order, but under the motive power of his own conscience and sense of duty, is higher than it ever was.

I say that is good.

Social agencies after the war will have this great reservoir of new, intensified interest in welfare endeavors to draw upon. Participation in community endeavors is one of the most fascinating and rewarding activities that human beings can have. I believe that a very large section of the men and women who have had their first taste of participation in this work will wish to go forward in it in the years after the war.

The expansion of the volunteer spirit is good in quite

another sense. The health and vitality of our American state lies not alone in the area of Government, though the responsibility of Government has increased, and may well continue to increase. The life blood of free America lies in what may be expected of the private citizen as a private citizen, and in what the private citizen expects of himself.

We must say it and say it again. The society which has completely abandoned all private enterprise, whether it be in business, education or social service, cannot any longer claim to be a free society. The fellow over whose head Government must, in all matters, hold a protective umbrella, is a frightened man, not a free man. It is the frightened man who is the source and raw material for regimentation and totalitarianism.

We hark back to the safeguarding of such fundamentals as the freedom to work; freedom to say what we believe to be true, to speak out against wrong as we see it; freedom to worship as we please; and freedom for enterprise to operate within the bounds of decency and social usefulness.

Broadly speaking, there are two kinds of people in the world—the kind that have things happen to them and the kind who make things happen. In a totalitarian state, there is a great preponderance of people who have things happen to them. They are pushed around, quite literally; they haven't the right to conduct their own businesses; they haven't the right to join trade unions; they are treated with official contempt if they worship God; they have no right to live their own lives in their own way—they do what they are told to do.

Free men are cut from quite another bolt of cloth. A free society must have an increasing number of people who do things for themselves and for others—people with starch in them, with initiative, imagination and vision.

I have stressed the vital role in our society of volunteer

work such as that of Federation, voluntarily financed by private citizens. I am equally convinced that government, too, in the name of all its citizens has its deep social obligations. Government, perforce, is responsible for the broad social securities. This is a basic responsibility. But we must always remember two things about these obligations of government: First, they must necessarily be financed out of the revenue drawn from all our people. Second, government can fulfill its responsibilities in this field only as it remains within the bounds of sound fiscal operations.

I have said in the past, and I cannot repeat too often, that the outstanding problem of government today is this: How can we maintain and expand the services of government without bankrupting both the state and the nation? To that there is only one answer. We must finance the advances of the future out of the savings achieved by better management. In the achievement of that better management, we must look, I think, to increasing cooperation between the social agencies of government and those of private enterprise.

Each must, in its own field, supplement the other. Neither should compete with the other.

A more effective and a more economical attack upon our present day and future responsibilities in the field of individual and family security requires that we do the following things as a minimum:

1. Bring related activities such as unemployment insurance, workmen's compensation, public welfare, employment and rehabilitation services, into an effective working team.
2. Simplify our administrative machinery.
3. Develop a more skilled corps of public servants to manage these services, selected and retained on a basis of merit.

4. Provide, through competent research, geared in with our industrial planning, sufficient foresight in social affairs so that we will meet changing conditions, not through the wasteful devices of "emergency" programs and agencies—but through the orderly use of flexible, permanent governmental machinery.

Private social agencies, acting alone and in cooperation with government agencies, will have much to do when readjustments come and the strain and tensions uncover new areas of need. As a matter of fact, social welfare and medical endeavor stand today only on the threshold of new fields of achievement.

One of the great areas where much remains to be done is the study and treatment of mental diseases, another fruitful area in which public and private agencies can join hands.

In our State, the system of mental hospital care had until recently become static, if it was not actually going backward. The State planned for the permanent custody of increasing numbers of mental patients rather than for the treatment and cure of mental diseases. It exploited new building programs while neglecting adequate reception, infirmary and modern therapeutic care. By putting so much into permanent, long-enduring construction, the State blocked the march of progress. Today we can hope to afford but little new construction and should plan better use of what we have.

The keynote of our program in the mental hospital field must be the better care of the patient through improved organization and professional management. I look for the day when internship by young doctors in our mental hospitals will be sought after as widely as in the best private hospitals. It is my hope that with largely increased internships, we may select from an ever greater group, those with the best skills and natural aptitude for mental institutional work.

Any sound program will require more accurate knowledge and classification of the individual patient, together with improved and individualized attention, earlier treatment, earlier and better managed discharges back to the community.

Here we need increased educational work with the family and relatives, particularly of convalescents, to promote earlier release to out-patient family care and follow-up status, and to prevent, as far as possible, readmission to institutional care. Greater attention must be paid to the use of modern dietetic methods in treating mental patients. There must be increased emphasis upon the work of rehabilitating patients through proper occupational therapy and other programs of physical instruction and training. All this necessitates the establishment of an up-to-date and better organization of hospital and institutional management.

In short, our effort to meet the problem of the treatment of mental diseases must call for increasing emphasis upon the cure and rehabilitation of the mentally ill rather than upon mere custody of large numbers of them in institutions that resemble prisons rather than hospitals.

There is also a vast work to be done in medical research and health education. We still have a health problem in this country; a serious one, which the war has merely thrown into bold relief, and which we are only just beginning to tackle. Delinquency will challenge our best thought and skill. For it must be said here that war is not a cause of delinquency; war merely gives prewar tendencies an opportunity to flourish. If this war proves no exception, and it surely will not, the high water mark in juvenile delinquency is still ahead.

Let me try to place this vast picture of widening horizons and new opportunities for medical and social service in its proper perspective. It was within your lifetime and mine that the handing out of a basket of food was our chief expression of "charity." We have come a long way from that narrow view. We no longer tolerate insensitive, unreflective care of people. We think of the family as a functioning unit in a free society that must go on day by day. We safeguard the child, and afford him the normal, full life that builds good citizenship. Having come so far, is it conceivable that the end of the road has been reached? Have all our resources and ingenuity been exhausted?

We in America are only at the beginning. Our history is the history of a quest for a continually improving economic and social life. It is in our nature to pursue the ultimate.

We are here to celebrate the spirit of voluntary cooperative effort, which is the spirit of democracy in action. We are here in the service of humanity, in the knowledge that no matter how sweeping our dreams and hopes for building a better life may be, they cannot be too bold or ambitious. It is fundamental of the common comradeship of all men and women of good will that "they build too low who build beneath the stars."

THE CASE AGAINST TAMMANY HALL

Address Delivered in Favor of Joe R. Hanley, Candidate for Lieutenant Governor, at a Rally at the St. George Hotel, Brooklyn, N. Y., October 28, 1943

I THINK you know what I am going to talk about tonight. The shocking tale of political debauchery on the front page of every New York newspaper requires that every man in public life take sides. There can be no shrinking from the age-old issue in our City and State whether the criminal underworld is to dominate our public affairs.

On this issue, every Republican I know is willing to stand up and be counted. If he is not willing, he is not a Republican so far as I am concerned.

Tragically enough, not one Democratic candidate in the City or State of New York has dared open his mouth about the disreputable leadership of the Democratic party in this City. There are fearful implications in the continuous silence from Democratic headquarters, most of whose candidates were also nominated by the American Labor Party. With an important election next Tuesday the criminal control of Tammany Hall cannot be ignored by any man who seeks to go before the people with clean hands.

Two years ago all the leaders of organized crime operating in New York were, so far as I know, dead or in prison. Most of the key leaders of Tammany Hall were also either in prison or driven from public office in disgrace. The Administrative Assistant District Attorney of New York County was unanimously selected by all parties for the office of District Attorney. One of the most fortunate things that ever happened to our City was that Frank Hogan became District Attorney of New York County.

Then, you remember, Tammany chose a new leader. It was to be a newer, a better Tammany. In fact, it was no longer to be Tammany Hall at all. It was to be just the Democratic Party. It moved uptown and sold Tammany Hall to the International Ladies' Garment Workers.

After twenty years of active opposition to that benevolent society, I almost began to believe that maybe there was something in Tammany's reformation. I am sure many others thought the same way. But thanks to Frank Hogan, we have all had a rude awakening. The Tiger does not change its stripes. We have learned once again that Tammany Hall, core of the Democratic organization of the City of New York, is, and apparently always will be, a criminal organization with larceny in its heart. Gangster control of that powerful political machine is something that new faces, new names, jail sentences and purges never cure.

Now, who is this present boss of Tammany Hall? Is he a new figure? Well, you might be interested to know a little about the history of Frank Costello. The real head of the Democratic machine in New York, as in Albany, holds neither public nor party office. Each is the shadowy boss behind the pawns in front, and each is a graduate of penal institutions.

Frank Costello is one of the top ranking gangsters in the United States. He has been for many years the national boss of the slot machine racket but so far as I know his business has not been conducted in the City or State of New York in the last ten years. He is an old timer in national as well as in local affairs. At the 1932 Democratic National Convention he was present in all his glory. He traveled from New York to that Convention with one James J. Hines, whose present address is Sing Sing, New York. At that Convention Frank Costello was the hotel roommate of Jimmy Hines.

When Lucky Luciano was arrested in Hot Springs, Arkansas, in the Spring of 1936, there was only one piece of paper on his person. That was the private, unlisted New York telephone number of Frank Costello.

So it is not surprising that when Tammany was due for a new face-lifting, it should turn to one of its oldest friends. Congressman Mike Kennedy already had the OK from the national headquarters of the Democratic Party. But that wasn't enough. So he took his hat in his hand and went to see Frank Costello. He asked Costello to make him leader of Tammany Hall. And Costello did.

Had any Republican made these statements on the radio just three months ago, every Democratic leader would have risen in horror and charged him with blackening the name of the local Democratic Party, the State Democratic Party and the national leadership of the Democratic Party. Today the silence from every one of those quarters is deafening.

Now, is this an individual matter or is it a system?

When Boss Tweed went to prison, everybody hailed the new Tammany. When Croker left the country with his boodle, everybody again hailed the new Tammany. Within the past ten years, there went to prison or were driven from office James McCormick, James J. Hines, William Solomon, Charles Schneider and Al Marinelli.

We were asked to believe that once again Tammany Hall had become respectable. And what does the new leader do? Having procured his election through the criminal underworld, he desecrates the White House by repeated personal visits. Then he goes for a holiday as the guest of Costello's partner, Dandy Phil Kastel, the Beau Brummell of five criminal trials and of two penitentiaries.

The faces change but the system remains the same. Leader after leader is driven out or goes to jail, and who takes his place? Whom have we seen in private conference within the past three months with Frank Costello, gangster boss of Tammany Hall? Here is just that part of the list in addition to Kennedy, the nominal boss, which has become public: James De Salvio, alias Jimmy Kelly, leader of the Second Assembly district West; Dr. Paul Sarubbi, leader of the First Assembly district East; Congressman James Fay, leader of the Twelfth Assembly district South; Clarence Neal, leader of the Twentieth Assembly district; Abe Rosenthal, leader of the Eighth Assembly district, and Bert Stand, still Secretary of Tammany Hall though now no longer Secretary of the State Athletic Commission.

One hundred and fifty years of Tammany history, from Aaron Burr to Frank Costello, proves one simple thing. No one can vote the Democratic ticket in the City of New York without knowing that gangsters have participated in the selection of that ticket. Let us not again be deluded by the "new Tammany" that emerges every few years with a brand new suit, its hair brushed and its face and ears glistening with soap.

Decent, honest government is something we have to fight for not just every four years, not just every Election Day, but every day in which you and I enjoy the privileges of a free country.

One of those who has worked every day for seventeen years for decent government in our State is the Republican candidate for Lieutenant Governor, Joe R. Hanley.

Upon the tragic death of Lieutenant Governor Tom Wallace, Joe Hanley automatically became Acting Lieutenant Governor of the State.

As Majority Leader of the Senate, he fought, with us, to humanize the income tax system of New York, saving the people of our State millions of dollars. He fought with us for reapportionment which had been denied the people of the State for 26 years.

He helped to clear up the chaos in civilian protection which was left to us by its former director, the Democratic candidate for Lieutenant Governor.

With the help of Joe Hanley, your State Administration

tackled the food crisis on a dozen fronts and helped save the crops of our State.

Every pledge we made to the people last year has been performed and more too. In all of this Joe Hanley has played a vital and moving part. A veteran of two wars, twice decorated for saving six lives in the last war, he knows the problem of the returning veteran. He knows the business of State government. He has never failed to speak out against crime and corruption wherever it appeared.

The Democratic Party cannot wash away by silence the major issue which recent evidence has posed in our civic life. The good people of the City and State must go to the polls and give one simple, resounding answer. I have absolute faith that an aroused electorate will give that answer next Tuesday.

UTOPIA, CHAOS, OR COMMON SENSE?

Address Delivered to the Herald Tribune Forum, November 16, 1943

THE other day a friend of mine was talking to his twelve-year-old daughter who is in the seventh grade at school. He asked her what they were taking up this year and she said, "We are taking up post-war planning." That makes it unanimous.

Now that everybody is engaged in making plans for the post-war world, let us take stock of the kind of thinking which is going into the planning. The two most common kinds of thinking we find are wishful thinking and fearful thinking. We have people who try to make us believe that after the war we shall be living in a kind of Buck Rogers Utopia. We shall all live in ultra-modernistic houses, ride in futuristic cars, be surrounded with miraculous new gadgets and each of us have a private helicopter in the backyard garage. It will be an era of full employment in which nobody has to work. Those are the wishful thinkers.

Then there are the fearful thinkers who seem to be frightened to death that peace may break out at any moment. They paint lugubrious pictures of chaos and collapse with 15 million unemployed—bread lines and soup kitchens and everybody dependent upon a dole from the Federal government.

I think both of these pictures are completely wide of the mark. I very much doubt we can hope for an immediate Utopia and I am firmly convinced that we need not fear chaos and collapse.

When this war is over we shall still be the same people, living in the same homes, working at pretty much the same

jobs. We shall, of course, be considerably poorer, with a debt of 250 to 300 billion dollars to pay off. We shall be I hope, a little wiser, a little more understanding, as a re sult of what we have passed through. And we shall still b a country of boundless resources, unlimited opportunit and above all a country made up of the most ambitiou daring and highly skilled human beings on earth. On thing is sure: 130 million people can produce enormous and can consume enormously, provided the channels of pr duction and consumption are kept free.

Naturally, it will not be all clear sailing when the war over. In the period of conversion from war to peace the will inevitably be lags. We shall face some temporary une ployment. We shall face some dislocations in prices, r materials and distribution. But all that, I am confident, c be overcome. We shall need determination, faith, and little patience. We shall need the thoughts and efforts everybody.

In seeking a solution to the problems that will face after the war, it is tempting to wish for some single formu But the truth is, no such formula exists. One of the thi we have learned in recent years is that magic formu solve no problems. A living standard is not created by l by honeyed words or by anything except the goods services that are produced by the people of a nation w ing in harmony and in productive peace.

In our country, as in the world at large, no magic form no single written document will bring a stable peace. peace of the world is something to be labored with, un stood and sacrificed for in all the years to come. In the way, the successful peace at home will be the result of and continuous effort. Certainly neither by manipula of government finances nor by any other single device possible for the nation to lift itself up by its own bootst

We must indeed plan for our domestic affairs in the

war period. All of the physical and spiritual realities of life are dependent on the success with which we plan to meet the problems ahead of us.

In New York State we are doing our planning with no effort to find the non-existent magic formula. We are aiming at a scheme of cooperation whereby every business concern in every community in the State will collaborate. First, we are finding out exactly what the problems will be. We know, for example, that in this State there will be six million people requiring employment after the war. That means one million more people than there were jobs for in 1940. We are setting about learning what this will mean translated into terms of cities, counties, towns and villages. We are helping the people of those communities to take stock of their own part in the problem and to mobilize their own resources and ingenuity to meet the conditions ahead. That is the way it will have to be done, community by community, industry by industry. That means that the businessman must plan now for the new methods, the new products, the new markets that will be available to him when peace returns. The individual must plan to take advantage of the new jobs that will be open to him. The community must plan for the new enterprises it can encourage, the new public works it can undertake.

In all this picture, government must also plan. Government must plan its policies so as to create the conditions under which private enterprise spurred on by the profit motive will plunge into peace-time production with all the energy and effectiveness that it has devoted to war. That means government must not only plan the things it should do, but most particularly the things it should refrain from doing.

Most of us are agreed that there must be a halt to the concentration of power in the national government. That means we must stop leaning wholly upon the national gov-

ernment. In the period ahead, the states will be strong. They alone will have survived the war without overburdening debt. They express the vitality and resurgence of a free people. They are unafraid of the future. They are untrammeled by the weariness and defeatism that comes from the repeated fumbling of over-centralized government which believed that this country was built to saturation in 1932.

Clearly, we shall need a new kind of equal partnership between national, state and local government. Every community in the nation will have its own special and different problems. By that token every community will have its own special and extraordinary opportunities.

The most conspicuous characteristic of the period we are about to face is that its challenge will present our greatest opportunity. During this war we have learned about the techniques of production in industry and in agriculture beyond the dreams of even five years ago. We have learned enormously about the art of living together in peace and in unity. We have learned about industrial relations and racial and religious good will. With the greatest demand for goods and services that ever faced our country and with the greatest skills we ever possessed, every single American has an opportunity to blaze new trails and to build as we have never built before.

Once we have determined to approach the problems that come after the war in this spirit we can go forward without fear. We need not be afraid of the future, for the future will be in our own hands. We shall need courage, energy and determination, but above all, we shall need faith—faith in ourselves, in our communities and in our country.

THE BEST INFORMED PEOPLE IN THE WORLD

Address Opening the Annual Exhibition of the Press Photographers Association of New York, March 24, 1944

WE are here to give fitting recognition to outstanding achievement in the field of news photography. The good reporter, whether he works with the camera and flash bulb or with notebook and typewriter, was never more necessary than he is today. It is impossible for us here in America to realize what a precious thing we have in a free press until we start reading the unashamed falsehoods offered to most of the rest of the people of the world by what they call newspapers.

We in America have learned to distinguish between fact and opinion, between gossip and actual events. We have come to doubt a news report when fact is adulterated with opinion.

The news and camera men who report to us through the newspapers, the radio and news reels, are the eyes and ears of America. Under our system they have to report truthfully or else they gradually die from public disrespect. Thanks to that system, they make us the best informed people in the world. And it is through knowing the truth that we can keep ourselves free.

Unfortunately there have been increasing signs of late that our newspapers are being denied the right to print all the news. Important matters have repeatedly been withheld for months until they leaked out and become the subject of such wide-spread gossip that they could no longer be suppressed.

Only now do we learn, because it leaked out, of the shooting down of 23 transport planes and the killing of 410 American paratroopers in Sicily, eight months ago. Even after a Presidential broadcast, we still know precisely nothing of what really happened at the much-heralded conference in Teheran. We only know of the disquieting evidences of disunity which have since occurred in the Pravda attacks on the British and the Vatican, followed by the startling repercussions brought out by the President's announcement of the three-way division of the Italian fleet.

All of us understand the necessities of military censorship. We expect the military authorities to withhold all news, such as that of troop movements, that could be of any aid to the enemy. But the events of which I speak have not been suppressed to keep information from the enemy so much as to keep it from our own people. One such incident might be charged to blunder; two such incidents begin to lay the unpleasant suspicion of administration policy. When we find the State Department requesting the British censor to suppress political news sent to American papers by American correspondents abroad, it begins to amount to a deliberate and dangerous policy of suppression of the news at home.

Despite millions of dollars spent on war information service, we are constantly being surprised. Often we learn of important events through the pronouncements of foreign statesmen or by reading dispatches cabled back to this country from foreign papers. After making all due allowances for war-time conditions, it still remains that we know far too little about our own foreign policies and practically nothing about our diplomatic commitments.

The press of this country has cooperated unanimously in voluntary censorship. It will continue to do so. But the stakes in this war are too high for it to be fought in the dark. The issues are too momentous. It is time we had light as we fight for freedom.

There seems to be too little recognition of the fact that free people cannot fight a war with blinders on their eyes. Knowing present dangers and the hardships ahead they will brace themselves to any task. They will sacrifice as deeply as the welfare of the nation demands. They can do neither if they are not told where they are going and why.

Our people can take the bad news with the good but they have a right to know the facts. We need a free, informed people to fight a war for freedom.

Whatever excuse may be made for the blunders of censorship in war-time, we must see to it that no vestige of censorship, either voluntary or enforced, shall continue for one moment when the war is over. Then we shall face the hard task of building a just and lasting peace. That task cannot be successful without the aid of an alert, courageous and unfettered press.

The building of a durable peace will not be simple. It will not be accomplished overnight by the mere signing of a treaty. It will certainly not be done just by an agreement made by a few men seated around a conference table. It will be achieved by the labor and willing sacrifice of people the world over for generations to come because they understand the conditions of peace and want them.

There have been studied efforts in recent months to make people believe that Congress will obstruct the building of a lasting peace. That is not true. That is a part of a continuing effort to discredit the Congress of the United States. I have confidence in the Congress because it is close to the people. I have eternal confidence in the good sense and the character of the American people.

If the peace we build is to succeed, it must reflect the will and understanding of our people. That understanding can be fostered and that will expressed through a free press. Certainly in the years to come, the peace will succeed only if our people have the information and the will to make it succeed as a living reality. For the sake of our sons and our sons' sons, we must have the determined, abiding will to build a better world.

REPORT TO THE PEOPLE

*To the People of the State of New York on the Work of the
1944 Session of the Legislature and the Accomplishments of
the State Administration, April 14, 1944*

TONIGHT I want to give you my second annual report on
the administration of your State government. When I reported to you last April, we had just made a fair beginning
on the task of cleaning out, from the departments and
agencies of the State, the accumulated cobwebs of twenty
years. In the last twelve months, without interrupting or
disturbing for a moment the day-to-day business of the State,
that job has made tremendous progress. We have now in
Albany a complete administration, infused with new blood
and new energy, filled with a spirit of teamwork between
the legislative and executive branches, working in cooperation with each other, with the people of the State, and with
the local units of government which are closest to the
people.

We are striving, in other words, to establish and maintain a genuinely competent and progressive government—
in sharp contrast with that type of personal government
which talks fine phrases of liberalism while seeking to im-
pose its will and its whims upon the people through cen-
tralized bureaucracies issuing directives from a distance.

Three immediate and fundamental purposes have guided
our work to strengthen the State government: first, to win
the war; second, to prepare for a rapid and smooth readjustment to peaceful pursuits, once complete victory is
won; third, to preserve and develop that freedom at home
for which our young men are fighting abroad. In the light
of that intent I want now to throw into perspective for you

the pattern and interrelated purposes of what we have been doing since last April.

When the year began it was clear we were going to have a large accumulated surplus in the treasury; actually, at the first of this month, starting the new fiscal year, that surplus amounted to $163,000,000. This money had piled up as a result of abnormal wartime conditions and of good State housekeeping. There were many suggestions of pleasant and useful ways in which we might spend it. But it seemed to me, and to the Republican leaders of the Legislature, that this money was not really ours to spend. Rather, it was a fund to be held in trust for the million young men and women of our State who are in the armed forces, for the millions of war workers who, when hostilities end, will be changing over to peacetime jobs. When that time comes, a great responsibility will fall upon the State, which it must be ready to meet without delay—to help industry convert itself to peace production and to contribute its own part through immediate launching of needed and deferred public works.

Accordingly, in my opening message to the Legislature— to forestall raids which were later vigorously attempted by pressure groups on this wartime surplus—I proposed to create a Post-War Reconstruction Fund and to lock up in it the entire surplus. This was done, as Chapter 1 of the Laws of 1944.

Our State Post-War Planning Commission has been working hard to prepare for the day of reconversion for peace. Blueprints are now being drawn for new housing projects. Plans are being made for urgently needed additions to our overcrowded state hospitals. Under a law passed this year we are now already at work, preparing to purchase rights of way for a great arterial highway system.

When the day of reconversion comes, New York State will approach it, not merely with blueprints and bond issues to create new debts; we will have, ready for instant use, a minimum of $163,000,000 cold cash. Moreover, the State Department of Commerce is working intensively with business, big and small, all over the State, for the new industries and quick change-overs, which will provide the great bulk of opportunity and employment for our people.

Some of you have now paid the first quarterly installment of the State income tax. You know, therefore, that we were able to salt away our surplus while continuing the 25 per cent reduction in the tax on personal incomes. Many of you did not have to pay any State tax at all, because we had been able to continue the high exemptions, $1000 for single persons, $2500 for married folk, and also to continue the deductions for medical expenses, life insurance premiums, and children in school. But the most gratifying thing about the income tax this year was that we were able to let the taxpayer make his return on a new and simpler one-page form.

When the President of the State Tax Commission first proposed that simplified form I realized once again how fortunate we now are to have a cabinet officer who is out to make taxation more simple, rather than to drape it in mysterious complexities.

When I spoke to you last April we were just hearing the first of that sordid history of corruption under the Workmen's Compensation Law which was revealed by a Moreland Act Commission. For many years groups of corrupt lawyers, doctors and laymen, licensed by the Department of Labor to represent claimants, had been siphoning off millions of dollars from benefits due to injured workers. There were also shocking delays by the Industrial Board in determining the case of injured workmen; the board was four months behind in its work.

Eighteen bills designed to correct these long-standing evils were proposed by me to the Legislature this year and are now law. Under this program the Industrial Board was enlarged from five to ten members so that determination of claims of injured workmen can be cleared within a month. Another bill increases benefit claims from $25.00 to $28.00 a week. Still others provide for increased benefits for disability and death resulting from dust—the disease we know as silicosis. Other bills will, I hope, under good administration drive the thieves permanently from the field of workmen's compensation.

The working men and women of our State can now know that they will receive full and prompt compensation for their injuries. They do not have to pay one cent for tribute to anyone.

Trade unionism is an increasingly important factor in the life of our State, but events of the last year have shown us that workers and employers alike have much to learn about the vast field of industrial relations. One of the most important things we did this winter was to create, through action of the Legislature, a State School of Labor and Industry at Cornell University. This school, blazing a great trail, will offer advanced studies in this rapidly expanding field, will prepare young men and women for useful careers of leadership in the solution of labor's perplexing problems. Such a school as this can become not only a training place, but also a meeting ground for industrial statesmanship.

One of our most grievous problems in industry has been that of discrimination against some groups because of race or religion and particularly because of color. I am deeply gratified at the progress we have made through a committee of the War Council, and New York State today leads the nation in employment regardless of race, creed or color. But with the end of the war, the fight against discrimination in employment will need new legal basis. Accordingly, the committee proposed legislation to me and to the Legislature to this end. Unfortunately, the bill came in just two weeks before the close of the session, and I was advised that, despite my interest in it, no action could be taken at this session. To make progress in the meantime, after consultation with the Chairman of the Committee, I recommended to the Legislature, and it passed, a bill creating a temporary State Commission for the purpose of drafting good sound legislation. Shortly the members of the commission will be appointed and I have every hope and expectation that they will be able to report to the next session of the Legislature a system and philosophy of law for the permanent elimination of discrimination in industry in peacetime.

Now, as in normal times, much of your State's daily work has to do with the health and social well-being of its people. Let us take a swift glance now at some of the things which have been happening in some of these basic State departments.

I am happy to report real progress in our program of providing care for the small children of women engaged in war industry. Through the Committee on Child Care, the State is contributing to forty-seven child care centers in New York City and to 105 centers upstate. Arrangements are now being made to speed the opening of new centers in war manpower shortage areas.

Most important of all, we are in the process of trying, at long last, to change the basic concept of our mental hospitals. We must not regard them as mere institutions of custody. We must and will make them into institutions not merely of care but of cure, not of despair but of hope—hope for restoration of mental health. Our State can have no more important long range objective—through research and sound administration—than the cure and conquest of mental illness.

The people of New York may well be proud of the way the farmers of this State met the crisis last year, with inadequate help, little new machinery, excessive regulation and, at times, not even gasoline for plowing or cultivating. Under the distinguished leadership of the Emergency Food Administration many obstacles were overcome. The crops of our State were harvested and processed without loss last fall with the extra aid of a volunteer army of 111,000 workers.

I have told you about our postwar fund and how it has been segregated and saved, to be used for the benefit of our returning veterans. Now, in conclusion, I want to explain in some detail our further plans for these young people who must be first in our hearts and plans.

One thing immediately at hand for the benefit of these veterans while they seek employment is unemployment insurance. Nearly half of the members of the armed forces from our State come from our farms and from small businesses, which are not covered by the unemployment insurance law. So today, as a result of action this year, and until the Federal government takes action, there is unemployment insurance for every returning New York veteran.

We have set up a temporary commission to study the various proposals for assistance to veterans and to help them and their families learn of the many provisions, both State and local, which exist for their assistance. The sum of $100,-000 was appropriated for this commission.

Your State Administration also took the lead in proposing a simple, workable formula for soldier voting. Under the new State law, adopted at this last session, every member of the armed services desiring to vote has simply to send in his name and his home and service address. He will then receive in the mail a ballot and self-addressed envelope.

This soldier ballot will not be the blank piece of paper which was sponsored in Washington. Nor will it, as the National Government tried to do, deprive the soldier of his Constitutional right to vote for every office to be filled. It will give every man and woman in the armed services, by the simple act of signing his name once, a valid vote for every candidate from President down to the local officers in his home town. Under this New York law voting is simpler for a soldier on foreign service than it is for a citizen here at home and the honest ballots cast by real soldiers will not be cancelled by the frauds which other proposals would have permitted.

The problem of the interrupted or incomplete education of our youth in the armed services is vital to them and to our country. We must not miss part of a generation of skilled men and women or of doctors, clergymen, lawyers, architects and engineers. To this end, the Legislature this year created 1200 scholarships for veterans to continue their studies. Those scholarships are available now for the veterans who are already returning from war this year and 1200 per year will be available after the war.

These, then, are part of the fruits of the labors of the past year. They are, of course, only the portion of which mention is possible in a summary report. But they show the purpose with which our war tasks are being met and the spirit and purpose of your State government.

Running like a thread through our every thought and act has been the sacred task of bringing this tragic war to a speedy and overwhelmingly successful end. No other consideration can be allowed to enter our minds until Nazism and Fascism are totally wiped off the face of the earth.

But, as we labor with singleness of purpose to this end, we can think and plan for the future. We must look to the day when free men everywhere, regardless of race, color or creed, can live in freedom, can work at occupations of their own choosing, can raise their children in the traditions of their parents, can worship God in the manner of their own choosing. We can, and we must, keep our own society clean of those within who would lead us into paths of narrow or bigoted selfishness.

REPORT TO THE PEOPLE

Our State will be strong to meet the great problems after the war. It will be clean of the poison of hatred or prejudice. It will be set on its course toward full peace-time production and employment for all the day the war ends. It will do its part in the Nation to the end that out of this war may come a happier day for all mankind and the beginning of a just and a lasting peace.

OUR FOREIGN POLICY

At the Annual Meeting of the American Newspaper Publishers Association Held in New York City, April 27, 1944

I AM very happy to speak before this wartime gathering of American newspaper publishers. Yours is an essential industry because in America the press is a vital part of our war effort, it is a vital part of our whole free system. It is an indispensable element of everything for which we fight.

The tragic history of recent years has shown us vividly that freedom of the press cannot exist where there is no political freedom, but the corollary to this basic truth is perhaps even more important; political freedom cannot exist without a free press.

An electorate, fully informed on issues, is as fundamental to representative government as the election itself. And full information through the press is the bulwark of the people's power to check up on their representatives between elections.

We saw it demonstrated in Germany that tyranny can rise to power by the elective process. But in order to stay in power the Nazis immediately set about destroying the freedom of the German press. In all countries men have been elected to office who proved unworthy of the trust. The strength of a free system is that such mistakes need never be fatal. They can be corrected at the polls. But these corrections can be made only if the people are informed.

The precious guaranty in our Constitution of freedom of the press is not a mere guaranty to the press. It is a guaranty to the people that their press shall be free. It imposes an obligation on government to permit free dissemination of news and a duty on the press to print honest news. The right resides in the people because it is basic to their liberties.

Freedom of the press today means more than freedom to print what information can be obtained. It means access to the news. It involves the right of information and a corresponding duty to print it.

All of us recognize the need for military censorship. But there is a dividing line between military news and political news, or, if you will, diplomatic news. It is a dividing line which can never be left without scrutiny—which throughout the war calls for vigilance. Once the fighting has ceased we must insist that all censorship of every description cease with it. We shall need then the uncorrupted word of truth.

I am confident of our future because we have, in fact, a great, free press. I believe our publishers generally are today more conscious of their tremendous responsibility than ever before. They will have much to do with the steadfastness with which we fight through this war. They will have much to do with the intelligence and determination with which we face the even more complicated problems of the peace.

The power of the written word lies in shaping the mind and spirit of man toward high achievement. There is, of course, a wide gulf between a statement of fact or of principles, on the one hand, and epithets or empty promises on the other. In recent years we have had good reason to learn that difference in our domestic affairs. It is not enough to talk about a more abundant life if the actions that follow the words leave millions unemployed and dependent upon government for bare existence. It is not enough to talk about economic security and then pursue policies which promote insecurity. It is not enough to talk about the enterprise system and then pursue a course of action that stifles enterprise.

These experiences with domestic policies cannot be forgotten when we think of foreign policies. All of us are aware that there is great concern and uncertainty among our people over our nation's foreign policy. Yet I think it is no more than fair to say that we have had some excellent expressions on that subject lately from the Secretary of State, Mr. Hull. In his address of April 9th, Mr. Hull certainly offered a statement of basic principles which deserves respect. His pledge to seek the advice and help of members of Congress from both parties is especially welcome. Nevertheless, these statements have done little to relieve the concern and uncertainty our people feel. That is not primarily because of dissatisfaction with the words Mr. Hull has used. It is because we see reported daily in your papers developments from abroad and other statements from high government officials at home which do not seem to fit in altogether with the words Mr. Hull has used. It is because we cannot be sure to what extent our foreign policy is actually being handled by the Secretary of State and to what extent it is being handled privately by the President.

What troubles us is not the main objectives of our foreign policy, but whether that policy will be effectively carried out in accordance with Constitutional methods. One way it will succeed. The other way it will surely fail. Foreign policy is not a mere matter of negotiations, of diplomatic maneuvering, or even of treaties and alliances. Foreign policy is the expression of the ideals, traditions and aspirations of a people in their relations with the people of other countries.

In a free republic there can be no such thing as an Administration having an effective foreign policy, unless that policy reflects the will of the people. Here we are, fighting, hoping, praying for a world in which we can have a lasting peace but in almost every discussion one simple fact is forgotten. No foreign policy that fails to represent the will of the people will ever last as long as two years. It will not last beyond the next Congressional election. Among our people there are differences of opinion with respect to details and methods; but I insist, there is overwhelming agreement upon the main objectives. Those major objectives are:

To carry on the war to total crushing victory, and in so doing to drive home to the aggressor nations a lesson that will never be forgotten;

To organize in cooperation with other nations a structure of peace backed by adequate force to prevent future wars;

To establish and maintain in our relations with other nations conditions calculated to promote world-wide economic stability not only for the sake of the world, but also to the end that our own people may enjoy a high level of employment in an increasingly prosperous world.

There is, I am confident, no real dissent from those major objectives on the part of any substantial portion of our people. They have been proclaimed by men of all parties and subscribed to by men of all walks of life in all parts of our country. They constitute the fundamental principles of our foreign policy because they represent the will of our people. But once again let it be said that these objectives cannot be attained by mere words.

As to the winning of the war the point needs no argument. We shall win the war only by the work and sacrifice of all our people. We shall win it by the courage, strength and suffering of our fighting men and by the unremitting effort of our war production forces at home. To win the peace will require equally great determination, and over a longer period of time. It will not be sufficient when the fighting ceases merely to draw up a treaty and then forget about it. We must not repeat the tragic error of twenty-five years ago.

The central error of our course in 1919 was the false assumption that words could create a peace. Then, as now, there was much wishful thinking. Men everywhere wanted to feel that a treaty which proclaimed peace would suffice to assure it and that from there on they could relax. The war leaders of the world wanted to feel that by signing their names to a treaty, they had brought their task to an end. The very idea that fine words made a peace bore within it the seeds of its own failure.

Within a few years the reality of Germany bore no relation whatever to the word picture of Versailles. This was because those who drafted the treaty were tired war leaders. They could not find within themselves the physical and mental strength to make the peace a living reality.

We have learned much since 1919. The experience of two world wars has taught us that we cannot remain unaffected by what happens elsewhere in the world. It has shown us also that unprovoked aggression against a freedom-loving people anywhere is an attack upon the peace of the whole world. We may again be tempted to feel that with the defeat of our enemies and a proclamation of peace, we can afford to rest on our oars. But the truth is, those years that follow will be decisive. The maintenance of peace will require continuing labor and forbearance. When we have ceased to wage war we shall have to wage peace.

Germany and Japan must not only be utterly defeated and completely disarmed—they must not be left in a post-war environment which might enable them to maneuver as a balance of power. After 1919, lethargy, jealousy and power politics resumed sway among the allies. In that environment Germany quickly eluded the controls of the treaty of Versailles. If after this war we reproduce that same political climate, we will get the same results. No initial measures against Germany and Japan, however drastic, will have permanent value unless they fall within the setting of a durable cohesion between Great Britain and ourselves, together, I hope, with Russia and China. To deal effectively with our enemies and also to solve many other post-war problems will, as I have said, require solid relations among the United States and Great Britain, Soviet Russia and China.

We have a long background of friendly working relations with Great Britain and China, which will make easy their continuation. As regards Russia, it would be stupid to ignore the fact that during the twenty-four years between the Soviet revolution and the German attack on Russia our relations were not of the best. There were faults on both sides. If after this war we relapse into the old suspicions, the future is indeed dark. But there has been genuine improvement growing out of our partnership in this war. The American people have sympathy and admiration for the peoples of the Soviet Union.

There are and will be fundamental internal differences between our countries. Our economic and social systems will not be the same. But our political dissimilarities from Russia need not be the source of friction if we seek and find the many practical ways in which we can work to a common end.

Russian affairs are in the hands of hardheaded, realistic leaders. That is nothing we should be afraid of, provided we are equally realistic and devoted to our country. If we are, the United States and Russia can deal with each other with candor, while building firm mutual respect and friendship.

Inevitably a major responsibility to work together will fall upon the United States, Britain, Russia and China in the first few years following the war. They will be the strongest nations. They will be the nations with the greatest power to preserve peace or to undermine it.

In some countries we may for a time face confusion. We must wisely and without intrusion into their domestic affairs seek to make that period as brief as possible. We shall need the participation of these nations. The peace of the world will require the support of all peoples. We are all agreed that there must be prompt measures to establish a system of general international cooperation. First came the Republican Mackinac charter, then the Moscow declaration and the Fulbright and Connally resolutions. All agree in proposing an arrangement which will regularly bring together the representatives of the nations to discuss, to plan and to seek agreement about matters of common concern. This will not be accomplished to perfection overnight, or in a few months. It must be a matter of growth and experience and everlasting hard work.

It will not be possible to solve immediately the economic problems of the world. It will take time and patience to restore currency stability and trade relationships and to promote the general economic well-being.

Here it cannot be too greatly emphasized that the role of the United States will be decisive. We will be truly effective in helping with the economic rehabilitation of the world only if we first restore at home a healthy, a vigorous and a growing economy.

There are false prophets who for years have been telling us that America has ceased to grow; that its period of vigor is over. They would have us believe that our economy has become mature. They say it is static, that it can continue to function only by constantly taking ever more expensive patent medicines. Yet these same people now talk glibly of a W.P.A. for all the rest of the world.

To hear them talk, Uncle Sam must play the role of a benevolent but slightly senile gentleman, who seeks to purchase the good will of his poor relations by distributing among them the dwindling remains of his youthful earnings.

I utterly reject that proposition. America is still young, still vigorous, still capable of growth. Certainly we shall play the part of a good citizen in the community of nations. We shall deal fairly and generously with our neighbor nations throughout the world. This we shall do because it represents the practical idealism for which America has always stood and because it is good hard common sense. Good will cannot be bought with gold. Good will flows irresistibly to the man who successfully manages his own affairs, who is self-reliant and independent, yet who is considerate always of the rights and needs of others.

Traditionally, America has occupied this role for 150 years. This country won the admiration of the world because we had here something to which the people of all nations aspired. We had a society of free men who believed in themselves and in the future of their country. We were in sober truth the land of opportunity. Here beyond everywhere else in the world there was a field for economic enterprise and human progress.

For the sake of the men and women who are working and fighting and dying to win this war, for the sake of their children and for the sake of the world, we must work to make America once more the land of opportunity.

It is particularly incumbent on us solemnly to view our obligations tonight. As we meet here, hundreds of thousands of the youth of America stand poised on the shores of Great Britain for the mightiest invasion of a defended coast line in history. Every one of those young men knows that the future of his country and of freedom itself may hang on the success of this terrible venture. Every man knows the price he may have to pay.

Nothing any of us has said here tonight will be of import unless the invasion is crowned by ultimate success. The infinite patience, preparation and training behind this gigantic effort may well serve us as a standard for our own acceptance of our future responsibilities. Surely it is a minimum standard for the infinite patience, preparation and toil we should be willing to give for peace. No sacrifice for peace will ever equal the ultimate sacrifice we expect of our young men in war.

OUR FOREIGN POLICY

The very least we can do, therefore, as we look ahead to-night to hopes of a peaceful world, is to pledge to ourselves and to those who die for our country that we shall accept the challenge they lay before us. We can resolve to accept the responsibility which our own greatness and importance as a nation place upon us—a responsibility which two world wars have shown is utterly inescapable.

Let us recognize that this peace we pray for and our young men die for will have to be worked for over many years. Let us be flexible, earnest, and devoted enough to make it a reality.

If the newspapers of America will accept the challenge of peace as they have of war, we shall have made a great beginning. The years of labor ahead will be successful only if an informed people support the effort—only if they know the size of the task. We shall need in these years, as never before, a courageous and a free press in the United States of America.

ACCEPTANCE

To the Republican National Convention, June 28, 1944

I AM profoundly moved by the trust you have placed in me. I deeply feel the responsibility which goes with your nomination for President of the United States at this grave hour of our nation's history.

That I have not sought this responsibility, all of you know. I told the people of my state, two years ago, that it was my intention to devote my full term as Governor exclusively to their service. You have decided otherwise. In accordance with the principles of our republican form of government you have laid upon me the highest duty to which an American can be called. No one has a right to refuse that call. With the help of God, I shall try to be worthy of the trust. I accept the nomination.

I come to this great task a free man. I have made no pledges, promises or commitments, expressed or implied, to any man or woman. I shall make none, except to the American people.

These pledges I do make:

To men and women of the Republican party everywhere I pledge my utmost effort in the months ahead. In return I ask for your support. Without it I cannot discharge the heavy obligation you lay upon me.

To Americans of every party I pledge that on January 20th next year our government will again have a Cabinet of the ablest men and women to be found in America. Its members will expect and will receive full delegation of the powers of their office. They will be capable of administering those powers. They will each be experienced in the task

344

to be done, and young enough to do it. This election will bring an end to one-man government in America.

To Americans of every party I pledge a campaign dedicated to one end above all others—that this nation under God may continue in the years ahead a free nation of free men.

At this moment on battlegrounds around the world Americans are dying for the freedom of our country. Their comrades are pressing on in the face of hardship and suffering. They are pressing on for total victory and for the liberties of all of us.

Everything we say or do today and in the future must be devoted to the single purpose of that victory. Then, when victory is won, we must devote ourselves with equal unity of purpose to re-winning at home the freedom they have won at such desperate cost abroad.

To our allies let us send from this convention one message from our hearts: The American people are united with you to the limit of our resources and our man power, devoted to the single task of victory and the establishment of a firm and lasting peace.

To every member of the Axis powers let us send this message: By this political campaign, which you are unable to understand, our will to victory will be strengthened, and with every day you further delay surrender the consequences to you will be more severe.

That we shall win this war none of us and few of our enemies can now have any doubt. But how we win this war is of major importance for the years ahead. We won the last war but it did not stay won. This time we must also win the purposes for which we are fighting. Germany must never again nourish the delusion that she could have won.

We must carry to Japan a defeat so crushing and complete that every last man among them knows that he has been beaten. We must not merely defeat the armies and

345

navies of our enemies. We must defeat, once and for all, their will to make war. In their hearts as well as with their lips let them be taught to say: "Never again."

The military conduct of the war is outside this campaign. It is and must remain completely out of politics. General Marshall and Admiral King are doing a superb job. Thank God for both of them. Let me make it crystal clear that a change of administration next January cannot and will not involve any change in the military conduct of the war. If there is not now any civilian interference with the military and naval commands, a change in administration will not alter that status. If there is civilian interference, the new administration will put a stop to it forthwith.

But the war is being fought on the home front as well as abroad. While all of us are deeply proud of the military conduct of the war, can we honestly say that the home front could not bear improvement? The present Administration in Washington has been in office for more than eleven years. Today it is at war with Congress, and at war with itself. Squabbles between Cabinet members, feuds between rival bureaucrats and bitterness between the President and his own party members, in and out of Congress, have become the order of the day. In the vital matters of taxation, price control, rationing, labor relations, man power, we have become familiar with the spectacle of wrangling, bungling and confusion.

Does any one suggest that the present national Administration is giving either efficient or competent government? We have not heard that claim made, even by its most fanatical supporters. No, all they tell us is that in its young days it did some good things.

That we freely grant. But now it has grown old in office. It has become tired and quarrelsome. It seems that the great men who founded this nation really knew what they were talking about when they said that three terms were too many.

When we have won the war, we shall still have to win the peace. We are agreed, all of us, that America will participate with other sovereign nations in a cooperative effort to prevent future wars. Let us face up boldly to the magnitude of that task. We shall not make secure the peace of the world by mere words.

We cannot do it simply by drawing up a fine-sounding treaty. It cannot be the work of one man or of a little group of rulers who meet together in private conferences. The structure of peace must be built. It must be the work of many men. We must have as our representatives in this task the ablest men and women America can produce, and the structure they join in building must rest upon the solid rock of a united American opinion.

I am not one of those who despair of achieving that end. I am utterly confident we can do it. For years, we have had men in Washington who were notoriously weak in certain branches of arithmetic but who specialized in division. They have played up minor differences of opinion among our people until the people of other countries might have thought that America was cleft in two.

But all the while there was a large, growing area of agreement. Recently the overwhelming majesty of that broad area of agreement has become obvious. The Republican party can take pride in helping to define it and broaden it. There are only a few, a very few, who really believe that America should try to remain aloof from the world.

There are only a relatively few who believe it would be practical for America or her allies to renounce all sovereignty and join a super-state. I certainly would not deny those two extremes the right to their opinions; but I stand firmly with the overwhelming majority of my fellow citizens in that great wide area of agreement. That agreement was clearly expressed by the Republican Mackinac declaration and was adopted in the foreign policy plank of this convention.

No organization for peace will last if it is slipped through by stealth or trickery or the momentary hypnotism of high-sounding phrases. We shall have to work and pray and be patient and make sacrifices to achieve a really lasting peace.

That is not too much to ask in the name of those who have died for the future of our country. This is no task to be entrusted to stubborn men, grown old and tired and quarrelsome in office. We learned that in 1919.

The building of the peace is more than a matter of international cooperation. God has endowed America with such blessings as to fit her for a great role in the world. We can only play that role if we are strong and healthy and vigorous as nature has equipped us to be. It would be a tragedy after this war if Americans returned from our armed forces and failed to find the freedom and opportunity for which they fought.

This must be a land where every man and woman has a fair chance to work and get ahead. Never again must free Americans face the specter of long-continued mass unemployment. We Republicans are agreed that full employment shall be a first objective of national policy. By full employment I mean a real chance for every man and woman to earn a decent living at a decent wage.

What hope does the present administration offer here? In 1940, the year before this country entered the war, there were still ten million unemployed. After seven years of unequaled power and unparalleled spending, the New Deal had failed utterly to solve that problem. It never solved that problem. It was left to be solved by war. Do we have to have a war in order to get jobs?

What are we now offered? Only the dreary prospect of a continued war economy after the war, with interference piled on interference and petty tyrannies rivaling the very regimentation against which we are now at war.

The present administration has never solved this fundamental problem of jobs and opportunity. It never can solve this problem. It has never even understood what makes a job. It has never been for full production. It has lived in chattering fear of abundance. It has specialized in curtailment and restriction. It has been consistently hostile to and abusive of American business and American industry, although it is in business and industry that most of us make our living.

In all the record of the last eleven years is there anything that suggests the present administration can bring about high-level employment after this war? Is there any reason to believe that those who have so signally failed in the past can succeed in the future? The problem of jobs will not be easily solved, but it will never be solved at all unless we get a new, progressive administration in Washington—and that means a Republican administration.

For one hundred and fifty years America was the hope of the world. Here on this great broad continent we had brought into being something for which men had longed throughout all history. Here, all men were held to be free and equal. Here, government derived its just powers from the consent of the governed. Here, men believed passionately in freedom, independence—the God-given right of the individual to be his own master.

Yet, with all of this freedom—I insist, because of this freedom—ours was a land of plenty. In a fashion unequaled anywhere else in the world, America grew and strengthened; our standard of living became the envy of the world. In all lands, men and women looked toward America as the pattern of what they, themselves, desired. And because we were what we were, good will flowed toward us from all corners of the earth. An American was welcomed everywhere and looked upon with admiration and regard.

At times, we had our troubles; made our share of mistakes; but we faltered only to go forward with renewed vigor. It remained for this past eleven years, under the present national administration, for continuing unemployment to be accepted with resignation as the inevitable condition of a nation past its prime.

It is the New Deal which tells us that America has lost its capacity to grow. We shall never build a better world by listening to those counsels of defeat. Is America old and worn out? Look to the beaches of Normandy for the answer.

Look to the reaches of the wide Pacific—to the corners of the world where American men are fighting. Look to the marvels of production in the war plants in your own towns. I say to you: our country is just fighting its way through to new horizons. The future of America has no limit.

True, we now pass through dark and troubled times. Scarcely a home escapes the touch of dread anxiety and grief; yet in this hour the American spirit rises, faith returns—faith in our God, faith in our fellowman, faith in the land our fathers died to win, faith in the future, limitless and bright, of this our country.

In the name of that faith we shall carry our cause in the coming months to the American people.